ASC
American Studies Center SCU
四川大学美国研究中心

American Studies Symposium
美国研究论丛

# Comparative Studies on Chinese & American Areas

# 中美区域对比研究

主编 陈 杰 王 欣

Sichuan University Press
四川大学出版社

责任编辑:余　芳
责任校对:周　洁
封面设计:米迦设计工作室
责任印制:王　炜

**图书在版编目(CIP)数据**

中美区域对比研究=Comparative Studies on Chinese and American Areas:中文、英文 / 陈杰,王欣主编. —成都:四川大学出版社,2015.5
(美国研究论丛)
ISBN 978-7-5614-8574-3

Ⅰ.①中…　Ⅱ.①陈…　②王…　Ⅲ.①中国-对比研究-美国-文集-汉、英　Ⅳ.①D6-53②D771.2-53

中国版本图书馆 CIP 数据核字(2015)第 114560 号

书名　**中美区域对比研究**
**Zhongmei Quyu Duibi Yanjiu**

主　　编　陈　杰　王　欣
出　　版　四川大学出版社
地　　址　成都市一环路南一段 24 号 (610065)
发　　行　四川大学出版社
书　　号　ISBN 978-7-5614-8574-3
印　　刷　郫县犀浦印刷厂
成品尺寸　170 mm×240 mm
印　　张　16
字　　数　300 千字
版　　次　2015 年 6 月第 1 版
印　　次　2015 年 6 月第 1 次印刷
定　　价　48.00 元



◆读者邮购本书,请与本社发行科联系。电话:(028)85408408/(028)85401670/(028)85408023　邮政编码:610065
◆本社图书如有印装质量问题,请寄回出版社调换。
◆网址:http://www.scup.cn

# 编者的话

美国研究是一个跨学科的广阔的研究领域，涉及人文学科和社会学科的多个方面，其研究对象、视角和方法具有极大的包容性和开放性。美国研究的跨学科性质，对我国高校传统的学科体制、科研运作和人才培养模式均提出了严峻的挑战。如何避免“大而全”的肤浅研究，如何兼顾美国研究的广度和深度，如何在研究中突出重点和特色，都是需要认真思考的问题。

四川大学美国研究中心自2012年6月成为教育部区域与国别研究培育基地以来，即将中美西南区域对比研究作为中心的一个重点研究领域，希望借此整合校内外的研究资源，构筑一个跨学科的学术平台。我们希望在研究中以跨文化和跨国界的视野，引入多元和比较的视角，通过中国学人的视角去观察美国，同时又通过研究美国来反思自身。2013年11月“中国和美国的西南区域比较研究”国际学术研讨会的召开，即是我们在这方面努力的结果。该会议由四川大学和美国亚利桑那州立大学联合主办，聚集了中美学者六十多人。参会学者就中美西南区域中的文学、文化、经济、旅游、教育及少数族裔等诸多话题进行了比较研究，并展开了热烈讨论。这部文集主要就是以参会学者提交的论文汇编而成。

本书以《中美区域对比研究》命名，是四川大学美国研究中心推出的“美国研究论丛”系列文集的第一部。今后，我们将陆续出版中心的学术研究成果。借此机会，我们感谢2013年四川大学“中国和美国的西南区域比较研究”国际学术研讨会参会学者的赐稿，感谢四川大学美国研究中心学术委员会对入编论文的审阅，感谢美国亚利桑那州立大学凯瑟琳·莫门（Kathryn Mohrman）教授为本书撰写英文前言，感谢外国语学院数位研究生同学对论文摘要的编译，感谢我中心项目主管洪舒老师在书籍出版过程中所做的联络与校稿工作，感谢四川大学出版社余芳、敬铃凌编辑为本书出版付出的辛苦努力！

陈　杰

2015年4月

# Foreword

Sichuan is located in the southwest of China and Arizona is located in the southwest of the United States. Sichuan University and Arizona State University are sister institutions, not just because of their geographic locations but because of their common commitment to creative, interdisciplinary research and teaching that are linked to the communities in which they reside.

The two universities are collaborating on a series of activities that look thoughtfully and comparatively at the southwestern regions of China and the United States. This volume is one result. A quick glance at the chapter titles reveals the wide range of topics that fall under the theme of Southwest Studies: American missionaries in China in the $19^{th}$ century, modern Chinese students in the United States, history of indigenous peoples in both southwestern regions, the development of high-tech industries in Sichuan and Arizona, immigration and population flows, and the impact of globalization in many spheres.

Many of these topics were first presented at the 2013 International Conference on Chinese and American Southwest Studies, held at Sichuan University and co-sponsored by Arizona State University. At that symposium, Wang Xiaolu from Sichuan University noted that comparative studies help us to develop new understanding of ourselves as well as of other cultures. The focus on the southwestern regions of the two countries is especially valuable in creating greater understanding, since both regions have been under-represented in scholarly explorations in the past. This volume adds an important set of perspectives to Sino-American comparative research.

This volume is also the first publication of the newly upgraded American Studies Center at Sichuan University. In existence since the 1980s, the American Studies Center was designated as a National Research Base in 2012 by the Chinese Ministry of Education. We look forward to further collaboration between Sichuan University and Arizona State University in the future.

The opening keynote speaker at the November 2013 conference on Southwest Studies was Dr. Huang Ping, Director of American Studies at the Chinese Academy of Social Sciences. He commented that the intersection of cultures can lead to new solutions for important social issues. By investigating the southwest of China and the southwest of the United States, using many different academic perspectives, we hope this volume will lead, not only to greater mutual understanding, but to real solutions to the challenging problems facing both countries.

Kathryn Mohrman
Professor, School of Public Affairs
Arizona State University, USA
10 June 2014

# 目　录
# CONTENTS

## 区域研究　Area Studies

Utopian Communities on the Southwestern Frontier of the United States and China ······ *J. Eugene Clay* 3

Deep History of Food in the American Southwest: Points of Convergence for Comparison with Southwest China ······ *Christine Szuter* 11

The Role of High Tech/Industrial Park in Leading Local Development: Tales in Chengdu and Phoenix ······ *Lan G. Zhiyong* 27

Globalization: A Response to Eduardo Pagan ······ *David Pickus* 45

A Comparative Study into the Eco-ethics Between North American Indians and Ancient Ethnic Minorities in China's Southwestern Regions ······ *Fang Yonglan* 54

美国亚利桑那州产业集群发展战略：模式、绩效与经验启示··· 路　征　李　唯 65

## 文化、文学　Culture & Literature

The Sichuan University-Arizona State University Center for American Culture: The Context of US Cultural Diplomacy ······ *Jannelle Warren-Findley* 89

美国文化外交的政治目标与非政治策略
——以国际访问者项目为例······ 杨　光 103

西南边疆在明清史研究中的地位
——美国现代学术视野下的中国西南边疆史研究······ 邹立波　李沛容 116

"文化碰撞"、墨西哥人北迁与心灵边界…… 卡洛斯·G. 维勒兹-艾巴那兹 134

中美文学作品中知识分子形象的对比研究
——以《赫索格》和《围城》为例…………………………………… 段丽斌 145

A Great Reality: Willa Cather and the American Southwest …………………… *Li Li* 155

## 教　育　Education

From China's Southwest to America's Midwest: Ethnic Minorities and Higher Education
……………………………………………………………… *MaryJo Benton Lee* 167

Motivation for Overseas Study: Chinese Students at Arizona State University
………………………………………………………………*Li Xiaojie Li Wei* 197

The Promises and Challenges of Teaching History through Television
……………………………………………………………… *Eduardo Pagán* 216

美国研究学科建设中的中美区域对比研究……………………………… 陈　杰 233

ASC

# 区域研究

*Area Studies*

# Utopian Communities on the Southwestern Frontier of the United States and China

J. Eugene Clay

(School of Historical, Philosophical, and Religious Studies, Arizona State University, Tempe, USA, 85287-5503)

**Abstract:** The frontier regions of Sichuan Province and the state of Arizona have long been separated by great distances from the centers of political and economic power; both of these regions have become the sites of unique communities, alternative ideas, and encounters among diverse cultures. On the frontier, utopian and heterodox groups have an opportunity to flourish away from the centers of orthodox authority; in both Sichuan and Arizona, new and alternative religious movements found the space to grow and develop. This paper compares two utopian communities: the Spiritual Christian Molokan Jumpers of early twentieth-century Arizona in the US and the Celestial Masters of late second century southwest China. Each of these movements constructed an alternative vision that challenged the orthodoxies of their respective societies.

**Key Words:** Sichuan Province; the State of Arizona; Utopian Communities; Comparison

Sichuan Province and the state of Arizona have both been frontier regions for long periods of time. Separated by long distances from the centers of political and economic power, both of these regions have become the sites of unique communities, alternative ideas, and encounters among diverse cultures. On the frontier, utopian and heterodox groups have an opportunity to flourish away from the centers of orthodox authority; in both Sichuan and Arizona, new and alternative religious movements found the space to grow and develop. Because frontiers are situated far from the centers of wealth and power, they offer an opportunity for religious and political dissenters to develop communities that offer alternatives to the dominant hegemonies. These southwestern regions of China and of the United States are both territories where settlers have formed new communities, developed new ideas about social organization, and created innovative networks of human and material resources to meet the difficult challenges of daily life. This paper compares two utopian communities: the Spiritual Christian Molokan Jumpers of early twentieth-century Arizona in the US and the Celestial Masters of late second century southwest China.

Many historians have argued that the peculiar features of frontiers have had a profound effect on religion. As Michael Khodarkovsky, a historian of Muscovy, has observed, a frontier—a "*region* that forms the margin of a settled or developed territory, a politico-geographical *area* lying beyond the integrated region of the political unit" (2002: 47)—must be distinguished from a border, which is "a clearly demarcated boundary between sovereign states" (2002: 47). Situated between two different ecologies, the liminal region of the frontier offers new opportunities and challenges to the peoples who contest it. Frederick Jackson Turner (1861-1932), who argued that the frontier had a democratizing effect on US history, has long dominated the study of the American frontier. Turner first advanced this thesis in his 1893 paper "The Significance of the Frontier in American History," which he published in four versions over the next three decades (Turner, 1938: 275-292). Extending Turner's argument into religious history, William Warren Sweet (1881-1958) suggested that free-church Protestants, including the Methodists and Baptists, helped to civilize, Protestantize, and Americanize the frontier, which in turn had a democratizing effect on American Protestantism (Sweet, 1964). More recently, Nathan Hatch, in his magisterial *Democratization of American Christianity*, also suggests that the frontier provided a space where radical egalitarians (such as the Methodist revivalist Lorenzo Dow) could challenge traditional notions of authority and leadership in ways that were not possible in Europe (Hatch, 1989). Likewise, Laurie Maffly-Kipp has both rejected and extended Sweet's arguments by suggesting that the classical Protestantism of the Eastern United States ultimately failed to take root in California—that Protestant values of hard work and community had little purchase in the western gold-rush. At the same time, however, Maffly-Kipp contends that the California frontier helped to forge a new and highly individualized form of religious life (Maffly-Kipp, 1994). These schools of thought emphasize the power of the frontier to shape religious experience and institutions.

Frontiers are liminal regions, where radically different cultural, social, and economic systems can come into contact and influence one another. For example, in the Southwestern United States, Native American farmers, such as the Hopi of north-eastern Arizona, dealt with a series of migrants, including the Athabascan-speaking Diné (or Navajo) who arrived in Arizona and New Mexico from the north roughly a millennium ago, and with Spanish settlers and missionaries, who came in the sixteenth century. These frontier societies engaged in a vigorous exchange of narratives, rituals, agricultural practices, and trade. The Diné adopted the farming practices of the Pueblo peoples that they met in northern Arizona as well as some of their cosmological narratives; the Diné emergence cosmogony is very similar to that of the Hopi. Likewise, the Hopi adopted Athabascan hunting technologies that the Diné introduced, including sinew-backed bows and arctic style microblades (Dykeman & Roebuck, 2008). Spanish explorers, such as the Franciscan father Marcos de Niza (1495-1598) who traveled to Arizona in 1539, also contributed to the interplay of languages, practices in the southwest. In the same way, the region now known as Sichuan Province was an ethnically diverse frontier region in the second century. The *Shu* culture that dominated the Sichuan region in the centuries before the unification of China under the Qin in the third century BC was probably not ethnically Han (Sage, 1992: 43; Farmer, 2007: 9-14). Later, Sichuan became one of the earliest sites of Chinese Chan (Zen or meditation) Buddhism (Adamek, 2006). In both the American and the Chinese Southwest, cultural diversity flourished.

Even into the early twentieth century, Arizona remained a frontier region where a variety of cultures came into contact. A booming mining industry attracted many Eastern European immigrants to the Southwest. Agriculture, promoted by irrigation projects such as the completion of the Roosevelt dam, also encouraged farmers to move to Arizona. In the late summer of that year, a group of 170 Russian immigrants arrived in Glendale, Arizona, to establish a Christian agrarian colony on the outskirts of the state capital, Phoenix. A persecuted movement of pacifist religious dissenters, the Spiritual Christian Jumpers (also known as the Molokans) had fled from Russia to Arizona by way of California to avoid military conscription. The Spiritual Christians had originally broken away from the Russian Orthodox Church in the 1760s when a group of state peasants in central Russia rejected the Orthodox sacraments, fasts, hierarchy, and rituals. Instead, they contended that the true church was made of ribs and flesh, not wood and stone; the true image of God was found in living people, not in icons; and the true sacraments were spiritual, not physical. Calling themselves "spiritual Christians," they were later tagged with the moniker "Molokan" because they drank milk [*moloko*] on fast days when dairy products were forbidden to Orthodox Christians. In the 1830s the Russian state began exiling these "most harmful" heretics to the Caucasian frontier, and it was from the Caucasus that the first Molokan settlers to the US arrived in California in 1904. Settling in Los Angeles and San Francisco, many Spiritual Christians longed to return to an agrarian life, and one such group decided to move to Arizona in 1911. They arrived with a strong eschatological hope, for one of their prophets, Maksim Gavrilovich Rudometkin (1832?-1877) had spoken in hauntingly beautiful images of the terrestrial kingdom that the faithful would inherit after struggling against the beast of false religion (Clay, 2011: 109-138; 2013: 221-243).



In many respects, the history of the Arizona Spiritual Christians echoes that of the early Daoist movement known as the Way of the Celestial Masters (*Tianshi Dao*) or, more pejoratively, as the "Five Pecks of Rice" (*Wǔ Dǒu Mǐ Dào*). This utopian community was formed by Zhang Lu on the southwestern frontier of China in the late second century. Zhang Lu's grandfather, Zhang Daoling, had moved from Jangsu Province on the eastern coast to the more remote and ethnically diverse Sichuan region. Attributing his doctrines to his grandfather, Zhang Lu, like the Spiritual Christians of Arizona, sought to create a virtuous communal society in which all would cooperate to care for the needy and advance the common good. Zhang's movement evolved into one of the most important forms of Daoism (Robinet, 1997: 53-77).

Both Zhang Lu's Daoists in the second century and the Spiritual Christians of Arizona represented alternative, textual communities that had settled far from the centers of power in order to construct their own utopias. Zhang Lu's community in what is today Sichuan Province, was centered on two important texts: the *Daodejing* (*The Way and Its Power*), attributed to the legendary sixth-century BC sage Laozi, and the *Xiang'er*, the community's authoritative commentary on Laozi's classic work. More than simply a scholarly exegesis of the *Daodejing*, the *Xiang'er* provided a radically new interpretation that sometimes went against the apparent sense of the original. Although the *Daodejing* was originally a handbook for rulers that questioned the efficacy of artificial rituals, the *Xiang'er* provided the new community on China's southwestern frontier with a panoply of rituals designed, in part, to strengthen social bonds. These included complicated rules for sexual hygiene, diet, and invocations of the emanations of the *Dao* (Bokenkamp, 1997: 1-148).

The Spiritual Christian Molokans, on the other hand, preserved the writings of the sacred prophets, especially those of Maksim Rudometkin, who provided an apocalyptic script for understanding their position in their new country on the eve of the First World War. Seeing their community as the Woman Clothed in the Sun of Revelation 12, the Spiritual Christians had fled into the wilderness to escape the pursuit of Satan, the seven-headed dragon. By establishing an agrarian commune in imitation of the early apostles who held all things in common, the Spiritual Christians in this way prepared themselves against the famines that the Antichrist would soon provoke. Like the Daoists, they maintained their own separate rituals that marked them as a unique community. Although Christian, they followed the Old Testament calendar of feasts, including Passover, Tabernacles, and Trumpets (Rosh Hashanah). The Molokans' strong pacifism and their direct connection to God through their prophets also distinguished their community as God's chosen bride, the Woman of the Apocalypse (Clay, 1928: 332-372).

Situated between two different ecologies, the liminal region of the southwestern frontiers in China and the US helped shape the "social imaginaries" of these two religious communities (Taylor, 2004). For both communities, the frontier provided a space for the development of their alternative visions of society. At the same time, neither of these utopian communities was able to escape entirely the power of the center. Zhang Lu's rebellion against the Han was crushed in 215, and the Spiritual Christian Molokans were compelled, despite their pacifist convictions and determined resistance, to register for the draft during the First World War (Moore, 1973: 281-302). Both communities survived these temporary defeats and adapted to their new conditions in ways that continued to enrich the frontiers where they had settled.

## Bibliography:



Adamek, Wendi Leigh. *The Mystique of Transmission: On an Early Chan History and Its Contexts*[M]. New York: Columbia University Press, 2006.

Bokenkamp, Stephen R. *Early Daoist Scriptures*[M]. Berkeley: University of California Press, 1997: 1-148.

Clay, J. Eugene. "Woman". *Bozhestvennye izrecheniia NASTAVNIKOV i STRADAL'TSEV za Slovo Bozhie, Veru Iisusa i Dukh Sviatoi Religii Dukhovnykh Khristian Molokan-Prygunov [The Divine Utterances of the Preceptors and Martyrs for the Word of God, the Faith of Jesus, and the Spirit of the Holy Religion of the Spiritual Christian Molokan-Jumpers]*. 2nd ed., rev. Los Angeles: Tipografiia I.G. Samarina s synom, 1928: 332-372.

Clay, J. Eugene. The Woman Clothed in the Sun: Pacifism and Apocalyptic Discourse among Russian Spiritual Christian Molokan-Jumpers[J]. *Church History*, 2011, 80(1):109-138; Russian Spiritual Christianity and the Closing of the Black-Earth Frontier: The First Heresy Trials of the Dukhobors in the 1760s[J]. *Russian History*, 2013(40): 221-243.

Dykeman, Douglas D., Paul Roebuck. Navajo Emergence in Dinétah: Social Imaginary and Archaeology[D]. Paper presented at the Society for American Archaeology, Vancouver, BC,

2008, available from http://drarchaeology.com/publications/navajoemergence.pdf.

Farmer, J. Michael. *The Talent of Shu: Qiao Zhou and the Intellectual World of Early Medieval Sichuan*[M]. Albany, N.Y.: State University of New York Press, 2007: 9-43.

Khodarkovsky, Michael. *Russia's Steppe Frontier: The Making of a Colonial Empire, 1500-1800*[M]. Bloomington, IN: Indiana University Press, 2002: 47.

Moore, William Haas. Prisoners in the Promised Land: The Molokans in World War I [J]. *Journal of Arizona History*, 1973, 14(4): 281-302.

Robinet, Isabelle. *Taoism: Growth of a Religion*[M]. trans., Phyllis Brooks. Palo Alto, CA: Stanford University Press, 1997: 53-77.

Sage, Steven F. *Ancient Sichuan and the Unification of China*[M]. Albany: State University of New York Press, 1992: 43.

Sweet, William Warren. *Religion on the American Frontier*[M]. New York: Cooper Square Publishers, 1964; Nathan Hatch, *The Democratization of American Christianity*[M]. New Haven: Yale University Press, 1989; Laurie F. Maffly-Kipp, *Religion and Society in Frontier California*[M]. New Haven: Yale University Press, 1994.

Taylor, Charles. *Modern Social Imaginaries*[M]. Durham: Duke University Press, 2004.

Turner, Fredrick Jackson. *The Frontier in American History*[M]. New York: Henry Holt, 1921; idem, *The Early Writings of Frederick Jackson Turner with a List of All His Works Compiled by Everett E. Edwards and an Introduction by Fulmer Mood*[M]. Madison, 1938: 275-292. For assessments of Turner, see Ray A. Billington, *Frederick Jackson Turner: Historian, Scholar, Teacher*[M].New York: 1973; Wilbur R. Jacobs (ed.), *The Historical World of Frederick Jackson Turner with Selections from His Correspondence*[M]. New Haven: 1968; Allan G. Bogue, Frederick Jackson Turner Reconsidered[J]. *The History Teacher*,1994, 27(2): 195-221.

# 中美西南边境的乌托邦社区

J. 尤金·克雷

（亚利桑那州立大学历史、哲学及宗教研究学院，美国坦佩 85287-5503）

**摘　要：**位于边疆的四川省与亚利桑那州长期以来都远离政治与经济中心。两个地区都产生了独特的团体、思想以及多元的文化。因为位于边疆，乌托邦与异端群体有机会偏离正统中心从而蓬勃发展。不论是在四川还是在亚利桑那州，不同的宗教运动都找到了发展的空间。本文对比了两个乌托邦群体：20世纪初美国亚利桑那州的莫罗康（Molokan）和2世纪后期中国西南地区的统治者。这两个时期的运动都建立了自己的体系，挑战着各自社会的正统思想。

**关键词：**四川省；亚利桑那州；乌托邦群体；对比

# Deep History of Food in the American Southwest: Points of Convergence for Comparison with Southwest China

Christine Szuter

(School of Historical, Philosophical, and Religious Studies, Arizona State University, Tempe, USA, 85287-5503)

**Abstract:** This exploratory essay makes large scale comparisons of food systems between the southwest regions of the United States and China based on syntheses of current research. The focus is on the deep history of food in both countries. Three topics are explored: water and irrigation; salt pilgrimages and production; and select foods of the Columbian Exchange, specifically tea, corn, and chile peppers.

The deep history of the American Southwest is shallow compared to the much deeper history of human occupation of Southwest China. Nonetheless, the food systems and landscapes of both regions were dramatically transformed by ancient irrigation systems. Today's world food systems are a direct result of what Alfred Crosby called the Columbian Exchange: the spread of animals, plants, insects, and diseases worldwide after Columbus "discovered" the Americas in 1492.

This first International Conference on Chinese and American Southwest Studies sets out to answer the question: How can connections be made between the southwest regions of China and the United States? This paper suggests answers to that question through the lens of food drawing examples from both countries. The examples from the United States include Hohokam irrigation canals, the Salt River Project, O'odham salt pilgrimages, corn domestication, and contemporary tea and salt companies. Examples from China are drawn from the Dujiangyan Irrigation System, Ba salt production, Pu'er tea, and the Sichuan pepper.

While the Columbian Exchange formed a global community of food, it also created problems in those food systems. Knowledge and understanding of food systems is a starting point for solving "wicked problems" associated with food security, food safety, food biodiversity, food globalization, food commodification, and food health. By returning to deep local traditions and histories of food, connections between both the Chinese and US southwests can be used to address current and future issues surrounding food.

**Key Words:** History of Food; American Southwest; Convergence; Southwest China

## 1. Introduction

The southwestern region of the United States and the southwestern region of China may at first glance appear to be unlikely areas of comparison. This first International Southwest Studies Conference is intended to explore what those connections might be and if those comparisons can be made. My presentation is no exception. It is exploratory in nature and makes large-scale comparisons on the topics of food exchange, food globalization, and food commodification. Each one of these topics is grand and unwieldy. In this essay, I do not reach definitive conclusions. I merely suggest ways of thinking about two diverse regions of the world through the lens of food. At its heart this essay remains the conference paper I presented at the First International Conference on Chinese and American Southwest Studies in 2013. It draws on synthetic works (Cordell & McBrinn, 2012; Fish & Fish, 2007; Sheridan, 2012) written by southwestern archaeologists and anthropologists and on Chinese works by scholars in these fields (Elvin, 2004; Falkenhausen & Shuicheng, 2008: 105-129; Falkenhausen, 2006: 61, 45-56; Hein, 2013; Lin, 2013; Yao, 2010: 18, 203-239). It draws its originality in making these comparisons with a focus on my own interests and research in southwest ancient food systems (Szuter, 1991; Szuter & Martin, 1999: 13, 36-45; Szuter & Bayham, 1989: 80-95).



The deep history of the American Southwest is shallow compared to the much deeper history of human occupation of Southwest China. Nonetheless, the food systems of both regions were dramatically transformed by what Alfred

Crosby (2003) called the Columbian Exchange: the spread of animals, plants, insects, and diseases worldwide after Columbus "discovered" the Americas in 1492. Charles Mann (2011) argues that this ecological revolution created the first wave of globalization and that China's landscape and agriculture were irrevocably altered by the introduction of corn and sweet potatoes, crops domesticated in the Americas.

The cuisines of both regions continue to change and evolve as influences from across each countries' borders influence the foods that ultimately define Southwestern cooking or Sichuan cooking. Through an examination of a very limited set of food systems of the American Southwest various questions will be posed as a way to approach a cross-cultural comparison with China. How did each regions' different deep histories impact the current food systems of each country? How did the diversity of cultures in these lands influence choices in food preferences? How did the Columbian Exchange of animals and plants fundamentally alter both societies? Finally, how are past food systems—gardening, farmers' markets, and local food production—able to be sustained or recreated today within a system dominated by worldwide agribusiness?

In this essay I propose several topics of discussion when examining the deep history of food in our respective regions: water and irrigation; salt pilgrimages and production; and select foods of the Columbian Exchange, specifically tea, corn, and chili peppers.

## 2. Southwest United States and Southwest China: How Do We Connect?

Chengdu in Sichuan Province is 11,938 kilometers (7,418 miles) from Phoenix, Arizona. Both cities are along similar latitudes: Phoenix at 33.45 degrees north latitude and Chengdu at 30.67 degrees north latitude. These numbers, however, are not necessarily informative of connections between these two areas.

Paul Hirt, professor of history at Arizona State University, in his 2005

PowerPoint presentation on "The US West and China's West: An Exploration of Similarities," pointed to comparisons of their respective geography: mountains, deserts, large rivers, and canyons. He also discussed the remoteness of these regions from political power, their ethnic diversity, lower population density, and water resources, including dams and irrigation. Many of these comparisons were echoed by the conference participants, including me, with my emphasis on water and irrigation and food resources.

The term "southwest studies," when used within a country, such as the United States or China, belies the fact that these regions are close to other international borders. If these regions are only examined with the current international borders in mind, then an understanding of the "deep history" is limited. The deep history of both of these regions actually took shape before current nation-states were formed. In the United States, scholars who work in the field of Southwest Studies will oftentimes make distinctions and clarifications, such as Southwest US/Northwest Mexico. For the Greater Southwest viewed from the United States perspective is the Greater Northwest when viewed from the Mexican perspective. The southwest region I discuss in this essay is focused on the southern southwest in the United States and parts of northwestern Mexico, and specifically on southern regions of the state of Arizona, where Arizona State University is located.



## 3. Physical Landscape and Climate of the Southwest United States

The physical landscape of the greater Southwest United States is one of vast differences—from mountain peaks, called "sky islands," that jut up from the desert floor to the broad valleys that stretch between them, called "basin and range" topography. As mentioned above, the term "southwest studies" when used within the United States actually crosses the current international border, so that the deep history of this area also encompasses northwest Mexico. The Sonoran Desert bisects this international border reaching from south-central

Arizona down through northwest Mexico. It is a hot, dry region where rainfall is only 20-30 centimeters (8-12 inches) per year and summer temperatures exceed 38 degrees Celsius (100 degrees Fahrenheit). Plant and wildlife species provide great biodiversity with most species adapted to this arid region.

## 4. Ancient History of the Southwest United States

The deep history of food in the American Southwest began with Pleistocene big-game hunters. They were hunters and gathers known for hunting megafauna, such as the mammoth, with Clovis fluted points. Incontrovertible evidence of human occupation of the American Southwest are recovered Clovis stone spear points embedded in the bones of a mammoth in southeastern Arizona dating to at least 10,000 years ago. Other archaeologists have argued for an earlier date for human occupation of the Americas, most recently with discoveries in Brazil (see Bower 2013 and Romero 2014 for news reports on these finds). These early hunters may have ultimately played a key role in the extinction of mammoths and other megafauna through overhunting, according to geoscientist Paul Martin (1967, 1984), while other scholars argue that climate change was a stronger factor in their extinction.



## 5. Southwest Archaeological Complexes

With the extinction of megafauna the native populations continued to hunt large and small game and gather plants, seeds, and nuts. Agriculture eventually became part of these early food systems when maize (corn) from Mesoamerica became part of the Southwest complex (Merrill et al., 2009) more than 4,000 years ago. Corn ultimately changed the desert southwest: irrigation canals were built, people became more sedentary, and population size increased.

Archaeologists have divided the Greater Southwest US into three main archaeological complexes: Hohokam, which is the focus of this paper, Mogollon, and Ancestral Pueblo, with many other smaller complexes dotting the land

(Cordell & McBrinn, 2012). The Hohokam people lived primarily in what is now south-central Arizona from 300 to 1450 CE (Fish & Fish, 2007). They traveled and extended their range into northwest Mexico, particularly through their salt pilgrimages and trade networks for shell and obsidian (Darling & Lewis, 2007: 13-140; Mitchell & Foster, 2011: 176-184).

The remains of Hohokam architecture include Great Houses, such as the mud adobe one south of the Phoenix area called Casa Grande (big house), subterranean pit houses, large storage pits for food, compounds, and earthen platform mounds. They made ceramic containers and figurines with a distinctive red-on-buff design, along with utilitarian wares that held and stored their foodstuffs. They walked from central-south Arizona to the Gulf of California where they found Glycymeris shell that they carved into animal shapes and or inlaid with turquoise. They ground corn and also possibly small rodents with manos and metates. Bone awls were used as hairpins or to work animal hides. The Hohokam used stone digging implements to build large oval shaped ballcourts where they played a game that might have been quite similar to the games played on ballcourts in Mesoamerica.



The Hohokam are known as the "Desert Farmers" because they harnessed water to grow corn, beans, and squash (Haury, 1976). These crops are affectionately called the "three sisters" because of their intertwined nature of growing with squash vines climbing up the corn stalks and bean plants growing below. Although they were desert farmers, the Hohokam never gave up their hunting and gathering ways. They hunted mule deer (*Odocoileus hemionus*) and big horn sheep (*Ovis canadensis*) in the mountains; small game in and near their agricultural fields, including jackrabbits (*Lepus californicus*), cottontails (*Sylvilagus audubonii*), and even small rodents (Szuter, 1991; Szuter & Bayham, 1989: 89-95; Szuter & Martin, 1999: 36-45). They gathered the seeds and fruit of the desert. Pods from the mesquite tree were collected, dried, and ground into a flour. The stately tall saguaro, an iconic plant of the Sonoran Desert, provided a luscious red fruit that was harvested using long poles made from the ribs of the saguaro cactus itself. This lush landscape provided great food biodiversity, food security, and food health that allowed the Hohokam to thrive in the Sonoran Desert for over one thousand years.

## 6. Comparison and Contrast: SW China and SW United States

How can this world form the basis for comparisons between SW China and the SW US? I suggest three main topics of comparison with a focus on water and irrigation, salt procurement and production, and foods of the Columbian Exchange, specifically tea, corn, and chiles. Water and irrigation are core for agriculture and energy in the Southwest US and in Southwest China from the ancient pasts to the modern urban areas of both countries. Salt provides a critical nutrient for human life. Salt pilgrimages in the prehispanic Southwest US and salt production in Southwest China were ways indigenous peoples from both areas fulfilled this need. The Columbian Exchange, where Christopher Columbus' exploits connected two worlds, led to globalization with various foods being part of that exchange. The crops of tea, corn, and chiles each tell a unique story, but one that weave themes of global food commodification with local food traditions.

## 7. Ancient Hohokam Irrigation Canals and Contemporary Salt River Project, Phoenix, Arizona

The Hohokam Indians built an extensive system of 14 irrigation networks allowing them to irrigate over 400 square miles of land (Doyel, 2007:83; Fish & Fish, 2007). These ancient canals were dug by hand using stone implements to remove tons of dirt without the use of metal tools or domesticated draft animals.

Although abandoned around 1450 CE, the Hohokam's irrigation systems were still visible (and some were used) when Omar Turney, a City of Phoenix, Arizona, engineer, mapped them in the 1920s. He proclaimed that this irrigation system represented "The largest single body of land irrigated in prehistoric times in North or South America and perhaps the world" (quotation on the map). The map of this system covers an area approximately 33 miles by 18 miles.

These ancient canals form a loose template for the Salt River Project, modern metropolitan Phoenix's system of nine canals that snake through the valley creating power and electricity for many. These canals provide a stark contrast to the surrounding desert environment. Water is one of the limiting factors to living today in the Greater Southwest United States, but this extensive SRP canal system allows for an urban oasis in the Sonoran desert.

## 8. Dujiangyan Irrigation System, Chengdu, China

Dujiangyan Irrigation system, a no-dam irrigation system and a World Heritage Site, was built in 256 BC along the Minjiang River outside of Chengdu. This irrigation system solved the problem of massive flooding when Li Bing created a system that divided the river by splitting it into two parts: one to control flooding and the other for irrigation. Over 668,700 hectares of farmland are irrigated thus allowing for greater agricultural production (http://whc.unesco.org/en/list/1001). I visited this site in November of 2013 and observed workers today carrying baskets of large boulders and stones that were then placed in bamboo cages hanging from wooden tripods. Large bulldozers in the shallow river bed were digging out the river bottom. This past irrigation system was built without dams and current maintenance is continued with human labor and mechanical force.



All of this landscaping of the natural environment created systems of controlled water flow allowing for extensive agricultural production in both Southwest China and in the Southwest United States.

## 9. Salt Pilgrimages and Salt Production

Salt was procured through songs, trails, trade, and labor by indigenous peoples in the SW of China and the SW US. The contemporary Tohono and

Akimel O'odham people live where the earlier Hohokam Indians did in south-central Arizona. Their landscape is one of songscapes—songs they sing about the landscape that in their earliest history provided pathways to natural resources. They walked nearly 300 miles from the Phoenix area south to Mexico and the Gulf of California to gather salt that formed flats along the gulf edges (Darling & Lewis, 2007: 13-140; Chabot & Bostwick, 2012; Mitchell & Foster, 2011: 176-184).

Today these traditions, such as the salt pilgrimages, are marketed and commodified to sell salt. The sea salt is collected from traditional lands in traditional ways and sold in traditional packaging, so that all consumers can be part of this authentic system of food production. Authenticity is assured even when these products are bought online from the comforts of one's home. Salt, a necessary nutrient, has become commercialized beyond Morton Salt (a common brand in the US) to become a boutique product produced in a traditional way. In Mexico, a company called *Sal de Mar* (Salt of the Sea) collects salt from the same region in the Gulf of California that the Hohokam and Tohono O'odham traveled to centuries ago (for a photograph of the region see http://sdmsaltsense.files.wordpress.com/2012/05/dsc02165.jpg).

Claudia Franklin Karafotas blogs about her company, "This is a photo I took a while back at the salt ponds where Sal del Mar is harvested. The coastline is pristine and characterized by 300 estuaries and other wetlands that are key components to the rich community of plant and animal life comprising a unique ecosystem... Archaeologists are able to use the songs to navigate as the Hohokam once did; along those same trails, which because of the desert landscape are still visible today" (http://sdmsaltsense.wordpress.com/tag/gulf-of-california/). This selling of salt is marketed with specific values observed in other markets: local production, locally made embroidered bags to hold the salt, and the authentic product based on ancestral traditions.

## 10. Ba Salt Production

Archaeologists excavating in Zhongba (Falkenhausen, 2006: 45-56; Falkenhausen & Li Shuicheng, 2008: 105-129; Rowan et al., forthcoming) found evidence of salt production from approximately 2000 BC to 200 BC. Small ceramic vessels were used for brining and the recovered salt was traded from the Ba region of the Upper Yangzi River basin to the Shu kingdom on the Chengdu plain. Scholars argue that this trade network provided economic interdependence and strong, enduring ties between these two regions. "Salt production and salt trade played a tremendously important role in the political, social, and economic history of all major culture areas" (Falkenhausen & Li Shuicheng, 2008: 107). This statement is applicable to both China and the Greater Southwest of the United States.

## 11. Columbian Exchange Corn, Tea, and Chiles



Alfred Crosby (2003) coined the phrase "The Columbian Exchange" in his 30-year old book of the same name. When Christopher Columbus landed in North America in 1492 he launched the first wave of globalization. The exchange of new foods spread from the New World to the Old World and from the Old World to the New. Corn, tea, and chiles were only some of these foods.

Corn, originating from the teosinte plant in Mesoamerica, made its way to the SW US and became a critical grain for the development and growth of the prehistoric Hohokam, as well as other peoples of the southwest (Cordell & McBrinn, 2012; Fish & Fish, 2007; Merrill et al., 2009, 2010; Piperno et al., 2014; Smithsonian Tropical Research Center press release, 2014). The corn was not the large yellow kernel corn we know today. It was small—only a few inches in length—and multicolored. Corn kernels were ground with manos and metates using traditional indigenous methods of preparation with manos and metates. Corn (as well as sweet potato) in China led to population growth, according to Charles Mann (2011), because it could be planted in somewhat marginal areas.

Thus, corn is an example of a food that originated in the Americas and made it way around the world changing food systems on a global level.

### 11.1 Pu'er Tea

Tea, originating in China, led to the creation of trade networks and large markets in Europe and then spread throughout the world from there. Zhang Jinghong (2013), lecturer at Yunnan University, writes about Pu'er tea from ancient caravan to urban chic. She traces tea from Imperial China and its status as a prized commodity to today's world of urban connoisseurs treating tea in the same way as those who appreciate good wine.

The commodification of Pu'er tea by various companies, such as Teavana (http://www.teavana.com), found in many shopping malls in the United States, relies on making the connection to ancient legends, Chinese princesses, and emperors from 641 AD. Selling tea today requires a story, a story about the origin of tea. Seven Cup Tea Company (http://www.sevencups.com) located in Tucson, Arizona, also sells Pu'er tea (and other Chinese teas) by promoting Chinese tea culture, direct sourcing of their teas, and building relationships with Chinese tea masters to supply real tea to their customers. They offer tea tours of China as a way to link the Tucson tea drinker with the ultimate source of their drinking pleasure. In this way, the commodification of foods from the Columbian Exchange continues to make connections back to the original source.

### 11.2 Chiles: Sichuan Pepper

Chiles originated in North America and have been a central component of Southwest US cuisine. But the chile is also closely identified with Sichuan cuisine. "Sichuan pepper (*hua jiao*) was used in Chinese cuisine well before black or white pepper was introduced by way of the spice route" (http://www.seriouseats.com/2011/02/sichuan-peppercorns-spice-roundup.html).

The Sichuan pepper's amazing flavor numbs the mouth and provides a sensation that is unique to this chile. According to Gary Paul Nabhan (2014), the Sichuan pepper can now be imported into the US. An exchange that began with the original chiles moving from the Southwest to China is now reciprocated by the cultivation of Sichuan peppers in China returning to the Americas. If this introduction is similar to past food introductions, the expectation is that the Sichuan pepper will become part of the Southwest greater cuisine—and not only in Chinese food.

## 12. Connections: The Wicked Problems to Solve

So returning to original question of this essay: How do we connect these two regions, the southwest of each of our respective countries? How do we bridge the nearly 12,000 kilometers that separate us? Over 500 years ago the Columbian Exchange connected these regions through the exchange of food. Before that time both southwests had their own water and irrigation systems that allowed for large scale food production. Both regions developed ways to obtain and produce salt, a basic and universally needed human nutrient.

While the Columbian Exchange, specifically the food exchange, formed a global community of food, it also created problems in those food systems. Today the global community grapples with the "wicked problems" (Rittel & Webber, 1973: 155-169) of food security, food safety, food biodiversity, food globalization, food commodification, and food health. Problems worth solving, but ones that are complex in nature, and therefore, complex to solve (www.wickedproblems.com). Knowledge and understanding of our food systems is a starting point for solving these problems. By returning to our respective deep local traditions and histories, we can provide the connections needed to address current and future issues surrounding food.

## Bibliography:


Austin Center for Design. Wicked Problems: Problems Worth Solving[EB/OL]. 2014. Accessed April 1, 2014 (https://www.wickedproblems.com/read.php).

Chabot, Nancy Jo, Todd Bostwick. The Verde Salt Mine Revisited: Sinagua Salt Mining and Ritual Burials[D]. Paper presented at the Arizona Archaeological Council and Verde Valley Archaeology. Center Verde Biennial Verde Valley Archaeology Conference. October, 2012.

Collins, Lauren. Fire-Eaters: The Search for the Hottest Chili[J]. The New Yorker, 2013. http://www.newyorker.com/reporting/2013/11/04/131104fa_fact_collins.

Cordell, Linda S., Maxine E. McBrinn. Walnut Creek, California: Left Coast Press, Inc., 2012.

Crosby, Alfred W. Jr. *The Columbian Exchange: Biological and Cultural Consequences of 1492* (30th Anniversary Edition)[M]. Westport, Connecticut: Praeger, 2003.

Crown, Patricia L. *Women & Men in the Prehispanic Southwest*[M]. Santa Fe: School of American Research Press, 2003.

Darling, J. Andrew, Barnaby V. Lewis. Songscapes and Calendar Sticks[M]// Suzanne K. Fish and Paul R. Fish. *The Hohokam Millennium*. Santa Fe: School for Advanced Research Press, 2007: 13-140.

Doyel, David E. Irrigation, Production, and Power in the Phoenix Basin Hohokam Society[M]// Suzanne K. Fish and Paul R. Fish. *The Hohokam Millennium*. Santa Fe: School for Advanced Research Press, 2007: 82-89.

Eleven Sichuan Peppercorn Recipes. 2011. Retrieved February 18, 2011(http://www.seriouseats.com/2011/02/sichuan-peppercorns-spice-roundup.html).

Elvin, Mark. *The Retreat of the Elephants: An Environmental History of China*. New Haven: Yale University Press, 2004.

Falkenhausen, Lothar von, Li Shuicheng. Salt Archaeology in the Upper Yangzi Basin: Some Preliminary Considerations[M]// *New Frontiers in Global Archaeology: Defining China's Ancient Traditions*. International Sackler Symposium, 2008: 105-129.

Falkenhausen, Lothar von. The Salt of Ba: Reflections on the Role of the "Peripheries" in the Production System of Bronze Age China[J]. *Arts Asiatiques*, 2006, 61: 45-56.

Fish, Suzanne, Paul Fish. *The Hohokam Millennium*[M]. Santa Fe: School for Advanced Research Press, 2007.

Flad, Rowan K., Wu Xiaohong, Lothar von Falkenhausen, Li Shuicheng, Sun Zhibin, and Pochan Chen. Forthcoming. Radiocarbon Dates and Technological Change in Salt Production at the

Site of Zhongba in the Three Gorges, China[J]. *Asian Perspectives*, 48(1):148-180. http://dash.harvard.edu/bitstream/handle/1/2920214/Flad_RadiocarbonDates.pdf?sequence=2.

Goldfield, Hannah. The Airborne Sriracha Event[J]. *The New Yorker.* 2013. Retrieved November 1, 2013(http://www.newyorker.com/online/blogs/currency/2013/11/the-sriracha-lawsuit-and-the-rise-of-the-chili-pepper.html).

Haury, Emil. *The Hohokam, Desert Farmers, and Craftsmen: Excavations at Snaketown, 1964–1965*[M]. Tucson: The University of Arizona Press, 1976.

Hein, Anke Marion. Cultural Geography and Interregional Contacts: Prehistoric Liangshan (Southwest China)[D]. University of California, Los Angeles, 2013.

Hill, Jane H. New Evidence for a Mesoamerican Homeland for Proto-Uto-Aztecan[M]// *Proceedings of the National Academy of Sciences USA*, 2013, 107: E3. Retrieved March 16, 2010.

Lin, Kuei-chen. Pottery Production and Social Complexity of the Bronze Age Cultures on the Chengdu Plain, Sichuan, China[D]. University of California, Los Angeles, 2013.

Mann, Charles C. *1493: Uncovering the New World Columbus Created*[M]. New York: Vintage Books, Random House, Inc., 2011.

Martin, Paul S. 1967. Prehistoric Overkill[M]// Paul S. Martin and H.E. Wright, Jr. *Pleistocene Extinctions: The Search for a Cause*. New Haven: Yale University Press, 1967: 75-120.



Martin, Paul S. Prehistoric Overkill: The Global Model[M]// Paul S. Martin and Richard G. Klein. *Quaternary Extinctions: A Prehistoric Revolution*. Tucson: University of Arizona Press, 1984: 354-403.

Merrill, William. L., Robert J. Hard, Jonathan B. Mabry, Gayle J. Fritz, Karen R. Adams, John R. Roney, and A. C. MacWilliams. The Diffusion of Maize to the Southwestern United States and Its Impact[M]//*Proceedings of the National Academy of Sciences USA*. 2009, 106 (50): 21019-21026.

Merrill, William L., et al. Reply to Hill and Brown: Maize and Uto-Aztecan Cultural History[M]// *Proceedings of the National Academy of Sciences USA*. 2010, 107(11): E35-E36. Retrieved March 16, 2010.

Mitchell, Douglas R., Michael Foster. Salt, Seashells, and Shiny Stones: Prehistoric Hohokam Resource Exploitation in the Papagueria and Northern Gulf of California[J]. *Journal of Arizona Archaeology*, 2011, 1(2):176-184.

Mount Qingcheng and the Dujiangyan Irrigation System. World Heritage Site, UNESCO. http://whc.unesco.org/en/list/1001.

Nabhan, Gary Paul. *Gathering the Desert*[M]. Tucson: The University of Arizona Press, 1985.

Nabhan, Gary Paul. *Cumin, Camels, and Caravans: A Spice Odyssey*[M]. Berkeley, California: University of California Press, 2014.

Newman, Jacqueline M. *Food Culture in China*[M]. Westport, Connecticut: Greenwood Press, 2004.

Piperno, D. R., Irene Hoist, Klaus Winter, and Woen McMillan. Teosinte before Domestication: Experimental Study of Growth and Phenotypic Variability in Late Pleistocene and Early Holocene Environments[J]. *Quaternary International*, 2014. http://dx.doi.org/10.1016/j.quaint.2013.12.049.

Rittel, Horst W. J., Melvin M. Webber. Dilemmas in a General Theory of Planning[J]. *Policy Sciences*, 1973, 4:155-169.

Sal de Mar (Salt of the Sea). http://www.saldelmar.com.

Sheridan, Thomas. *Arizona: A History* (revised edition)[M]. Tucson: The University of Arizona Press, 2012.

Smithsonian Tropical Research Center. Greenhouse "Time Machine" Sheds Light on Corn Domestication[EB/OL]. 2014. Press Release. February 1, 2014. http://www.eurekalert.org/pub_releases/2014-02/stri-gm020114.php.

SRP Canal History. http://www.srpnet.com/water/canals/history.aspx.

Szuter, Christine R. *Hunting by Prehistoric Horticulturalists*[M]. New York: Garland, 1991.

Szuter, Christine R., Frank E. Bayham. Sedentism and Prehistoric Animal Procurement Among Desert Horticulturalists of the North American Southwest[M]// S. Kent. *Farmers as Hunters: The Implications of Sedentism*. Cambridge: Cambridge University Press, 1989: 80-95.

Szuter, Christine R., Paul S. Martin. War Zones and Game Sinks in Lewis and Clark's West[J]. *Conservation Biology*, 1999, 13:36-45.

Yao, Alice. Recent Developments in the Archaeology of Southwestern China[J]. *Journal of Archaeological Research*, 2010, 18:203-239.

Zhang, Jinghong. *Pu'er Tea: Ancient Caravans and Urban Chic*[M]. Seattle: University of Washington Press, 2014.

# 美国西南部食物深度史：与中国西南部对比的趋同点

克里斯廷·祖特

（亚利桑那州立大学历史、哲学及宗教研究学院，美国坦佩 85287-5503）

**摘　要**：这一探索性文章主要是在现有研究的合成基础上，就美国和中国西南地区间的粮食系统做出了大规模对比。重点在于这两个国家深远的食物历史。本文针对三个主题进行了探讨：水和灌溉，盐的生产和发展，哥伦比亚交换中的食物选择，特别是茶叶、玉米和花椒。与中国西南地区人类居住的悠远历史相比，美国西南部的历史则显得不太长。然而，这两个地区的粮食系统和景观都因为古老的灌溉系统产生了明显改变。今天的世界粮食系统是由阿尔弗雷德·克罗斯主张的哥伦比亚交换所产生的直接结果：1492年哥伦布“发现”美洲之后，动物、植物、昆虫和疾病在全世界范围内进行传播。

第一次中美西南研究国际会议提出了这一问题：如何在中美西南地区间做出联系？本文将以两个国家的食品为例来给出答案。美国的例子包括霍霍卡姆灌溉运河、盐河项目、欧欧德汉姆盐发展、玉米驯化、现代茶和盐公司。中国的例子包括都江堰灌溉系统、巴盐的生产、普洱茶和四川花椒。

哥伦比亚交换形成了全球性社区，但也在这些食品系统中产生了问题。食品系统相关知识和理解是解决“恶劣问题”的一个起点。这一问题涉及食品保障、食品安全、食品生物多样性、食品全球化、食品商品化和食品卫生。基于食品的当地传统和历史，中国和美国西南地区的联系可以用于解决食品当前和未来的问题。

**关键词**：食物史；美国西南部；趋同；中国西南部

# The Role of High Tech/Industrial Park in Leading Local Development: Tales in Chengdu and Phoenix

Lan G. Zhiyong

(School of Public Affairs, Arizona State University, Tempe, USA, 85287-5503)

**Abstract:** Chengdu is a large city in China's west. In the past thirty years, especially after the 1990s, it built a number of industrial and high tech parks to boost its local economic development. These parks have been proven to be pivotal forces leading change. Phoenix is a large metro area in America's west. It has been a fast growing city since the 1990s, driven by property development and high tech development efforts. Starting from the beginning of the new century, together with ASU president's initiative in building collaborative university-industry-government relationship, a series of efforts have been made in promoting technology driven research/industrial parks to lead local development. What are their developmental tracks? What are their experiences and lessons? What do these stories tell us? What can be learned from one another? This paper is an effort answering these questions in the hope to identify patterns, motifs, and environment for change and innovation.

**Key Words:** Chengdu; Industrial and High Tech Parks; Phoenix; Innovation

## 1. Introduction: the Background of Science and Technology Park Efforts in Chengdu and Phoenix

Chengdu and Metropolitan Phoenix are two large metro areas in the US and China's west respectively, with Chengdu city proper and the city of Phoenix as their urban centers. Chengdu is one city but has multiple counties including its rural areas under its jurisdiction. Phoenix is the fifth largest city in the United States with many satellite cities such as Tempe, Chandler, Scottsdale, Glendale, Gilbert surrounding it. While China's geographical longitudes and latitudes are very similar to that of the United States, albeit on the opposite side of the globe, the geographical locations of the "westness" of these two cities are not quite the same, with Chengdu more in the heartland of China as Kansas was in the United States. However, they are both considered western by their countrymen because of their remote locations from national political and economic centers. They share a number of similarities. They both are large urban centers in relatively less developed regions of their nation; they both have more laid back inland culture compared with their counterparts in other regions of their country; they both have nationally reputable universities, more or less because of their hard to penetrate geographical locations; and they both are actually not as backward as most people would normally think. When China opened up to the world in its reform initiative and was looking for a sister city in the United States, the city of Phoenix responded by reciprocally choosing Chengdu as its international partner. When Arizona State University president was visiting China and looking for an academic partner, China's academic leader un-hesitantly hand-picked Sichuan University in Chengdu for it. These two large and reputable universities hence started to work together to explore their meaningful relationships. What is most interesting is in today's globalized high tech world, both cities are seeking to develop themselves through high technology growth and innovation, with partnerships among their regional institutions of higher learning, local governments, and businesses. High Tech Parks are their platforms.



As we know, high tech park is a phenomenon started in as early as the late 1950s. It was an attempt to use cheap land for real estate development to attract the concentration of R & D labs, Industries, technologies, and human resources for innovative or productive activities (Massey & Wield, 2004; Castells & Hall, 2009; Wang & Cheng, 2013). They quickly build up new research or industrial constellations, and help with the transformation of industrial structures. It should be noted that many places build separate industrial parks from R & D focused parks. The high Tech Parks boomed as an innovative way to boost economic development after the 1990s. The famous high tech parks in the United States include Triangle Park in North Carolina, Sillicon Valley in Palo Alto, California, biosquare in Boston, Massachusetts.

Silicon Valley (USA) was a pioneer in the development of science parks in the world. Originally known as Stanford University Science Park, Silicon Valley dates back to the early 1950s. It was followed by Triangle Park in North Carolina domestically, and Sophia Antipolis (France) in Europe in the 1960s and Tsukuba Science City (Japan) in Asia in the early 1970s. This trio represents the oldest and the most well-known science parks in the world. Other famous high tech parks in the world include Cambridge Science Park in UK, Heidelberg Technology Park in Germany, Tsukuba Science City in Japan, Daedeok Innopolis in South Korea, Kent Ridge in Singapore, and Software Technology Parks of India, Bangalore.

The Triangle Research Park in North Carolina tells of a very telling story. Created in 1959 by state and local governments, nearby universities, and local business interests, it turned a backward and one of the poorest state in America in the 1950s into an internationally reputable technoples. It is by now one of the most prominent high-tech research and development centers in the United States. Karl Robbins bought the land where the park is now built. The park covers 7,000 acres (2,833 hectares) in a pine forest with 22,500,000 square feet (2,090,318 $m^2$) of built space. It is managed by the Research Triangle Foundation, a private non-profit organization, hosting over 170 companies employing 42,000 workers and 10,000 contractors, including the second largest IBM operation (14,000) in the world. Other famous companies include Glaxo Smith Kline, Cisco Systems, etc. The park is an unincorporated area, and state law prohibits municipalities from annexing areas within the park. As of October 2012, both zoning areas are in the process of being revised to allow higher density development.

China started its effort to build research parks after it initiated its massive economic reform. Zhongguancun in Beijing is by far the earliest science park in China. As its initiation, Li Lanqing, the Premiere at the time, clearly stated that the most important thing for Zhongguancun Science Park is not to attract high tech businesses, but to explore new systems of management. Other well-known ones include Zhangjiang Technology Park in Shanghai, Binghai New District in Tianjin, Suzhou Industrial Park in Suzhou. In fact, due to the Torch project sponsored by China's National Government, China is literally building science and technology parks in all its major cities. In a short few decades, these high tech parks are turning into the centers for innovation and industrial productivity, and contribute significantly to national economic development. By 2012, 88 major science parks in China produces 5.22 trillion RMB, 10.1% of the Chinese GDP (July 26, 2012, Ministry of Science and Technology, *Qinhuangdao News*, July 26, 2014).

Today, there are over 400 science parks worldwide and the number is still growing. At the top of the list is the USA, which is reported to have more than 150 science parks. Japan comes next with 111 science parks. China began developing science parks in the mid-1980s and now has around 100, 52 of which were approved by the national government and the remainder by state and local governments.



Against this large international and domestic background, both Phoenix and Chengdu metro worked hard to ride the tide and made their own efforts in creating innovation and productivity through the high tech park strategies. This paper provides a snapshot of the efforts made in each city and comparatively studies the viability and impact of these efforts. Hopefully, it can enlighten our perception on what lessons each can be learned from the other.

## 2. Efforts Made in Phoenix Metro

Phoenix is the largest central city in its metro area and the seat for both the state and the county governments. For a long time, Phoenix has been an exotic tourist city for transient populations, although it had some history in mining and gold rush. The growth of its large state university in the area—Arizona State University, is perhaps the major reason for its eyeing of high technology.

Its adjacent geographical location close to California helps attracting high tech business spinoffs into the valley, especially after the Los Angeles Earthquake in the 1980s. The cheap land, dry and warm weather, and fresh air made it the love of electronics manufacturers such as Intel, Microchips, and Motorola. Airplane industries such as Honeywell, Michael Douglas also found their homes in the metro area. With a population of over 3 million in the metro area, Phoenix experienced dynamic growth since the 1990s.

In as early as the 1980s, ASU started to think of a science and research park (Innovation.asu.edu). In fact, in 1956, Arizona State College Foundation (Now ASU Foundation) acquired the 320-acre Jones farm and utilized it as experimental farm. In 1979, the University disbanded its agricultural program and began to formulate a plan for re-use of the farm. The actual formation of the Research Park took several years, and required collaboration by a number of governmental agencies. In April, 1983, the State enacted a legislation authorizing the use of improvement bonds for infrastructure, and prescribed the formation of the park authority. In July of 1983, the Arizona Board of Regents authorized ASU to form a not-for-profit research park corporation. In May, 1984, under the leadership of ASU President J. Russell Nelson and Dean Roland Haden of the College of Engineering, the experimental farm became the ASU Research Park. Municipal improvement bonds were issued by the City of Tempe to construct the Park's infrastructure, with repayment generated from long-term ground leases of park land. The infrastructure improvements included streets, utilities, landscaping and lake system that users of the Park enjoy today. The official groundbreaking occurred in December of 1984, and the first ground lease was executed with Transamerica in April of 1985. Currently the Park has ground leases in place with 18 different lessees in 20 buildings totaling 1.8 million square feet. The Park is currently home to 48 companies employing over 4,000 people. This trajectory shows that science has not been a big thing for Arizona's past. It took 25 years for something to happen. The Park, just like the valley, laid low and dormant for quite a number of years.

The change of the ASU president in 2002 made ASU a different place, so are its science and technology park concept. The New President called for the building of a New American University on his 8 design aspirations: (1) Leverage the Place, embracing the local cultural, socioeconomic and physical setting; (2) Transform Society, catalyzing social change by being connected to social needs; (3) Value Entrepreneurship, using its knowledge and encouraging innovation; (4) Conduct Use-Inspired Research, having a purpose for research and striving for impact; (5) Enable Student Success, committed to the success of each unique student; (6) Fuse Intellectual Disciplines, creating knowledge by transcending academic disciplines; (7) Be Socially Embedded, connecting with communities through mutually beneficial partnerships; (8) Engage Globally, engaging with people and issues locally, nationally and internationally (www.asu.edu).

Driven by these aspirations, ASU took the initiative to engage the local community. Among many of its efforts, one is to work with the city of Phoenix to expand the University's downtown Center. It acquired the development privilege from the city of Phoenix to develop its run-down downtown center. It is a 4 billion in kind partner contribution from the city of Phoenix. ASU started by refurbishing a building donated by a local business to host its School of Public Affairs, and gradually built new buildings to host the Chronkite School of Journalism and Communication, and the School of Nursing together with the building of student dormitories. Businesses and light rail construction completion followed in suite. High tech companies such as Mayo clinic moved in, ready to collaborate with ASU researchers to build medical research facilities. In a short couple of years, a transportation link is built in between ASU's major Tempe Campus and its Phoenix down center, where the Phoenix government locates. The 20,000 some students and faculty plus the business services came with them revitalized the downtown community, and turned what used to be rundown donut center into an active, lively, and energetic center for education, research, and entertainment. The university expanded its student enrollment, the social sciences faculty found it easier to engage the Phoenix government for research, and many local government officials could receive continuing education because of the adjacency of the quality education facilities. It is a win-

win situation through collaboration between the university, the government, and the businesses. Interestingly, the university leadership is the main driver for all these.

Another major undertaking is ASU's SkySong, a 42 acre mixed use development. It is a partnership between Scottsdale, Arizona State University Foundation, the Plaza Cos. and USAA Realty Co. It is located in between Tempe and Scottsdale, a rundown area characterized by low income residents, junk yards, garages, storages, and red-light businesses. A one-time prosperous mall was deteriorating because of the Scottsdale's northbound growth and Phoenix's southbound growth. ASU engaged the Scottsdale city leaders and initiated a project to turn into this area into a high tech park—SkySong, meaning only Sky is the limit to imagination. The mission of the SkySong is to:

1. Create an ecology of collaboration and innovation among high-profile technology enterprises and related researchers;

2. Advance global business objectives of on-site enterprises;

3. Raise Arizona's profile as a global center of innovation through co-location of ASU's strategic global partners; and

4. Create a unique regional economic and social asset (www.asu.edu).

It is meant to be a unique high tech center attracting knowledge workers and corporations from around the world, creating a working community integrating academia with commerce, and developing an interactive relationship among mentor, supplier, and start-up technology companies and professional support. Resident businesses' easy access to ASU's engineering and human capital resources is a unique hallmark of this high center. It is a place where the architecture, lifestyle and amenities in and around the center stimulate and encourage creativity and new ideas. Where ideas and university research become new technologies and commercial enterprises. A place where imagination shapes reality and networks between university innovations, regional progress and global technology industry built strength and productivity.

According to a study by the Greater Phoenix Economic Council, SkySong has pumped $113 million into the state's economy since it opened in 2009.

The venture has pulled in companies from startups to established firms such as Ticketmaster, despite a challenging economy. It has pulled in 733 direct jobs from the grouping of companies at the south Scottsdale location (www.gpec.org/node/1085).

The study also found that Scottsdale and the Valley benefited from the construction and opening of SkySong with a total of 1,118 direct and indirect jobs to go along with 620 direct and indirect jobs from the construction of the two-building complex.

It is projected that over the next 30 years, with 1.2 million square feet of space, SkySong will have a $9.2 billion regional impact, with $8 billion of that centered on Scottsdale. A finished facility will account for 5,361 direct and indirect jobs (ibid.). Even SkySong has existed for less than a decade; it has already made a national reputation to be an innovation center leading change.

## 3. What Has Happened in Chengdu?



Chengdu is the capital city of Sichuan Province, and its political, economic, cultural and educational center. It is at the same time its center for science and technology, commerce, finance, transportation, and communication. Contradictory to conventional thinking that it is a very laid back city, it has been rated as China's Most Economically Dynamic City, China's Best City for Commerce, Best Tourist City, Environmental Protection Model City respectively. A 2007 World Bank Report rated Chengdu as China's Best City for Investment.

Chengdu also has science and technology parks. The most prominent is the Chengdu Hi-Tech Zone (CDHT), first established in 1988. It ranks 4th among all China's national-level hi-tech zones and is strongly supported by national provincial and municipal authorities. With an area of 130 km², CDHT comprises of the south park and the west park. There are 33,237 companies registered in the CDHT, among which 1,115 are foreign invested enterprises including 87 Fortune 500 companies.

In recent years, Chengdu has been working diligently to promote international standard service for its businesses and investors. It established many one-stop service stations to serve the businesses and help them quickly getting through the complicated labyrinths of China's administrative approval systems.

Built in 1988, CDHT was approved in 1991 by China's State Council as the one of the first groups of National High Technology R & D Zone. In 2000, it was approved as China's APEC Science Park, passed ISO14001 accreditation in 2011, and was recognized by the British Royal UKAS. After 20 years' development, in 2011, it became the home of 420 startup companies, attracting over 1,000 talents into it (500 overseas PhDs). In 2012, it realized 87 billion yuan GDP, surpassing 10% of Chengdu's GDP. 100 of fortune 500 (Intel, Texas Instruments, Dell, Lenov) and 13 of top 20 leading software companies found their homes here. Electronics, bio and pharmaceutical, precision machinery manufacturing. It has 760 incubating companies, 10 venture capital companies with 14 billion yuan, 140 thousand employees (9,000 masters and above, 600 overseas returned students, and over 2,000 PhDs). It works hard to promote its living environment, striving to build it to be a most liable place. What is particularly interesting is that the high tech area's effort to management build new urban communities in China. Were these efforts to be successful, it would start a new type of community life in China.

Other than this high technology parks, Chengdu has multiple industrial parks including those engaged in automobile and light-rail train manufacturing. It is a city that tries to combine history with future, and compete globally while maintaining its local culture.

## 4. Comparative Observations

The tale of two cities tell us a great deal of the efforts each made in seeking development through science and technology. While on the one hand, these two cities are known as large metro areas in remote places, on the other, they are both well-known star cities racing in the high tech arena for global prominence.

Things are not always as seem to be. And the world is no longer too big. Globalization is in our backyard, competition and innovation are already our normal way of life.

Also, the great changes are brought about because of the changes in the larger environment. The idea of high tech and its successfulness in other areas created pressure for innovation. An amicable large environment seems to be a necessary prerequisite for changes of such scale.

Third, change and innovation, although designed and top-down, have brought about great benefits including new products, income, jobs, and technological progress. It also greatly benefited regional and community development, changed rundown areas or under-developed areas into business site for the future.

Fourth, vision and leadership are critical for technological innovations to happen. Science and research parks, just as science and technology themselves per se, are human creations. They are not results of natural evolvement. Instead, they are human product of design—a human craftsmanship. ASU president once considered public administration as a design science, and he has been promoting innovation science and innovation since. Indeed, in both cities, the development of high tech parks have their champions and leaders. Without vision and leadership, what are already in operation are not possible.



Innovation requires design, support, and assistance. Both government provided large sum of support, in kind or financial resources, to support innovative activities.

However, Arizona developed its high tech parks through a market approach, building networks and partnership among institutions of higher learning, local governments, and business investors while in Chengdu, governmental efforts are the mainstay. In Arizona, the leadership comes from the university, while in Chengdu, the leadership comes from the government. In Arizona, relatively speaking, fewer federal dollars are pumped into local innovation, and a comprehensive long term national policy on local high tech center's development is lacking. In Chengdu, as a national government certified high tech zone, the high tech parks receive annual budget for its operation and tax incentives for its businesses. A significant amount of money is pumped into incubating new startups. These have enabled fast growth of the businesses.

Unexpected by many is that the Science and Technology Park in Chengdu has been developing in a larger scale and a faster speed than those in Phoenix, in spite of Phoenix's known innovation ability and the presence of well-known innovators locally. China's science and technology innovation has governmental mandate and strong governmental support, both in terms of policy and financial resources, while in America, the market operation tradition forces innovation to tread along the traditional mode of change, and its innovation leaders have to constantly fight political, economical, and social battles in local politics against the conservative forces. The advantage of this process is it may make less strategic mistakes amidst the highly political and scrutinized environment. The disadvantage is it is costly, exhausting, and things may have to happen slower than what the leaders wanted even though they already have a clear goal of where it should go. The massive effort made in China, in spite of its lower developmental stage, quickly brought China forward in a significant scale in high tech related growth and development. It also left many service loopholes to be patched later on. Nonetheless, the changes it has made outshines those in what is always known the most innovative country.

Nonetheless, China's high tech zone development is not without criticism. In one comprehensive study on China's high tech parks, Tang and Ying concluded that while many of China's science parks have demonstrated high growth, their actual innovation level is low (Tang, 2012). They attract businesses and talents and produce, but relatively fewer true innovations do happen. The high tech park is a way for China to upgrade its industry, importing and learning new technology, but not a real place for research and innovation generation. In contrast, the Phoenix research parks are manned and managed by a consortium in which Arizona State University plays an important role. The university has built a technology transfer team including scientists, technicians, entrepreneurs, and attorneys. It strives to tap into the innovation happened in university labs and turn them into production. It models the Stanford Science Park, emphasizing research based innovation. In the long run, this model may be the one with a sustainable future.

As we all know, the United States have always been a front runner in science and technology innovation. The founding fathers paid close attention to education and science and technology and made efforts to protect them from governmental interference. The federal government established Science and Technology council to provide consulting to the president. Federal support for science and technology development is strong. As a result, 40% of Nobel Prize Laureates are from the United States, over 30 percent of patents are generated by the United States, and between 2000 and 2010, its research papers have been referenced 41 millions times, topping all the other nations. The three most important technological revolution in the $20^{th}$ century: automobiles, electronics, and information technology have all happened in the United States. With a population of less than 5%, the country creates 24% of the wealth and 40% of the high tech products globally. Between 1929 and 1941, the contribution to economic growth made by science and technology is 33.8%. By the end of 1980s, the science and technology contribution to economic growth has reached 80%. As Jeffrey Lacker of the Federal Reserve said, in recent years, it is not trade, but the progress made in science and technology, that drives income and job growth (Anthony, 2012).



However, a great past may not necessary mean a future win. Just as China's past achievements could not guarantee its $20^{th}$ century prominence, America's traditional innovation pattern may not be without challenge. While with powerful local leadership, Arizona's institution of higher learning has positioned it self as a forerunner in the next round of research such as life sciences and internet based visual technology research. It is not without challenges, both domestically and internationally. A more comprehensive federal policy and strategic federal support may be a desirable feature really wanted in America. After all, the $21^{st}$ century competition is a different ballgame. To maintain its technological supremacy, the United States still have a lot to do.

In the same vein, China's high tech park development has already brought about great changes and social benefits. Nonetheless, it lacks ethos that can enable it to deliver its true promise—indigenous innovation. For a number of years, Chinese government has already made the seeking of indigenous innovation a national science policy priority. It shall take time for its science and technology sector to make it a reality.

## 5. Concluding Remarks

The tales of these two cities gave us a good picture that when compared at the city level, Phoenix lacks behind in terms of scale and growth speed in spite of its reputable university and ambitious academic leaders. Chengdu's institutions of higher learning, though also work in Chengdu's science and technology parks, have relatively less say in steering the direction of development of the entire park. Because of this, the major universities in town such as Sichuan University and Southwest University of Electronics Science and Technology are also building their own university research parks. Nonetheless, the two cities are both placing due emphasis in science and technology. Indeed, science and technology has been a primary force for growth and development in the United States since the beginning of the last century. Clusters of universities and high tech companies partner with local and regional governments to boost tech-based economic growth and create jobs. Now that the secret has been learned by China, the United States found itself a partner as well as a formidable competitor (Anthony, 2009). Many challenges still lay ahead. The traditional science park model of using low-cost land as a lure and lens for technology companies is showing signs of aging. Big science park projects from Russia to Nevada are in financial trouble as public funds for speculative development dries up. New variants of the science park model, such as technology incubators, are starved for funds as the venture capital industry retreats to safer bets on late-stage start-up companies with identifiable exit strategies. Also, many areas of uncertainty exist for future science and technology development. For one, the University's role in technology transfer is still under debate. Whether they could serve both as ivory tower research institutions engaged in basic research or as an economic growth engine transferring scientific discovering into economic gains remains to be seen. Some universities have embraced entrepreneurialism while others have rejected it. For two, how ecological economics or sustainable growth mandate will affect economic growth is still a hazy prospect due to the difficulties in estimating the cost of carbon dioxide emission control. Also, to what extent life sciences research will have economic pay-off remains to be a question. Industry observer Gary Pisano of Harvard Business School, once noted that over the past 30 years the biotechnology industry has yielded $300 billion in revenue, but consumed just as much investment capital. It is to say, while biotech firms created numerous new technologies, what they have not created are profits for their investors.

As to the future of the science parks, how to connect the people, companies, networks, and know-how for cooperation and innovation, rather than build a mere constellation of offices and workshops for sight remains to be a challenge. New research constellations, with or without physical working spaces, may become a new reality.



To properly answer these challenges, not just science parks and local leaders, but a consorted efforts made by local, state, and national leaders have to be in place. The global attention on science and technology created an impetus for countries to via with one another to build science and technology parks. The fast development in China is creating pressure for the United States—the traditional leader in science, technology, and innovation—to look hard into its self to see whether it has the right science and technology competition strategy. In the same vein, the Chinese leaders will still have the need to see how the United States is answering its own challenges in continuously pressing the boundaries of its own limitation. Chengdu and Phoenix, the two sister cities and science and technology development outposts in these two great nations, are two excellent cases for us to examine how these dynamics may happen. The competition as well as the collaboration between these two cities may help contribute to the building of a new science and technology reality for our human civilization. The tales of the two cities are just unveiling.

## Bibliography:


Anthony, Townsend. Is There a Future for Science Parks. Research Director in the Technology Horizons Program at the Institute for the Future. 2009. Http://www.iftf.org/innovation.

Castells, M., Hall, P. Technopoles of the World: The Making of Twenty-first-century Industrial Complexes, 2009.

Massey, D., Wield, D. High-tech Fantasies: Science Parks in Society, Science and Space[M]. London: Psychology Press.

Tang, Zhilin, Ying Cunyi. Governance Structure and Technological Innovation in STPs[M]. Beijing: Social Sciences Academic Press, 2012.

Wang, Shengguan, Cheng Yu. Report of Innovation and Development for China's National High-Tech Industrial Development Zones (NHIDZ)[M]. Beijing: China Economics Press, 2013.




## Appendix
## List of Innovation Clusters

1) Arizona State University Research Park, Arizona
2) Biomedical Research Park, Louisiana
3) Cape Charles Sustainable Technology Park, Virginia
4) The Research Triangle Park, North Carolina
5) CURI North Charleston Research Park, South Carolina
6) Clemson Research Park, South Carolina
7) Cummings Research Park, Alabama
8) Dandini Research Park, Nevada
9) Delaware Technology Park, Delaware
10) EverGreen Technology Park, Pennsylvania
11) First Union Science Park, Colorado

12) Florida Atlantic University Research Park, Florida
13) Francis Marion Research Park, South Carolina
14) Fontaine Research Park, Virginia
15) Indiana University Research Park, Indiana
16) Innovation Depot, University of Alabama
17) Innovation Park at Penn State, Pennsylvania
18) Innovation Park Tallahassee, Florida
19) Innovator.net University of North Dakota, North Dakota
20) Iowa State University Research Park, Iowa
21) Kapolei Business Park, Hawaii
22) Los Alamos Research Park, New Mexico
23) The Northwestern University Evaston Research Centre
24) The Olentangy River Wetland Research Park, Ohio
25) NASA Research Park, California
26) The Arrowhead Business and Research Park, New Mexico State University
27) Massachusetts Biotechnology Research Park
28) The High Technology Development Corporation (HTDC), Hawaii
29) Maui Research & Technology Park, Hawaii
30) Michigan Centre for High Technology, Michigan
31) Mililani Technology Park, Hawaii
32) Milwaukee Technopole, Wisconsin
33) Milwaukee County Research Park, Wisconsin
34) Thad Cochran Research, Technology and Economic Development Park, Mississippi State University, Mississippi
35) Missouri Research Park, Missouri
36) Oakdale Research Park, University of Iowa
37) Piedmont Triad Research Park, North Carolina
38) Purdue Research Park, Indiana
39) Rensselaer Technology Park, New York
40) The Washington State University Research Foundation (WSURF), Washington, DC
41) Research Park at University Illinois
42) Rheology Research Centre, Wisconsin
43) River Front Research Park, Oregon

44) Riverside Regional Technology Park

45) Sandia Science & Technology Park, New Mexico

46) Stanford Research Park, California

47) Sorrento West Life Science Park

48) Stout Technology Park, Wisconsin

49) Sunset Science Park, Oregon

50) Texas A & M University Research Park, Texas

51) Texas Research Park Foundation, Texas

52) Tri-Cities Science and Technology Park, Washington

53) UAB Research Park at Oxmoor

54) UMBC Technology Centre, Maryland

55) University Corporate Research Park, Michigan

56) University Heights Science Park, New Jersey

57) University of Virginia Research Park, Virginia

58) University of Arizona Science and Technology Park, Arizona

59) University of Colorado Research Park, Colorado

60) University of Idaho Research Park, Idaho

61) University of Maryland, Technology Advancement Program, Maryland

62) University of Minnesota Valley Technology Park, Minnesota

63) University of Nebraska, Nebraska Innovation Campus, Nebraska

64) University of New Orleans Research and Technology Park, Louisiana

65) University of Utah Research Park, Utah

66) University Park SIUE, Inc. on the campus of Southern Illinois University Edwardsville, Illinois

67) University Research Park Wisconsin-Madison

68) University Technology Park at IIT, Illinois

69) Utah University - Innovation Campus

70) Virginia Bio Technology Research Park, Virginia

71) Virginia Tech Corporate Research Centre, Virginia

72) WMU Technology & Research Park, Michigan

# 高新技术/产业园区对当地发展的领导作用
## ——成都和凤凰城的故事

兰志勇

（亚利桑那州立大学公共事务学院，美国坦佩 85287-5503）

**摘　要：**成都是中国西部的一个大城市。在过去的30年，特别是20世纪90年代后，一批产业和高新技术园区的建成促进了地方经济发展。这些园区都被证明是变革的关键领导力量。凤凰城是美国西部的一个大城市，自20世纪90年代以来快速发展，以房地产开发和高新技术的发展为驱动。从新世纪开始，亚利桑那州立大学倡导大学、产业、政府一起建立协作关系。在促进以技术为基础的研究或工业园区引领地方发展上，已经做出了很多努力。他们的发展轨迹是什么？他们的经验和教训是什么？这些故事告诉了我们什么？我们可以从中学习什么？本文试图回答这些问题，希望能找出变革与创新所需的模式、主题和环境因素。

**关键词：**成都；产业和高新技术园区；凤凰城；创新

# Globalization: A Response to Eduardo Pagan

David Pickus

(Arizona State University, Tempe, USA, 85287-5503; People's University, Beijing, China, 100872)

**Abstract:** Globalization is a very common and familiar topic. But precisely because it is so familiar it is often difficult to decide what the key issues are, and how to approach them. This paper provides a short overview of how I think that the complex problems of globalization can be grasped and taught. It responds to a question posed to me by ASU professor Eduardo Pagan as to whether globalization is always good. Of course, the immense problems faced by the world today are not "always good," but the place of globalization in contributing to, and possibly solving these problems needs a further look. To supply this overview of what we can and cannot expect of globalization, I return to the theme of this conference: regionalization, and use it as a way to understand and teach globalization itself.

**Key Words:** Globalization; Regionalization



It may seem like the topic of globalization is somehow antithetical to the subject of regionalism, and that the notion of "comparative Wests;" that is, Sichuan as a western region in China and Arizona as a western region in the USA only could be discussed as something somehow opposing globalization. By this I mean that someone might say "as opposed to the standardization of globalization, the two regions of the west..." In other words, globalization is associated with things that are entirely the same and regionalism is associated with things that are entirely different.

Short reflection, of course, shows that such oppositions are never as pure and neat on the ground as they are on paper. For instance, in studying the rise and spread of nation-states historians have often shown that the centralizing projects of the metropolitan center not only failed to eliminate the counter trends toward regionalism in nation-states, but often accommodated and even reinforced it. For example, no one studying the political system of the Federal Republic of Germany today can fail to note the special accommodating given to regions like Bavaria. Indeed, these kind of accommodations (as well as aggressive responses against them) have characterized internal German politics since Bismarck's unification in the mid 19th century.

If this is true of a single country, which at least has recognized boundaries and a single capital, it will be even more true of a trend like globalization, which does not admit of simple boundaries, or an agreed upon definition of success. Here, instead of looking only at history, I think we should also look at a relevant problem in philosophy, namely what to do about "antimonies," or situations when it is possible to produce equally valid but opposing and countervailing answers. For instance, what should we do if it is equally viable to say that knowledge comes from the evidence of our senses as well as from the categories of our mind. Alternately, what should we do if globalization seems to level out and "flatten" the world, while simultaneously allowing for all sorts of differences? There is no simple answer, but one profitable suggestion philosophers have made is that when you get equally viable opposing answers it might mean that there is something wrong with the basic premise of the question. Specifically, a question that presumes that a phenomenon is either exclusively one way or exclusively another way might be badly formulated. Let's not talk about either globalization or regionalization, but about the processes that hold the two together.



Here, I want to bring up a point rightly emphasized by geographers: activity is "spikey". This means that just as most physical features tend to be clustered areas where they are highly concentrated, the "spikes" and lightly or not at all represented everywhere else, so too, human activity tends to its "spikes," e.g., much or something at some point, and much of something else at another—and a pattern or logic, natural or human, linking and connecting them. With this notion in mind, it stands to reason that globalization and regionalism fit together as part of a single process.

But how can we describe this "process" and once we do so how can we go on to discuss and teach it more effectively? Let's begin by defining globalization more carefully, and relate this definition to the "spikiness" of things.

As Barrie Axford noted, "The fact is that there are many definitions of globalization clustered around common indicators and themes" (Axford, 2013: 1). This is a valuable observation and one of the most prominent clusters is the notion of speed, rapidity and acceleration. Yet, taken in itself, the idea that the world is moving faster explains little about what globalization might mean. I daresay that people in the midst of change, no matter where they are, and when they lived, always feel that the world is moving faster. Likewise, those that long for change, but cannot obtain it, always feel that the world is stultifying or confining. What accounts for the changes brought by globalization, and why, specifically, should we label this change as being due to globalization, and not something else? Here, I think that it is better to argue that what the cluster has in common is the notion of sharing, primarily by people who in other circumstances would not be sharing. Globalization, when you come to specify it, most commonly means different people sharing the same things.



This allows for a more succinct definition of globalization, namely one revolving around shared practices. As people in different parts of the world are linked into the same "systems," they take up the same practices. Thus, airports tend to operate the same way the world over. They have standardized regulations for the ways that runways and luggage handling should be organized, etc., and employees tend to be trained in similar ways, and the airline companies tend to adopt business strategies from a shared suite of goals and techniques.

There is nothing unusual about this. There are ever so many global practices that link different regions together, allowing them to share basic systems. Thus, not only do ATM's function the same way in most countries, but people tend to use them in the same ways, even when many other aspects of their lives are different such as income level, religion, language, and so forth. In country after country you can chart similarities: the people who use the machines in a measured fashion, before shopping and after payday. Those who visit it several times when on nights that they celebrate; those who impulsively empty their accounts to visit gambling casinos, and so on. My point is that you can find this sort of behavior in country after country. The same way that you can find standardized airports in so many places.

It is from this perspective of sharing systems that we can grasp the full implications of what it means for the world to be "linked." For instance, when the historian Peter N. Stearns seeks to provide a pithy overview of what globalization means he provides this sketch of linkage:

> It refers (in the financial crisis of 2008) to Americans who wake up at 3 a.m. To check Asian stock markets, because they know these will influence and and foreshadow Wall Street later in the day. It refers to global McDonald's, with 31,000 locations worldwide, all with common emphasis on fairly greasy food served quickly and (in principle at least) cheerfully. It refers to a quarter of the world's population (regardless of time zone) glued to televised accounts of World Cup soccer. It refers to the millions of American kids playing with Japanese toys like Hello Kitty or (not too long ago) Pokemon, or the charitable contributions from around the world pouring into disaster areas like tsunami-hit southeast Asia or Katrina-devastated New Orleans. It refers...the list is long indeed, with an impressive range of arenas and activities.
>
> (Stearns, 2009: 1)



The reason that there is such an impressive range of activities is that systems are shared. The stock markets not only function on similar principles, but they have become so integrated that it is impossible to tell which is influencing the other. Fast food restaurants look similar in many nations because they share basic techniques about supply chain and franchise operation and design. Children play with similar toys in different countries because toy designers understand what is appealing to children in general, irrespective of borders. When we speak about globalization in the 21st century we typically mean the accelerating integration of people from different countries and places into the same system.

How does this affect the overall discussion of regionalism in relationship to globalization? We can begin with an obvious objection to the notion of globalization as sharing. Perhaps "sharing" is not quite the right word, as it is clear that different people and places participate unevenly and unequally in shared global systems. Yet, the fact that we must be careful about how we use the term "sharing" does not mean that it is proportionally sharing. I never said "equal sharing," and grasping the meaning of inequality in the notion of unequal sharing will help us formulate conclusions on the topic as a whole.

First, it must be emphasized that even if there were no globalization whatsoever, if history is any guide, we can see that sharing of systems is only likely to be egalitarian in highly limited circumstances. In every other society, no matter how isolated, sharing the system—whether economic, educational, military, social, etc., meant participating in hierarchical arrangements that were often much more severe in their inequality than the inequality in the globalized world today. I say this with a slightly polemical edge because it is common today to hear the academic opinion that inequality is at all times high, and only getting worse. In one common version the reason inequality is only getting worse is because of the workings of neo-liberalism. As the matter is so grave, and since the charges are so extreme, it is worthwhile to look at them from more than one perspective.

On the one hand, the point about high inequality must be by definition true, very poor people today remain extremely poor. However, wealthy people today have considerably more wealth than they did even 50 years ago, to say nothing about the distant past. Indeed, from the standpoint of the past as a whole (but not from a possible happy future), the amount of wealth in the world today is staggeringly high. The difference between haves and have-nots must also be staggeringly high. So far we cannot argue with the critical point. However, we should consider what it was like to be poor in ancient Greece or the Tang Dynasty. Not only was the difference between the bottom and the top enormous, but there was almost no way to aspire to even a relative increase in wealth. The middle levels were tiny, and the number of those confined to (legal) bondage, huge. In almost every society, the gap between top and bottom was immense. Even societies characterized by a high degree of egalitarianism, if you looked close, were not altogether equal, since they had outcaste groups and other permanently subordinated members of the society. Egalitarianism typically meant sharing deprivation, not abundance, and even then there were many privileges that the unpopular and non-dominant could never hope to share.[1]

Saying this is not meant to settle any issues about social justice. The fact that there are more middle levels in world societies today also means that there is likely to be more suffering and frustration at visible and invisible barriers to advancement. Questions and poverty and inequality are extremely important and need to be discussed in detail. But we will misunderstand globalization if we continue to speak about the current gap between rich and poor as being uniquely severe. In my own judgment, the situation in previous societies was worse, rather than better than the present age. Precisely because globalization erodes efforts to fix society into unchanging patterns. It is true that the rich and powerful can find ever so many ways to entrench themselves, but they cannot find ways to arrest change. Indeed, the more middle levels there are in the world, the more likely there is to be change. One of the key challenges of sustaining globalization today consists in ensuring that societies do not shut themselves off from change.



Where does this leave us then in understanding globalization as a whole, as well as globalization in relationship to regionalism? The first thing that can be said about regionalism is that we no longer mean what humanity used to mean when it thought about a region. Region no longer means self-contained, and it does not necessarily even mean different. In fact, the meaning of region is more akin to what we mean when we speak of phenomena in the globalized word being "spikey." Put differently, regions can be seen abstractly and schematically as variegated inputs and outputs. That is, from geography to culture a different

1 I am aware that this view is disputed by some scholars. Thus, the matter is best studied in reference to specific historical examples. This is a good exercise for Chinese students.

"mix" will work on the region, as well as provide resources for continued activity. As regions by definition must be different, the process of globalization will simply accentuate the "spikey" or uneven character of the way it relates to the world as a whole.

Some of this may seem obvious, but it leads to two further considerations about the nature of globalization that are not so self-evident. First, the meaning of "standardization" in globalization needs to be treated with more sophistication. The fact that the same "system" is used in a very large number of places, almost everywhere with some key technologies, etc., does not mean that experience is standardized. In fact, the mere presence of the extensive inequalities found throughout the world guarantees that there will be divergent attitudes toward these systems. If you combine this with the fact that development is never even, then it becomes obvious that globalization's standardization does not mean "leveling."

What does it mean then? To answer this question it is necessary to think about globalization in long-term historical perspective. Here, I want to say something that is not so common in the literature, namely that globalization efforts were implicit in all large civilizations, not matter how ancient. A look at Egypt of the Pharaohs shows the intensity of the efforts to unite the disparate regions, particularly the Upper and Lower Nile, and create one "system." In another respect, China and its history is one large "globalization" attempt. The reason that we do not think of it thusly is that conditions made it impossible for these empires to realize their full ambitions. Had they been able to expand further, and maintain their authority and control, they would have. The Ming Dynasty shutting down of Zheng He is an example of anxieties about keeping order and authority trumping the desire for global expansion. The reason we do not think of these civilizations as global civilization is because a) we tend to forget how far they aimed to expand at the time of their greatest reach and b) more importantly, they simply couldn't achieve the degree of conquest, growth and organization that Western imperial civilizations obtained. This round of globalization, therefore, begins in Western expansion. Where it will end is anyone's guess.

I am now ready to conclude by giving an answer to Eduardo Pagan, and summing up my ideas on globalization. Upon giving a first version of this talk at the Chengdu conference, Professor Pagan asked in response "So is globalization always good?" This is a legitimate question, but it cannot be taken at face value because the question actually means two different things. On the one hand, it means whether or not I am somehow happy with the bad things of the world and somehow defending them. Articulated this way we can say that globalization is part of history and only a lunatic thinks that history is always good. Indeed, one of the main points of history is the realization of how horrible it is. But my point was not the madness that history was always good, and the path we have taken the most desirable. My point is that given the horrors of history, what is the most honest and viable goal for humanity to strive for. Here, I see no better option than a globalized world, unified by the same systems and seeking to alleviate the miseries of its uneven development. This, I think, is what students should be taught about, if only to give them a worldview they can respond against.



## Bibliography:

Axford, Barrie. *Theories of Globalization*[M]. Cambridge: Polity, 2013.

Stearns, Peter N . *Globalization in World History*[M]. London, N.Y.: Routledge, 2009.

# 全球化——基于爱德华多·蒲甘问题的回答

大卫·皮卡思

（亚利桑那州立大学，美国坦佩　85287-5503；中国人民大学，北京　100872）

**摘　要：**全球化是一个十分常见的话题，我们都很熟悉它，但正因为耳熟能详，我们很难把握它的关键及实现全球化的方法。本文简要概述了全球化的一系列问题以及怎样去理解和把握这些问题，并且回答了亚利桑那州立大学的爱德华多·蒲甘教授提出的问题——全球化是否总是好的。诚然，当今世界正面临巨大的问题，但全球化为解决这些问题做出的贡献不容忽略。全球化能够带给我们什么？为回答此类问题，我将本文的重点回归到本次会议的主题上来，即区域化以及利用区域化来理解和指导全球化问题。

**关键词：**全球化；区域化

# A Comparative Study into the Eco-ethics Between North American Indians and Ancient Ethnic Minorities in China's Southwestern Regions

Fang Yonglan

(Foreign Language Department, Chengdu Sport University, Chengdu, China 610041)

**Abstract:** Today's ever worsening eco-environment and ever serious eco-crises make people attach more importance to eco-ethics. Amid their long-term contact with and conflict against nature, North American Indians and ancient ethnic minorities in China's southwestern region have developed their own eco-ethics. This paper attempts to make a comparative study into the eco-ethics between North American Indians and ancient ethnic minorities in China's southwestern regions from such perspectives as their views of nature, religious philosophies, lifestyles, and modern reflections. Meanwhile significance of their eco-ethics on the environmental protection in modern context is also discussed in this paper.



**Key Words:** Eco-ethics; North American Indians; Ancient Ethnic Minorities of China's Southwestern Regions; Environmental Protection

## 1. Introduction

After WWII, American federal government, in view of the national integral interests, explored the economically comparatively underdeveloped southwestern regions. With the support of the federal government, local governments in the southwestern regions implemented and adopted a series of policies and measures to nurture an environment conducive to high-tech investment. Coupled with natural endowments and aided by high-tech investments, American southwestern regions developed at a rapid rate. Likewise, China's southwestern regions have been experiencing the great exploration advocated and supported by the state council. The great exploration provided incentive to the prosperous development of China's southwestern regions. As a consequence of the thriving economy, an array of newly-risen metropolises were generated. A good case in point is Chengdu.

However, following close behind the rapid economic development are a variety of prominent environmental crises, which is a common problem confronted by the southwestern regions of both the USA and China. In 2012, a record-breaking number of forest fires broke out in more than one western American states, with the forest fire in Colorado being the largest and most destructive one ever happened to the state. Meanwhile, the western part of China is confronted with such environmental problems as low precipitation, severe drought, increasing deforestation and desertification and the extinction of more and more species. As we look ahead to find measures to solve these environmental problems, we might as well look back on the eco-ethics of North American Indians and ancient ethnic minorities living in present China's southwestern regions. Throughout history, both North American Indians and ancient ethnic minorities in China's southwestern regions have developed their unique eco-ethics which is still of significance when it comes to the cause of environmental protection in modern context.





## 2. A Comparative Study into the Eco-ethics between North American Indians and Ancient Ethnic Minorities of China's Southwestern Regions

Eco-ethics is a system to regulate the ethical standards and behavioral norms between man and nature as well as between man and the environment. Eco-ethics summarizes behavioral norms and evaluation standards of man in the community of different life forms. Being the evolution from human ethics to nature ethics, eco-ethics has wide connotations, involving all forms of ideologies on the relationship between man, nature and the environment, restraining and supervising human behaviors, and guiding human beings in handing their dialectical unity with nature. Eco-ethics is formed on the basis of eco-ethical thoughts which are gradually developed along with man's understanding and reform of nature. Eco-ethical thoughts are shaped on the basis of man's understanding of the ethical relationship between him and nature, capable of constant changes along with the changes made by man in his practice of reforming nature. It is generally believed that these changes undergo three periods. The first period begins with the ancient times and lasts till the embryo of civilization. In the first period, man was powerless in the face of nature and all he could was to submit himself to nature. At that time, man was submissive and humble to nature and hence, nature worship was developed. The second period begins with the early stage of civilization and lasts till the modern times. In this period, man developed no sense of fear towards nature, taking precedence over nature. The last period ranges over the modern times. Over this period, man, confronted with various natural disasters, begins to reflect on his own behaviors and hits upon the true position he can hold and the real role he should play in nature. He has gradually realized the consistence between maintaining the rights of natural substances and securing the rights of man. More and more importance has been attached to eco-ethics along with the ever-worsening ecological environment and the ever-increasing ecological crises. Amid their long-term contact with nature, North American Indians have developed their own eco-ethics which highlights the holistic and organic connection between man and nature. Such concepts as "respecting human lives" and "unity of man and nature" are valued in their eco-ethics. Likewise, ancient ethnic minorities living in present China's southwestern regions, during their long-term social production and practice, have developed their unique eco-ethics which centers on preserving nature. Their eco-ethics are represented in their religious beliefs, folk tales, production means, festival celebrations, burial customs and civil stipulations. In the following, the thesis writer is going to discuss the eco-ethics of North

American Indians and ancient ethnic minorities of China's southwestern regions from such aspects as their views of nature, religious philosophies, lifestyles and modern reflections.

### 2.1 The Eco-ethics of North American Indians

For thousands of years, North American Indians have been observing and exploiting their surrounding environments. They have gained a deep understanding of the mutual relationship between their surrounding environments and different life forms. The eco-ethics of North American Indians is characterized with rich and traditional ecological wisdom; therefore, modern society has generally embraced their eco-ethics.

*Chief Seattle's Manifesto* is said to be the declaration of North American Indians' ecological holism, the belief that all things are interrelated and they together form the life as a whole. In his manifesto, Chief Seattle expressed North American Indians' deep love for earth and their close relationship with the land and all other things on earth in affectionate words. He said: "Earth is the mother of the red man. We are part of the earth and it is part of us."(Yang, 2012:14) He also designated man's responsibilities to nature, considering it wrong to conquer and pillage nature.

Generally speaking, North American Indians believed that man and nature were interdependent and interrelated. Man could not afford to be separated from nature, for nature held the key to man's development. Thus, respecting and loving nature was incorporated and highlighted in the ecological ethics of North American Indians. As a consequence of this plain ecological ethics, North American Indians could live in harmony with nature.

In the first place, animism is carried through the view of nature of North American Indians. They believe that great spirits and supernatural powers are embodied in various creatures. Under the influence of animism, North American Indians take it as a matter of course that all creatures are equal. In their eyes, all things on the earth have their own living souls. Undoubtedly, their animism-based eco-ethics is conducive to protecting the environment, especially the biodiversity. Many North American Indian tribes have their unique rituals concerning animal-hunting and food-gathering activities. They have strict protocols to guarantee that animals won't be hunted to extinction and food won't be unnecessarily wasted. Why have they developed the unique rituals and followed the strict protocols? Part of the reason is that they are sympathetic with and grateful to the animals and plants used as their food sources. Another part of the reason is that they have developed a sense of fear toward nature, afraid that they might be punished if they hunt animals and waste food without any checks.

In the second place, religion plays an important role in the life of North American Indians. Religious influence can be found in every aspect of their production and life. Their religious activities highlight the important position of mother nature. Totem worship is the primitive religious belief of North American Indians. It helps them to develop the plain eco-ethics of maintaining a harmonious relationship between man and nature. For example, the North American Iroquois have more than 30 clans. Each clan have its own animal totem. They have formed a strong reverence towards such animals as the wolf, bear, eagle, beaver, for these animals are regarded as their totems. It is stipulated by the Iroquois that animals regarded as totems should not be eaten, killed, hurt or touched. They respect and worship these animals. If any clan member dare to hurt or kill these animals, which is a violation of the stipulation, they will be severely punished and in extreme cases, put to death.



Besides totem worship, North American Indians believe in shamanism. The shamanism they believe in is subjected to animism and characterized with a worship for and reverence towards ancestral spirits of their clans or tribes. Safely speaking, the shamanism advocated by North American Indians combines nature worship with totem worship. This unique shamanism helps to designate the various objects for North American Indians to worship in their religious consciousness. The religious mechanism of shamanism embodies a pack of systems to strike an ecological balance, and maintain a harmonious relationship between man and nature. In the name of spirits, shamanism requires people to love, respect and protect nature, which indirectly contributes to protecting the ecological environment and maintaining the ecological balance. It is evident that the shamanism upheld by North American Indians pertains to their worldly eco-ethics. They believe that human beings must adapt to and coexist with nature before they can secure their existence and survival upon the earth.

Last but not least, North American Indians attach importance to the holistic, coordinated and organic link between man and nature in their daily life. In their opinions, the earth is sacred. They worship and appreciate the land beneath their feet as well as the creatures upon the earth. Not only do the North American Indians worship the land, but also they have a clear understanding of their dependence on the land. In the late $19^{th}$ century, when the whites tried to seduce the Shah Hap Martin Indians living in present Washington DC into clearing the land, Smohalla, the initiator of the Dream Sect, strongly opposed to the move. He reacted to the greedy move, saying "You want me to clear the land? I will rip open the chest of my mother with a sword?... You want me to cut the grass and turn it into the fodder? You want me to grow rich in your white people's way! But how can I cut the hair of my mother?" Generally speaking, North American Indians led a comparatively pure and plain, though not perfect, life. They were attached to the land, likening them to mountains, rocks, trees, and animals. They considered themselves affiliated to the land. For them, the land is their hometown and burial ground as well. The land is the born religious shrine, too holy to be tempered with. The lifestyles of North American Indians give priority to nature and their eco-ethics center on respecting life and the unity of man and nature, which is significant in and relevant to today's environmental protection cause.

The animism-based eco-ethics developed and advocated by North American Indians is indeed instructive and constructive to today's ecological preservation.

### 2.2 The Eco-ethics of Ancient Ethnic Minorities in China's Southwestern Regions

The eco-ethics of ethnic minorities refers to the ethical standards and behavioral norms of ethnic minorities concerning their reflections upon the universe, nature and life. It includes all ideologies of ethnic minorities in their handling of relationships between man and nature as well as between man and the environment. The views of nature of ancient ethnic minorities in China's southwestern regions are mainly reflected in their eco-ethical thoughts concerning their understanding and perception of the universe, the origin of human beings as well as the elements of natural environment. There are chiefly three views concerning their understanding of the universe and the origin of human beings. The first view is that the universe and human beings are created by some mysterious power; the second view is that the universe and human beings evolve from certain things in the natural world; the third view is that human beings, deities and animals are descendants of the same ancestors, with human beings taking precedence over deities and animals. When it comes to the religious culture of ancient ethnic minorities in China's southwestern regions, the eco-ethical thoughts of revering nature, loving nature, and protecting nature are deeply impressed on their religious culture. In terms of the lifestyles of ancient ethnic minorities in China's southwestern regions, they have exploited such agricultural production means as the "slash-and-burn" cultivation, the terrace cultivation, and the dam cultivation which can fit perfectly into the warm and damp climate of southwestern regions. Besides these eco-friendly agricultural production means, ancient ethnic minorities in China's southwestern regions have formed their unique nomadic and hunting lifestyles that are also conducive to protecting the local environments. Last but not least, the civil stipulations of ancient ethnic minorities in China's southwestern regions can also reflect their environmental protection awareness.



The eco-ethical thoughts of ancient ethnic minorities in China's southwestern regions can be dated back to the times when their productivity is pretty low and they have to gather foods and hunt animals to survive. Their food-gathering, fish-catching and animal-hunting activities are largely dependent on nature. As a consequence of their strong dependence on nature, they develop the unique view of nature—"unity of man and nature," which is also the eco-ethics of ancient ethnic minorities of China's southwestern regions. The concept of "unity of man and nature" points to the holistic harmony between man and nature. In other words, man and nature are an inseparable whole. From the viewpoints of ancient ethnic minorities in China's southwestern regions, nature is the mother of all creatures; man is part of nature, originating and evolving from nature and man and nature should not be separated. They revere nature to such an extent that they even go to great lengths to sanctify nature. Thus, they develop a worship for and taboo against such natural stuffs as the heaven, earth, mountain, water, tree and stone, which contributes to the formation of their nature-revering eco-ethics.

The existence of holy mountains, holy lakes, holy springs, holy rivers, holy trees and holy stones can be found everywhere in the dwelling places of ancient ethnic minorities of China's southwestern regions. Their long production history helps them understand that every creature in the natural world has its spirit, the power of nature is sacred and solemn, and thus human beings must respect and worship nature. The deep understanding of ancient ethnic minorities in China's southwestern regions towards man's dependence on nature can be reflected in their various forms of nature worship and totem worship. For example, the Tibetans worship holy mountains and sacred lakes; the Dong minorities worship many creatures upon the earth, and the Bouyei minorities have their unique totem worship. Furthermore, many an ancient ethic minorities in China's southwestern regions have their own taboos on animals and plants (李良品，2008：139–140).

Ancient ethnic minorities of China's southwestern regions generally have religious beliefs. Buddhism has exerted a wide and deep influence upon each ethnic minority in ancient ethnic minorities of China's southwestern regions, with the Naxi minority, Tibetans, Dai minority and Zhuang minority commonly believing in Buddhism. It is maintained in Buddhism that all creatures are equal and partake of the Buddha wisdom and therefore due respect must be paid to them. It is also advocated in Buddhism that life should be respected and cherished. Under the influence of Buddhism, ancient ethnic minorities in China's southwestern regions tend to give comparatively good protection to the animals and plants in their surrounding areas. The religious taboos of ancient ethnic minorities in China's southwestern regions show that they have developed a plain nature-preserving eco-ethics. Their taboos are seen through in such aspect of their daily production and living as eating habits, dressing customs, behavioral norms, wedding ceremonies, burial rituals and festival celebrations. Though these taboos have a superstitious flavor, they, in an objective way, contribute to protecting the ecological environment and maintaining the ecological balance. The taboos of ancient ethnic minorities of China's southwestern regions are listed as follows. Firstly, it is forbidden that forests are ruined and mountains are destroyed. In the cultural philosophies of ancient ethnic minorities in China's southwest regions, forests and mountains are too pure and holy to be tempered with. At ordinary times, people are not allowed to hunt or even walk in the sacred forests and mountains. Tending sheep and horses in these holy places are far from being permitted. Such a taboo is definitely contributive to protecting local environments. Secondly, hunting animals is also a taboo. This taboo, to some extent, helps preserve biodiversity and maintain eco-balance. Finally, it is tabooed that water sources can be contaminated, as water is indispensable to their existence. Through the experience and observation of one after another generation, ancient ethnic minorities of China's southwestern regions have been too well aware of the importance of water in their daily life to allow the destruction of trees and plants near the water sources (佟宝山，2007：100–103).



A set of civil stipulations with a religious flavor are also laid down by ancient ethnic minorities in China's southwestern regions to well manage forest and water resources and further protect the local environment. For instance, it is stipulated in the civil rules and regulations of Miao ethics that if trees in the mountain are burned down and roots in the valley are wiped out, local people would call a civil meeting to condemn the perpetrators and decide on the punishment and they would take effective measures to guarantee that the perpetrators cannot get away with the punishment. It is evident that the civil stipulations of ancient ethnic minorities in China's southwest regions embody their plain nature-preserving eco-ethics.

The environmental protection awareness of ancient ethnic minorities in China's southwestern regions is also reflected in their traditional production means. In order to adapt to the eco-environment, they adopt many positive measures in their production means. Over their long-term production and survival, they have drawn on their own life experiences to develop different farming and nomadic cultures, many of which are closely related to environmental protection. Their traditional farming and nomadic cultures help them form the eco-ethical thought of reasonable and sustainable development. They hold the view that if man's exploitation of nature exceeds a certain limit, man will be punished by nature.

Along with the historical development, the eco-ethics of ancient ethnic minorities in China's southwestern regions also gets enriched and developed, rendering it an organic part of their traditional culture.

## 3. Conclusion

Unfortunately, North American Indians quickly absorbs the negative elements in the white culture during their contact with the white society, especially in their fur trade with whites. To satisfy the increasing demand of the whites on fur, North American Indians soon degenerate into weapons of slaughter, wreaking havoc upon nature.

Similar problems can be found among the ancient ethnic minorities in China's southwestern regions. Some indecent and inappropriate behaviors and actions accompany the modern development of these ethnic regions. On the one hand, the economic development of these ethnic regions are promoted and local people's living conditions are improved. On the other hand, the traditional eco-ethics of ancient ethnic minorities in China's southwest regions gradually dysfunctions, which leads to the severe destruction of the local environment as well as serious crises of these ethnic regions. If the situation is not improved and the mistake is not corrected, the further development of these ethnic regions will be hindered.

Despite of this or that kind of problems, the eco-ethics of both North American Indians and ancient ethnic minorities in China's southwestern regions center on respecting nature and achieving a harmonious development between man and nature. It is of great significance to understand, explore and carry on their plain eco-ethics when human beings are faced with various environmental problems and ecological crises in the 21st century.

## Bibliography:

Yang,Tingting. Analysis on Ecological Cultural View of American Indians and Its Enlightenments[D]. Master's Dissertation of Beijing Forestry University, 2012:14.

李良品，等. 论古代西南地区少数民族的生态伦理观念与生态环境[J]. 黑龙江民族丛刊，2008, 3：139-140.

佟宝山. 西南少数民族传统文化中的生态环保观[J]. 辽宁大学学报：哲学社会科学版，2007, 6：100-103.



# 北美印第安人和中国古代西南少数民族之生态伦理观比较研究

方永兰

（成都体育学院外语系，四川成都　610041）

**摘　要：**现代社会生态环境的恶化和生态危机的加剧使得人们越来越重视生态伦理。中国古代西南少数民族和北美印第安人在与大自然长期艰苦的斗争中，形成了自己的生态伦理观。本文拟从他们的自然观、宗教观、生活方式、现代审视等方面来比较中国古代西南少数民族和北美印第安人的生态伦理观，并进一步探讨他们的生态伦理观对现代生态环境保护的借鉴意义。

**关键词：**生态伦理；北美印第安人；中国古代西南少数民族；环境保护

# 美国亚利桑那州产业集群发展战略：模式、绩效与经验启示[1]

路征[1] ［美］李唯[2,3]

（1 四川大学经济学院，四川成都 610064；2 亚利桑那州立大学社会转型学院，美国坦佩 85287-5503；

3 亚利桑那州立大学地理科学与城市规划学院，美国坦佩 85287-5503）

**摘　要：**20世纪80年代末90年代初，美国亚利桑那州经济遭遇严重衰退，地区经济发展面临转型压力。1992年，亚利桑那州实施了产业集群战略，这一战略成功推动了地区经济的复苏和转型，并使亚利桑那州成为之后十余年中美国经济增长最快的地区之一。本文深入分析了亚利桑那州产业集群战略的制定、调整和发展特征，并利用统计分析和QLR检验对战略的总体绩效进行了评价。结论显示，亚利桑那州产业集群发展得益于科学的战略设计和以技术密集型中小企业和企业网络组织为核心驱动因素的发展模式，地方政府只发挥“组织者”和“协调者”的作用。

**关键词：**产业集群；亚利桑那州；发展模式

## 1．引言

亚利桑那州地处美国西南边陲，受经济基础、地理区位等因素的影响，长期以来，亚利桑那州的经济发展主要依靠农业、矿产资源开采和旅游业，这一经济结构被形象地称为“5Cs”，即主要生产棉花（Cotton）、奶牛（Cattle）、铜（Copper）、柑橘类水果（Citrus）和依托自然气候（Climate）

1　本研究得到了教育部国别研究基地四川大学美国研究中心项目（项目批号：ASC201209）和四川大学引进人才科研启动经费资助项目（项目批号：YJ201342）的资助。

发展起来的旅游业（MIPP，2009）。这一传统的经济结构在20世纪30年代大萧条时期遭受重大打击时崩溃，亚利桑那州开始通过工业化道路来实现经济复苏，制造业尤其是矿产资源开发与加工、农产品加工、航空航天以及其他一些制造业取得了巨大发展。然而，在20世纪70年代的美国经济“滞涨”和80年代全球经济疲软的冲击下，亚利桑那州经济再次面临挑战，这也促使其开始思考如何在新形势下实现经济复苏，进而寻求一种新的模式来促进经济发展和提高竞争力。

1988年，亚利桑那州开始调动政府、民间机构等多方面力量，着手研究新形势下的经济发展策略，并于次年成立了州商业部来专门负责研究促进本州岛经济发展的策略。1990年，企业网络组织（Enterprise Network）联合州商务部、州经济委员会、大凤凰城（Greater Phoenix）经济委员会和大图森（Greater Tucson）经济委员会共同出资19万美元，用于研究亚利桑那州的经济战略规划。与此同时，迈克·波特通过对工业化国家的研究，于1990年首次提出了“产业集群”的概念（Porter, 1990）。这一概念很快被应用到实践当中，成为区域经济发展的新理念和新模式。1991年，亚利桑那州成立了一个名为“亚利桑那州经济发展战略规划”（Arizona Strategic Plan for Economic Development）的规则编制小组（以下简称ASPED规划组），专门负责研究和编制规划。该组织吸收了产业集群的发展理念，确定采用产业集群战略来重振经济。1992年，州政府正式发布了《创造21世纪：亚利桑那州经济发展战略规划》（Creating a 21$^{st}$ Century: Arizona’s Strategic Plan of Economic Development，以下简称ASPED战略规划），这使亚利桑那州成为美国最早将产业集群作为区域经济发展战略的地区。在产业集群发展战略下，亚利桑那州经济得以快速复苏，并成为20世纪90年代全美最具竞争力的地区之一。

自20世纪90年代末，中国政府和学界开始关注产业集群发展，随后成为国家和地区经济发展的重要指导理念。目前，中国已经形成了数百个产业集群或“准集群”，成为地区经济发展的重要推动力（吴利学、魏厚凯和刘长会，2009）。与此同时，中国目前正处于经济转型时期，尤其在2007年爆发的全球性经济危机的冲击下，经济转型和产业结构调整升级迫在眉睫。因此，对亚利桑那州产业集群发展的模式和经验进行总结和分析，对指导中国地区经济发展和产业集群建设有十分重要的意义。

## 2．研究方法

本文旨在分析和总结美国亚利桑那州产业集群发展战略的模式，包括战略的设计和调整、战略的特征以及该战略带来的经济成效，以期亚利桑那州产业集群发展的经验可为中国尤其是内地各地区近年来热衷于构建产业集群来引导地区经济发展制定战略提供参考。

在研究方法上，本文首先通过整理和分析各类相关政府公开材料、实证研究报告和学术文献，提炼出亚利桑那州产业集群发展战略的模式；然后，通过分析亚利桑那州在产业集群战略实施前后的经济表现，以及利用Quandt依然比（QLR）断点检验方法，检验亚利桑那州相对劳动生产率是否在产业集群战略前后发生突变，进而判断产业集群战略是否对亚利桑那州经济生产效率带来了实质性影响；最后，给出研究结论与亚利桑那州产业集群发展经验对中国大陆地区产业集群发展的启示。

## 3．亚利桑那州产业集群战略的基本框架及调整

制定地区经济发展战略是一个浩大的工程，需要对经济形势和本地状况进行深入研究。为此，亚利桑那州战略规划的制定分为三个阶段：第一阶段的主要任务是研究如何更好地发展地方经济和创造就业，并最终提出战略框架；第二阶段的任务是编制战略规划；第三阶段是战略规划发布后的进一步实施、调整和优化。

首先，亚利桑那州成立了由专业咨询机构和研究机构联合组成的ASPED咨询组，主要负责提供咨询支持和安排第一阶段任务。通过深入研究，ASPED咨询组提出用“集群”和“基础”为两轴的核心框架来编制ASPED战略规划。进而，亚利桑那州专门成立了由政府、企业组织、专家等各方面力量组成的大型规划组，包括由政府机构和企业组织构成的ASPED执行委员会，由各界专家组成的9个产业集群顾问小组（每个顾问组都有来自大学的专家代表），6个基础工作组和由州市政厅、地方市政府和公共论坛构成的公共部门组织。据统计，整个战略的研究和设计过程有一千余亚利桑那州人参与其中，共耗时一年时间研究新国际形势下的产业选择。研究过程主要采用了定量和定

性两种分析方法：通过数量分析，对主导产业的规模、集中度、出口、就业和生产率进行分析，以明确就业和商业发展的地区模式；定性分析则主要通过商务会谈、专题讨论和集群工作组三种形式来进行（Waits，2000）。

在整个战略规划研究中，集群顾问组发挥着核心作用。首先，它们需要明确集群的构成和企业之间的相互联系，并且提出未来10到20年中什么样的集群才是可行的，这一步的主要目的是针对当时国际经济形势和本地经济发展的基础优势，甄选出适宜并且能够带来长期效应的主导产业，进而发展产业集群；第二步任务，就是围绕确定下来的产业集群，提出发展和壮大这些产业集群的方案，包括如何发展壮大本地已有的企业，如何建立新企业和如何吸引地区外的相关企业；第三步任务，关注单个集群内的联系机制，明确发展集群必备的具体经济基础条件和战略措施。



表1　ASPED战略规划的阶段及组织构成

<table>
<tr><th>阶段</th><th>组织</th><th colspan="2">构成及任务</th></tr>
<tr><td>第一阶段</td><td>ASPED咨询组</td><td colspan="2">与SRI国际和亚利桑那州立大学Morrisson公共政策研究所联合构建公私合作伙伴关系组织，主要负责提供咨询支持和研究如何更好发展地方经济和创造就业，并提出战略编制框架。</td></tr>
<tr><td rowspan="4">第二阶段</td><td>ASPED联盟</td><td>由亚利桑那州商务部、州经济委员会、大凤凰城经济委员会和大图森经济委员会和企业家构成的企业网络5个组织构成，是ASPED的执行委员会。</td><td rowspan="4">完成《创造21世纪：亚利桑那州区域经济发展战略规划》（ASPED）编制（1992年3月发布）。</td></tr>
<tr><td>集群顾问组</td><td>由不同领域专家组成9个产业集群顾问小组，包括信息、生物医药、旅游、商业服务、交通运输、航空航天、采矿、农业和光电产业。</td></tr>
<tr><td>基础工作组</td><td>由人力资源、技术、资本、税收和管理、物质性基础设施、信息基础设施6个基础工作组构成。</td></tr>
<tr><td>公共部门组织</td><td>包括州市政厅、18个地方市政府和6个公共论坛（Public Forum）。</td></tr>
<tr><td>第三阶段</td><td>GSPED</td><td colspan="2">GSPED成立于1992年6月，作为原来的ASPED规划组的替代组织，是一个由公共部门和私人部门共同构成的伙伴组织，主要负责ASPED战略规划的后续优化调整和管理，其成员包括州长、企业和企业家、立法领袖、州商务部、经济发展专家、商会组织和来自少数族裔（包括美洲原住民）、小企业、大学、社区学校的代表。</td></tr>
</table>

数据来源：根据Breault，Hald & Kraver（1996），Waits，Rex & Melnick（1997）和Waits（2000）的描述整理。

经过全面而深入的分析，ASPED战略最初确定了8大产业集群，包括3个新兴产业集群（信息、健康与生物制药和交通与配送）、2个扩展产业集群（商业服务业和旅游业）和3个转型产业集群（航空工业、采矿业和农业与食品加工业）。三种产业集群充分体现了强化基础优势、着眼未来趋势的基本原则，航空工业、采矿业和农产品加工业是亚利桑那州的传统优势产业，但传统的生产模式已不能满足新形势的要求，需要进行转型和提升来增强产业竞争力，而对于已有一定基础的商贸服务业和旅游业，则需进一步扩大规模和提高服务能力。最重要的是，规划提出了具有前瞻性的三个新兴产业集群，这是在充分研究当时世界经济发展趋势的基础上决定的，这也为后来亚利桑那州在高科技领域处于国际领先地位奠定了基础。最初提出的8大产业集群虽然是基于科学的定性和定量研究得出的结论，但战略规划组认为，理论研究得出的结论并不一定是最优方案，于是就此进一步征询其他公共领域尤其是企业界的意见。通过公共论坛、专题讨论等形式，其他社会参与者尤其是企业领导人也提出了自己的看法。企业界认为，航空航天产业和信息产业集群应该合并成为高科技产业，软件产业应该成为独立的新兴产业集群，而不是作为信息产业集群的一部分，环境科技和光电产业也应被视为一种新兴产业集群。与此同时，商贸企业、金融机构和法律等咨询机构认为，它们是为其他产业集群和社会提供服务的行业，并不适合以一个独立产业集群的形式存在。工商企业界基于自身对市场趋势的判断提出的这些建议，得到了战略规划组的认同，重组后的产业集群变为9个。

1992年3月，政府正式发布了ASPED战略规划，ASPED规划组也完成了其使命。鉴于后续对产业集群战略的实施和管理，同年6月政府又牵头成立了GSPED（Governor's Strategic Partnership for Economic Development）。这是一个由州政府官员（一般是州长）、企业和企业家、立法领袖、州商务部、经济发展专家、商会组织以及来自少数族裔（包括美洲原住民）、小企业、大学、社区学校的代表组成的动态组织，该组织主要负责ASPED战略规划实施后的优化、调整和管理（Breault, Hald&Kraver, 1996）。1994年，为退休人员服务的企业和专业机构提议组建养老产业（Senior Living）集群并进入战略规划，这一提议经过GSPED的讨论和评估后得到批准，成为亚利桑那州的第11个产业集群。养老产业主要通过吸引退休人群定居亚利桑那州而带动的服务于养老小区的产业，例如医药、金融、法律服务、房地产和财务等。1998年，又组建了塑料及高级复合材料产业集群，主要致力于发展具有高科技含量的新型材料产品（Carrie，2000：289-298）。2002年，GSPED批准在线教育产业（E-Learning）成为第12个产业集群（PR Newswire，2002）。2003年，企业和亚利桑那州大学等相关机构又共同发起成立了纳米科技产业集群（KMK Consulting Team, 2006: 14）。

**表2　亚利桑那州产业集群和集群发展基础**

| 产业集群 | 传统的集群发展基础 | 新的集群发展基础 |
|---|---|---|
| 1. 高科技产业（航空航天和信息）<br>2. 食品、纤维和自然产业（Natural Product）<br>3. 环境科技产业<br>4. 矿产与采掘产业<br>5. 软件产业<br>6. 旅游与体验产业<br>7. 健康与生物制药产业<br>8. 光电产业<br>9. 运输及配送产业（物流产业）<br>10. 养老产业（Senior Living）<br>11. 塑料及高级复合材料产业<br>12. 在线教育产业（E-Learning）<br>13. 纳米科技产业 | 1. 资本<br>2. 教育与劳动力发展<br>3. 人力资源<br>4. 信息和通讯基础设施<br>5. 物质性基础设施<br>6. 生活质量<br>7. 税收和管理<br>8. 技术 | 1. 联络设施（Connecting）：完善的电子信息基础设施<br>2. 电子政务（E-Government）：通过电子化政府提供更快更好的服务<br>3. 在线教育（E-Learning）：远程学习和教育技术<br>4. 新型小区（Creative Communities）：创建具有优质空间和便利设施的小区<br>5. 知识型领导者、企业家和资本（Knowledge Leaders, Entrepreneurs and Capital）：高水平的教育、研发、技术转移、孵化和风险资本 |

数据来源：根据Waits（2000），Carrie（2000），Pavlakovich-Kochi（2010）等的资料整理。



为了促进产业集群的发展，还需一定的基础条件作为支撑。鉴于此，战略规划还明确了8个支撑产业集群发展的基础，包括资本、教育、人力资源、基础设施、生活、税收与管理以及技术。不过，最初的这8个基础并不是固定的，在新的条件下，亚利桑那州还对其进行了调整。20世纪90年代后半叶，全世界都在讨论“新经济”，为更好地让政府和社会公众理解新经济的内涵，亚利桑那州立大学Morrison公共政策研究所于1999年发布了一份研究报告——《新经济：亚利桑那州指南》（The New Economy: A Guide for Arizona）。这份报告给出了新经济的8个基本特征：①新技术的涌现和应用。正如迈克尔·波特所指出的，“没有低技术产业，只有低技术企业”（Porter，1998）。在新经济时代，新技术不断涌现，对于企业来说，在不断开发和销售新技术的同时，更重要的是如何应用新技术来提高自身的生产力和竞争力；②全球化趋势。在全球化趋势下，即使不以国际市场为目标的企业，也必须应对全球化；③知识创造财富。在新经济时代，知识是推动经济发展的主要动力，经济发展越来越依赖研发、知识产权、客户关系等知识资产，对建筑、交通、机器等实物资产的依赖程度降低；④人力资本最重要。传统经济更多地依赖于低技能工人通过体力劳动来完成基本的生产工作，而新经济中则更需要高技能工人来完成物流、信息生成、研发设计、提供高质服务等工作；⑤变化。在新经济中，竞争激烈，变化迅速，生存取决于应变能力，变革已成为常态，因而企业也需要通过不断的变革来应对不断变化的环境；⑥残酷的竞争，并且是全球范围内的竞争；⑦合作。传统经济中的自力更生已不适应新经济环境，企业需要与供应者、需求者以及其他机构深入合作，形成紧密的联系；⑧区位仍然重要，但影响因素更加复杂，企业倾向于把核心部门放在能提供竞争者、供应者、需求者、人才储备、特色机构和优质生活条件的地方。

基于对新经济的理解，在亚利桑那州政府的支持下，于1999年成立了亚利桑那州新经济伙伴组织（Arizona Partnership for the New Economy, APNE），并在2001年对支持集群发展的基础进行了调整，确定了包括联络设施、电子政务、在线教育、新型小区、知识型领导、企业家和资本在内的5个基础。与原来的基础相比，这5个新基础给出了更加具体的策略，例如通过建设新型小区来提供高质量的生活环境，通过提高教育、研发、技术转移、孵化和风险资本水平来满足产业集群对资本和人力资源的需求。最终，最初的战略框架经过重组和发展后，形成了由12个产业集群和5个产业集群发展支撑基础构成的战略框架。

表3 亚利桑那州的战略调整

| 调整时间 | 战略愿景 | 机构支撑 |
| --- | --- | --- |
| 1991/1992 | ASPED战略规划：通过发展产业集群振兴经济 | 亚利桑那州经济发展伙伴组织（Arizona Partnership of Economic Development） |
| 1993 | 建立跨国界合作区 | 亚利桑那州-墨西哥委员会（Arizona-Mexico Commission） |
| 2001 | 基于“新经济”理念优化支撑集群发展的基础 | 亚利桑那州新经济伙伴组织（Arizona Partnership for the New Economy） |
| 2002 | 提出发展生物科技产业的路线图 | 巴特尔纪念研究所（Battelle Memorial Institute） |
| 2005 | 提出将亚利桑那州建设成“全国最好的适宜生活和生产的地区之一” | 亚利桑那州未来中心（Center for the Future of Arizona） |
| 2008 | 提出建设“阳光走廊”；到2035年将亚利桑那州建设成为世界第一可持续发展区和全美领先的创新中心 | 亚利桑那州立大学Morrison公共政策研究所 |
| 2009 | 提出建设拥有“优质经济、社会和自然环境”的亚利桑那州 | 亚利桑那州未来中心（Center for the Future of Arizona） |

数据来源：Pavlakovich-Kochi（2010：24）。



在确定采用发展产业集群作为振兴经济的基本战略之后，亚利桑那州后续的战略调整都围绕着如何促进产业集群发展和提高整体经济的竞争力这一问题。鉴于与墨西哥索诺拉州（Sonora）接壤，亚利桑那州开始思考如何充分发挥边境区位优势和利用与索诺拉历史悠久的商贸、文化关系（Pavlakovich-Kochi，2010：23）。1993年，在亚利桑那州-墨西哥委员会的资助下，建立了跨国界的亚利桑那州-索诺拉经济合作区（Arizona-Sonora Region），开始开展跨境区域经济合作，以提高双方的全球竞争力和居民生活质量。2002年，在专业研究机构巴特尔纪念研究所的协助下，亚利桑那州提出了生物科技产业的路线图，明确了生物科技产业集群的具体发展路径，同时，巴特尔纪念研究所还继续对生物科技产业进行跟踪研究，每年都会对产业发展进程进行评估。此外，亚利桑那州近年来还重新调整了发展的战略愿景，这些愿景都致力于构建有利于产业集群发展的基础。例如，2008年，提出建设“阳光走廊”（Sun Corridor），“阳光走廊”是从普雷斯科特（Prescott）开始，经凤凰城和图森一直到墨西哥边境的一个大都市带，其发展目标是到2035年，将亚利桑那州建设成为世界第一可持续发展区和全美领先的创新中心，并为居民提供无与伦比的优势生活环境（MIPP，2008：10）。

## 4．亚利桑那州产业集群战略的特征

### 4.1　集群战略的科学性和动态性

前面的分析已经表明，亚利桑那州产业集群战略的制定，是由咨询机构、科研机构、专家、企业家等组成的庞大专业团队来完成的，采用了科学的方法来提出和编制规划，并吸收了社会各界的有益建议，这保证了规划的科学性和前瞻性。最初的亚利桑那州产业集群战略只提出了3类共8个产业集群，后来，在企业和社会各界的建议和推动下，不但对原设产业集群的名称和结构进行了重组，还形成了养老、新材料、在线教育、纳米科技等新的产业集群。与此同时，在研究机构的帮助下，通过对新经济的特征进行分析，对原来支撑产业集群发展的基础进行了浓缩和具体化。这些调整表明，亚利桑那州的产业集群发展战略并不是一个固定不变的战略设计，它是一个基于经济形势的变化和企业、研究机构等组织机构的推动而不断调整和优化的动态战略。值得注意的是，整个策略的调整和优化过程，都体现出行业组织的巨大推动作用。一旦行业组织自发形成并提出构建产业集群的诉求，产业集群战略的框架和内容也将做出相应调整，从而使这些新的产业集群与原有产业集群享受同等地位，而政府是很难从政治上拒绝这一诉求的（Waits，2000）。这也可以看出，亚利桑那州产业集群战略的主导者是市场而非政府。

### 4.2　中小企业是产业集群的核心主体

亚利桑那州产业集群体现出的重要特征之一，就是所有产业集群都是以中小企业为主体。例如，在产业集群集中的图森地区，高科技企业的全职雇员只有8人，年收入中位数为110万美元（KMK Consulting Team, 2006：17）。而在整个亚利桑那州，有超过41.2万个居民企业（Resident Firms），其中96.6%的企业雇员人数少于100人，而这些雇员少于100人的小企业雇佣了当地超过78%的劳动力，并且对1998至2008年间就业增长的贡献达到了92%（C2ER，2011：1）。在1998至2008年的10年间，居民企业总数年均增长8.1%，其中贡献最大的就是自营企业（1个职员）和职员数介于2至9人的小微企业，自营企业数年均增长了11.6%，而2至9个职员的小企业年均增长了7.5%，在从业人数方面亦体现出类似特征（表4）。此外，亚利桑那州还涌现出一批“瞪羚公司”（指那些增长很快的小企业，一般是指连续4年年收入超过10万美元并且年均增长20%的小企业）。据统计，2006至2009年期间，亚利桑那州共有43家“瞪羚公司”，其中38家来自私人部门，而这38个私人部门的“瞪羚公司”在4年里创造了550个新工作岗位，是其职员的两倍多（C2ER，2011：17）。由此可见，中小企业构成了亚利桑那州产业集群发展的核心主体，是促进地区经济增长和创造就业机会的主要贡献者。

表4　亚利桑那州企业增长情况（1998-2008）



| | 企业 | | | 从业人数 | | |
|---|---|---|---|---|---|---|
| | 1998 | 2008 | 年变化率 | 1998 | 2008 | 年变化率 |
| 居民企业总数 | 174 211 | 412 158 | 8.1% | 1 364 679 | 1 922 015 | 3.1% |
| 1个职员的企业（自营企业） | 44 317 | 149 591 | 11.6% | 44 317 | 149 591 | 11.6% |
| 2-9个职员的企业 | 103 463 | 231 370 | 7.5% | 378 242 | 671 794 | 5.3% |
| 10-99个职员的企业 | 25 037 | 29 561 | 1.5% | 571 657 | 684 911 | 1.6% |
| 100-499个职员的企业 | 1 261 | 1 488 | 1.5% | 216 692 | 259 750 | 1.6% |
| 超过500个职员的企业 | 143 | 148 | 0.3% | 153 771 | 155 969 | 0.1% |

数据来源：YourEconomy.org，转引自C2ER（2011：12）。

### 4.3　企业网络组织而非政府发挥着主导作用

尽管亚利桑那州政府在产业集群发展战略的制定中发挥了重要作用，但其并没有在产业集群的发展和壮大过程中过多地参与和干预。事实上，主导产业集群发展的是企业、科研机构等自发建立的网络化（Networking）组织，政府只鼓励和协助这些机构聚集在一起（Carrie，2000）。例如，在亚利桑那州南部的图森地区，聚集着高科技产业（航空航天和信息）、生物科技、在线教育、环境科技、纳米科技、光电和塑料及高级复合材料等产业集群，这些产业集群由各自领域的企业共同组建了非盈利的产业集群组织，产业集群组织又一起构成了南亚利桑那州科技委员会（Southern Arizona Tech Council, SATC），各级组织都为自己的会员提供信息交流平台、教育项目、专业咨询等服务（KMK Consulting Team, 2006：9-10）。SATC类似一个跨集群的联盟组织（Umbrella Organization），它由图森地区各个产业集群的负责人共同管理，运作资金来源于州、市、县政府拨入的用于发展劳动力、网络建设和维护等专项项目资金以及会员缴纳的会费，政府对产业集群的支持也主要通过这一平台来实现，会员可以向SATC申请项目经费（Sydow, Lerch, Huxham & Hibbert, 2007: 20）。

表5　南亚利桑那州产业集群组织

| 产业集群 | 集群组织 | 会员构成 | 组织使命 |
| --- | --- | --- | --- |
| 航空航天、先进制造和信息产业集群 | AMIT（Aerospace, Advanced Manufacturing and Information Technology） | 企业、教育机构和活跃于经济发展、科技研究的非盈利组织 | 为会员和亚利桑那州以外的企业创造商业机会；通过促进经验交流、培育专业人士团体、提供社交机会、统一与政府和公众对话和推进本地劳动力发展等措施来促进产业集群发展。 |
| 生物科技产业集群 | BIO-SA（Bioindustry Organization of Southern Arizona） | 企业、高校和研究机构以及对生物产业感兴趣的个人 | 通过社群建设、提供教育、识别联邦政策、促进技术转移和其他商务支持来促进地区生物产业发展。 |
| 在线教育产业集群 | GAZEL（Greater Arizona E-learning Association） | 提供在线教育的企业、企业家、教育工作者、在线教育参与者和消费者 | 通过帮助提供在线教育业务的企业开拓新业务、提升技术水准和服务水平、发展战略伙伴、与客户和其他专业人士建立联系、将技术和服务向全国和全球推广等方式来促进产业集群发展。 |

续表5

| 产业集群 | 集群组织 | 会员构成 | 组织使命 |
| --- | --- | --- | --- |
| 环境科技产业集群 | ETIC（Environmental Technology Industry Cluster） | 环境科技企业、科研机构 | 通过提供公共和私人资源的动态网络来促进环境科技产业的发展，最终把将亚利桑那州建设成为全球可持续发展科技的领导者。会员业务涉及碳管理、分布式发电、环境法、污染控制、资源回收、水域治理等所有环境科技领域。 |
| 纳米科技产业集群 | ANC（Arizona Nanotechnology Cluster） | 纳米技术企业、半导体、微电子领域的企业、高校、科研机构和研究人员 | 通过聚集纳米技术、半导体、微电子产业领域的个人、研究人员，向公众推广纳米科技，创造高收入工作机会，参与地区纳米实验室建设以促进纳米产业发展。 |
| 光电产业集群 | AOIA（Arizona Optics Industry Association） | 光电企业、研发及其他服务机构 | 通过市场推广和营销、构建成员及其他机构交流的网络、推动战略合作、提供教育等方式来促进光电产业发展。 |
| 塑料及高级复合材料产业集群 | PACMC（Plastic and Advanced Composite Material Cluster） | 企业、研发机构、政府、经济发展机构和其他私人非盈利机构 | 通过发展供应及分销网络、提供教育、发展劳动力、推进研发和技术转移等方式促进本产业集群的发展。 |

数据来源：根据KMK Consulting Team（2006：10–16）的描述整理。



### 4.4 以降低税收负担为主要激励措施

亚利桑那州主要通过构建更具竞争力的税收环境来实现地区经济发展。在20世纪90年代初，亚利桑那州开始实施大规模的减税措施，这使得亚利桑那州的个人税收和企业税收负担都远低于全国平均水平。根据霍夫曼和雷克斯（Hoffman & Rex, 2010: 56-57）的测算，1991年每1 000美元个人收入的综合税收负担超过了117美元，而到2001年，税收负担降到了100美元以下，2006、2007年税收负担有所上升，但这是由当时的经济繁荣导致的。尽管如此，这两年的税收负担也明显低于20世纪70年代、80年代晚期和90年代早期的税收负担。同时，与全国平均水平相比，亚利桑那州的税收负担长期以来也呈现出下降趋势，尤其是在20世纪90年代进行减税之后，人均税收负担一直低于全国平均水平，1993年以后，人均税收负担低于全国平均水平的90%（图1）。总的来看，亚利桑那州的税收负担相对较低，特别是个人税收负担和小企业税收负担非常低（Hoffman & Rex, 2010: 60-61）。而前述分析已经阐明，中小企业是亚利桑那州产业集群的核心力量，相对更轻的个人税负和小企业税负，无疑有利于中小企业的发展壮大和吸引优秀人才。显然，创造更具竞争力的税收环境是政府促进产业集群发展的主要手段。此外，亚利桑那州还不征收企业营业税（Corporate Franchise Tax）、商业库存税（Business Inventory Tax）和全球单一税（Worldwide Unitary Tax），也不对企业来自其外地附属公司的股息征收所得税（AZDC，2013），这使得亚利桑那州的税收环境在引进外来企业壮大产业集群时亦更具比较优势。

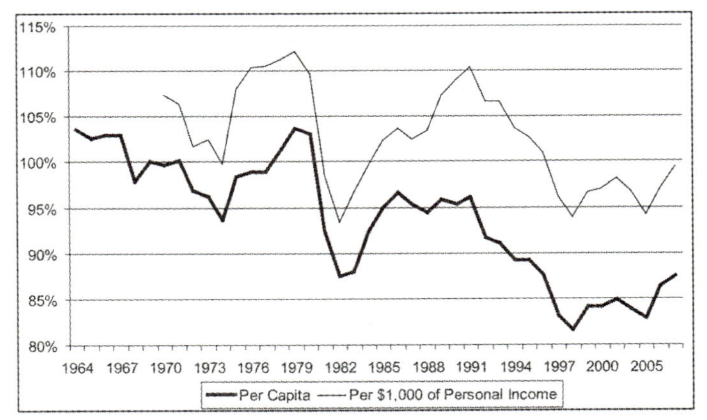


图1　亚利桑那州综合税收负担占全国平均水平的比（1964-2007）

数据来源：Hoffman & Rex（2010：57）。

### 4.5　跨境经济合作与跨境产业集群

前面已经指出，基于特殊的边境区位优势，亚利桑那州和墨西哥索诺拉州建立了跨境经济合作区，其具体目标是在北美自由贸易协议（NAFTA）的框架下，通过正式的协作和更有效地利用互补性资源来加快两个地区的经济发展和区域增长。两个地区特殊的历史、地理和经济关系，使得双方可以共享资本、人力资源、基础设施等资源，这些资源的共享也进一步使双方通过跨境产业集群之间的竞争和合作来促进地区经济增长。例如，就生鲜农产品产业而言，在NAFTA框架下，美国和墨西哥的生产者可以通过产品、金融、包装、仓储、信息、人力资源等领域的自由贸易和共享来实现竞争或合作。在亚利桑那州，生鲜农产品产业主要在运输和仓储等领域创造就业，而在索诺拉州，则主要在装载、货运等领域创造就业。此外，边境旅游业也是双方合作的重要领域。由于各自独特的自然环境，亚利桑那州与索诺拉州每年都有大量游客出入边境。据统计，2008年，来自墨西哥的游客共消费了27亿美元，这些消费为亚利桑那州创造了23 400个直接就业岗位和7 000多个间接岗位，并为州政府和地方政府贡献了超过2.35亿的税收（Mwaniki-Lyman，2010：101-104）。

## 5．亚利桑那州产业集群战略的经济效应

### 5.1 经济绩效的统计描述



自实施产业集群战略之后，亚利桑那州经济得以快速复苏，并成为20世纪90年代全美最具竞争力的地区之一。良好的工作和生活环境，成功吸引了大量外地人口到亚利桑那州工作和定居。据统计，在1990至2000年期间，亚利桑那州人口增加了150万，增速位列全美第二位，而且全州65%的人口是其他州或国外移民（Franciosi，2002）。亚利桑那州产业集群发展模式的成功经验，也得到了美国联邦政府和媒体的高度关注。国家发展政策委员会（National Growth Policies Board）和州长政策顾问委员会（Council of Governor's Policy Advisors）建议其他州借鉴亚利桑那州的产业集群发展模式，《世界贸易》（*World Trade*）杂志也对亚利桑那州的发展经验进行过专题报道。鉴于应用产业集群发展带动出口的显著效果，国家城市经济发展委员会还把“1996国家经济发展出口贸易奖”（1996 National Economic Development Export Trade Award）也授予了亚利桑那州（Waits, Rex & Melnick, 1997: 4）。

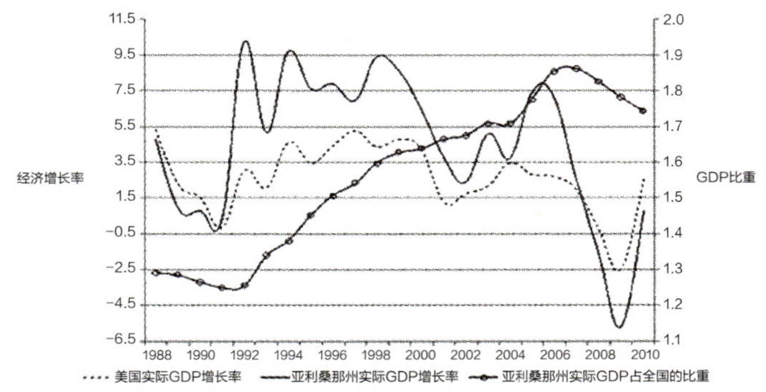


图2　美国和亚利桑那州GDP增速（1988−2010）

注：1988-1997年资料根据SIC标准计算（实际值以1997年为基期），1998-2010年资料根据NAICS标准计算（实际值以2005年为基期）。

数据来源：美国商务部经济分析局。

从经济增长情况来看，20世纪80年代末期，美国经济整体增长速度快速下降，亚利桑那州的实际经济增长率从1988年的4.78%快速下降到1991年0.42%，州国内生产总值（GDP）占全国的比重也由1988年1.29%下滑到1991年的1.25%。而在1992年的实施产业集群发展战略以后，亚利桑那州经济增长速度明显加快，尤其是1992至2000年期间，经济增长率长期保持在6%以上，年均增长率高达7.9%，远高于全国平均水平，这使得亚利桑那州GDP占全国的比重由1992年的1.26%上升到2000年的1.64%（图2）。与此同时，人均实际GDP增速在这期间也显著提高，年均增速达到4.3%。1992年，亚利桑那州人均GDP只有全国平均水平的83.84%，到2000年，这一指标达到了89.45%（图3）。

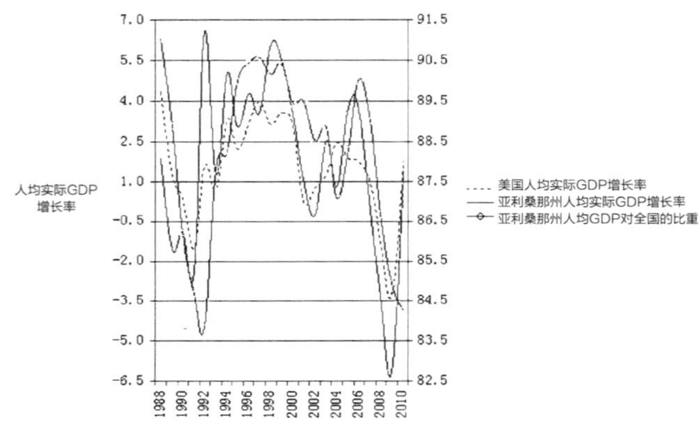


图3　美国和亚利桑那州人均GDP增速（1988-2010）

注：1988-1997年资料根据SIC标准计算（实际值以1997年为基期），1998-2010年资料根据NAICS标准计算（实际值以2005年为基期）。

数据来源：美国商务部经济分析局。



经济总量和人均产值在1992年前后的快速扭转，主要得益于实施产业集群战略后制造业的快速发展，这也充分体现了产业集群战略对亚利桑那州经济发展的积极影响。2000年亚利桑那州制造业和批发业产值在1991的基础上分别增长了178%和130%，采掘业和农业产值同期则只分别增长了58%和42%。而相比之下，就业增长的贡献主要来源于建筑业和金融、保险与房地产业，制造业和批发业就业增长分别只有22%和47%（表6）。制造业产值贡献和就业贡献的差异，也充分反映了亚利桑那州大力发展高科技产业带来的成效，产业重心逐渐由原来的劳动密集型产业转型为技术密集型产业。

表6　亚利桑那州产业增长速度（1991-2000）

| 就业增长 | | 州内生产总值（GSP） | |
|---|---|---|---|
| 产业 | 变化率 | 产业 | 变化率（扣除价格因素） |
| 建筑业 | 95 | 制造业 | 178 |
| 金融、保险与房地产 | 73 | 批发业 | 130 |

续表6

| 就业增长 | | 州内生产总值（GSP） | |
|---|---|---|---|
| 服务业 | 61 | 交通、通讯和公用事业 | 85 |
| 批发业 | 47 | 零售业 | 82 |
| 交通、通讯和公用事业 | 46 | 建筑业 | 76 |
| 农业 | 36 | 金融、保险与房地产 | 61 |
| 零售业 | 39 | 服务业 | 60 |
| 制造业 | 22 | 采掘业 | 58 |
| 政府 | 21 | 农业 | 42 |
| 采掘业 | -19 | 政府 | 21 |

数据来源：产业研究中心（Center for Business Research），转引自Franciosi（2002）。

## 5.2 经济绩效之断点检验

为了充分说明战略转型对经济运行效率的影响，下面对亚利桑那州经济长期表现（单一时间序列）进行突变断点检验，以判断经济效率是否在产业集群战略实施前后发生了显著变化。在指标选择上，考虑到人均国内生产总值不能真实反映劳动生产效率，因此选择每个雇员创造的GDP来（GDP per Employee）表示劳动生产率（记为EP）。同时，考虑到美国国民经济统计分类标准由NAICS标准替换原来的SIC标准，很难获得长期的GDP实际值，故而本文采用平均每个雇员创造的GDP占全国平均水平的比重来反映亚利桑那州的相对劳动生产率：

$$REP_t^{AZ} = \frac{EP_t^{AZ}}{EP_t^{US}} \qquad (1)$$

在式（1）中，EPtAZ和EPtUS分别代表亚利桑那州和美国的劳动生产率。由于还不能确定产业集群战略是否对亚利桑那州经济生产效率带来实质性影响，故不宜预先假设1992年前后经济效率发生了根本性改变。所以，本文运用Quandt依然比（QLR）统计量来检验未知的突变点。

QLR统计量在Chow检验的基础上进行了一定修正，它是所有Chow统计量中最大的那个统计值。假设F（τ）表示τ时期回归系数中存在突变假设的

Chow统计量，QLR检验的是一定时期内（ ττ ≤τ≤τ）的最大Chow统计量（斯托克和沃特森，2005：303），

$$QLR = Max\left[F(\tau_0), F(\tau_0+1), \ldots, F(\tau_1)\right] \quad (2)$$

首先，通过自相关性检验，设定REPtAZ为一个滞后4阶的自回归过程，进而对其进行Chow检验并获得Chow统计量，然后计算在区间内最大的Chow统计量，即获得QLR统计量。在5个约束条件（4个滞后项和1个截距项）、10%置信水平下的QLR统计量的临界值为3.26。利用STATA11.0程序设计来对1969至2010年亚利桑那州的相对劳动生产率进行QLR突变检验。结果显示，过去40余年中存在3个突变区间共8个突变点，分别是1975至1977、1991至1993和2003至2004（图4）。这说明，在产业集群战略实施的1992年前后，亚利桑那州经济生产效率确实发生了结构性突变，而经济发展的战略转型很可能就是导致突变的原因。



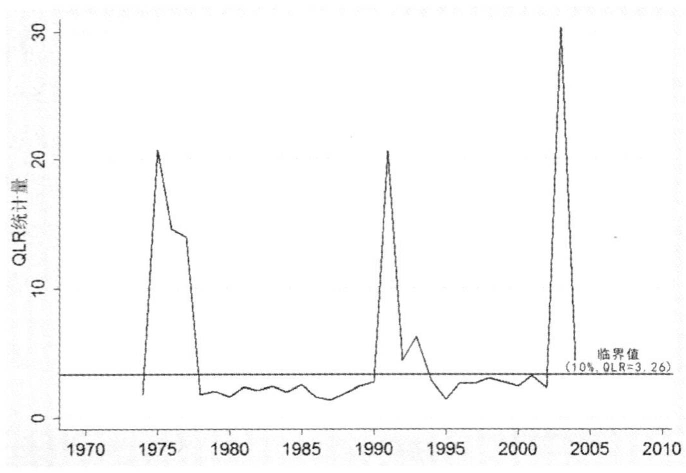


**图4　相对劳动生产率断点检验（1969-2010）**

注：此处的相对劳动生产率是指亚利桑那州平均每个雇员创造的GDP（GDP per Employee）占全国平均水平的比重；运用STATA11.0检验并制图。

综上所述，对经济增长速度、人均GDP增速、劳动生产率的分析都表明，1992年实施产业集群战略之后，亚利桑那州经济得以快速复苏，并且在很长一

段时期内，其经济增长速度都显著快于美国平均水平，并且实证分析也证明了1992年前后经济结构出现了突变。因此，从总体上来看，产业集群战略的实施对亚利桑那州经济复苏和快速发展起到了十分重要的作用，它快速提高了亚利桑那州制造业的生产水平和全球竞争力，实现了由传统劳动密集型产业为主的产业结构向技术密集型产业为主的产业结构的转型。

## 6．结论与经验启示

通过上文对美国亚利桑那州产业集群战略的制定、调整和特征进行的分析可以发现，亚利桑那州产业集群发展是以技术密集型中小企业和企业网络组织为核心驱动因素的发展模式，地方政府无论是在战略制定、实施还是后续调整和优化过程中，主要发挥“组织者”和“协调者”的作用，并且主要致力于创造领先的工作和生活环境来促进产业集群发展。亚利桑那州产业集群战略的实施，对地区经济复苏和发展起到了巨大的促进作用。目前，中国内地产业集群发展在空间分布上主要集中在长三角、珠三角、浙东南、环渤海湾等东部沿海地区，在产业类型上多以劳动密集型产业集群为主，缺乏自主创新能力，很多产业集群尤其是中西部地区发展还不成熟（吴利学、魏厚凯、刘长会，2009；向永胜，2012）。与20世纪90年代初的亚利桑那州一样，中国内地也面临经济结构转型的压力，而促进产业集群发展也成为很多地区促进经济转型的重要战略。借鉴亚利桑那州产业集群战略形成和发展的成功经验，我们认为，中国内地地区产业集群发展应重视以下几个方面：

第一，科学制定产业集群发展战略。亚利桑那州产业集群战略的制定过程中，专业性咨询机构、科研机构和专业人士发挥着关键作用，通过对本地优势、外部环境的深入研究和分析，最终才提出了具有长期可持续发展潜力的产业集群，并且整个战略是动态的，在后续的调整和优化过程中，又充分吸收了专业机构、专业人士和企业及企业家的建议。因此，亚利桑那州产业集群战略的成功，首先是从科学的战略设计开始的，政府的推动作用虽然不容忽视，但并不是关键因素，更重要的是，政府通过这个过程更加深入地掌握了当时的国际经济环境和发展趋势。亚利桑那州的经验无疑为中国内地试图通过发展产业集群来促进经济发展的地区提供了宝贵的经验，即必须通过科学的研究和分析，才能制定出具有长期效应的发展战略。

第二，重视创新型中小企业发展。中小企业是亚利桑那州产业集群发展的两个驱动因素之一，大量创新能力强的科技型中小企业引领着产业集群的发展和壮大。比较而言，中国内地的产业集群则以劳动密集型和资本密集型产业集群为主，这类集群中的企业需要通过规模化经营来实现利润提升，因此大多数地区的产业发展战略，都热衷于引进和发展大型企业，并围绕这些大型企业来发展产业集群，很多政府扶持政策也将这些大型企业作为重点对象，对中小企业发展的扶持力度很小。“一企独大”产业集群模式，实际上压抑了其他关联企业的发展，不利于企业间的竞争与合作。因此，有必要加大力度扶持具有发展潜力的、创新能力强的中小企业，以这些中小企业作为产业集群的核心力量。

第三，强化企业网络组织的作用。企业自发组建的强大企业网络组织是亚利桑那州产业集群发展的另一个核心驱动力。可以说，各个产业集群的企业网络组织和跨集群网络组织才是亚利桑那州产业集群的具体管理者和推动者，它们通过分享资源、提供专业咨询及教育等措施来强化彼此的联系、竞争与合作。而中国内地目前的产业集群发展过程中，企业网络组织发挥的作用有限，从而导致集群内企业之间、集群之间的联系不够紧密，企业间和集群间既缺乏竞争又缺乏合作，影响了地区产业的整体竞争力。



第四，加强跨区域产业合作。亚利桑那州地处美国西南边陲，独特的地理区位促使其把跨境经济合作和跨境产业集群作为战略方向之一，并取得了积极效果。这为中国内地边境地区产业集群发展提供了宝贵经验，例如中国内地西部的部分地区，就可以充分发挥区位地理优势，通过建立跨境经济合作区和发展跨境产业集群来促进地区经济发展。

## 参考文献：

吴利学，魏厚凯，刘长会. 中国产业集群发展现状及特征[J]. 经济研究参考，2009(15): 2-15.

向永胜. 我国产业集群发展的模式、现状与问题：一个全国范围的样本调查[J]. 科技管理研究，2012(10): 176-192.

斯托克，詹姆斯·H.，沃特森，马克·W. 经济计量学[M]. 王庆石，主译. 大连：东北财经大学出版社，2005.

AZDC. Arizona Nanotechnology Industry Profile: Science Crossing Traditional Boundaries[EB/OL].Available:http://www.azcommerce.com/assets/Nanotech%20Industry%20Profile_English.pdf, access date: 2013-4-2.

Breault, R., Hald, A., Kraver, T. The Governor's Strategic Partnership for Economic Development (GSPED) and Its Future[J]. *The International Society for Optical Engineering Journal*. Global Networking of Regional Optics Clusters, 1996: 11-20.

Carrie, A. S. From Integrated Enterprises to Regional Clusters: The Changing Basis of Competition[J]. *Computers in Industry*, 2000, 42: 289-298.

C2ER. Small Business & Entrepreneurship in Arizona: A Sector Profile. Arlington, VA, USA: Council For Community and Economic Research(C2ER), 2011.

Franciosi, R. Assessing Arizona's Economy: Boom or Bust?[M]//*Arizona Issue Analysis*. Phoenix, AZ: Goldwater Institute, 2002: 172.

Hoffman, D., Rex, T. R. *Improving the Fiscal System of Arizona State Government*[M]. Tempe, AZ, USA: W. P. Carey School of Business, Arizona State University, 2010.

KMK Consulting Team. Section 6: Industry Cluster Analysis[M]//Tucson Regional Economic Opportunities, ed. *Tucson Economic Blueprint: Strategic Analysis Report*. Tucson, AZ, USA: Tucson Regional Economic Opportunities, 2006.

MIPP. *The Road to Recovery: Lessons from Arizona's First Economy*[M]. Phoenix, AZ, USA: Morrison Institute for Public Policy, Arizona State University, 2009.

MIPP. *The New Economy: A Guide for Arizona*[M]. Tempe, AZ, USA: Morrison Institute for Public Policy, Arizona State University, 1999.

MIPP. *Megapolitan: Arizona's Sun Corridor*[M]. Tempe, AZ, USA: Morrison Institute for Public Policy, Arizona State University, 2008.

Mwaniki-Lyman, L. Uniqueness of Arizona[M]// Pavlakovich-Kochi, V. and McCormack, J. E. *Building Arizona's Future: Jobs, Innovation&Competitiveness*. Phoenix, AZ, USA: Ninety-Sixth Arizona Town Hall, 2010.

Pavlakovich-Kochi, V. Visioning Arizona: Where Do We Want to Be? [M]//Pavlakovich-Kochi, V. and McCormack, J. E. *Building Arizona's Future: Jobs Innovation&Competitiveness*. Phoenix, AZ, USA: Ninety-Sixth Arizona Town Hall, 2010.

Porter, M. E. Clusters and the New Economics of Competition[J]. *Harvard Business Review*, November/December, 1998.

Porter, M. E. *The Competitive Advantage of Nations*[M]. New York: Free Press, 1990.

PR Newswire. GSPED Recognizes E-Learning as New Arizona Industry Cluster. PR Newswire Association LLC, 2002, May 17.

Waits, M. J., Rex, T., Melnick, R. *Cluster Analysis: A New Toll for Understanding the Role of the Inner City in a Regional Economy*[M]. Tempe, AZ, USA: Morrison Institute for Public Policy, Arizona State University, 1997.

Waits, M. J. The Added Value of the Industry Cluster Approach to Economic Analysis, Strategy Development and Service Delivery[J]. *Economic Development Quarterly*, 2000, 14(1): 35-50.

Sydow, J., Lerch, F., Huxham, X., Hibbert, P. *Developing Photonics Clusters: Commonalities, Contrasts and Contradictions*[M]. London, UK: Advanced Institute of Management Research, 2007.

# Industry Cluster Development Strategy of Arizona, USA: Pattern, Efficiency and Lessons for China

[1]Lu Zheng [2]Li Wei

(1 School of Economics, Sichuan University, Chengdu, China, 610064; 2 School of Social Transformation, School of Geographical Science and Urban Planning, Arizona State University, Tempe, USA, 85287-5503)



**Abstract:** In the late 1980s and the early 1990s, Arizona's economy suffered a terrible recession which impelled Arizona to change its developing strategy. In 1992, Arizona's cluster strategy, ASPED, was implemented. This strategy successfully promoted the recovering and transforming of regional economy, and then it made Arizona to be one of the fastest growth regions of USA. This paper analyzed the decision-making, improvement and characteristics of ASPED strategy. This paper also assessed its overall effects as well by statistical analysis and QLR test. Conclusions show that Arizona's successful cluster development benefited from the scientific strategy making, the dual drive of high-tech small enterprises development and the networking between firms. The local government just exerts its effects as an organizer and a coordinator.

**Key Words:** Industrial Cluster; Arizona; Regional Development

# 文化、文学

# Culture & Literature

# The Sichuan University-Arizona State University Center for American Culture: The Context of US Cultural Diplomacy

Jannelle Warren-Findley

(School of Historical, Philosophical, and Religious Studies, Arizona State University, Tempe, USA, 85287-5503)

**Abstract:** The Sichuan University-Arizona State University Center for American Culture began operations with funding from the partner universities and the US Department of State through the American Embassy in Beijing in 2010. This account of its origins traces back in both the US and China to earlier days of diplomacy and educational exchange. This study maps the origins of "cultural diplomacy" through developments in twentieth-century US programs of international contact. Those programs, initially developed and funded by the private philanthropic community in the United States, later moved to national government status although nongovernmental groups (NGOs, private foundations, universities) continued to play a part in overseas diplomatic efforts. A brief mention of earlier US cultural diplomacy efforts and an account of their near-defeat by the US Senate in the late 1990s will frame the role of China's Confucius Institutes of the early 2000s as a spur to new efforts at cultural interaction between the two countries. The building of American Culture Centers, such as the SCU-ASU for example, can be seen at least partly as an American response to the development of Confucius Institutes worldwide.

**Key Words:** SCU-ASU Center; Cultural Diplomacy; Confucius Institutes

The Sichuan University-Arizona State University Center for American Culture began operations with funding from the partner universities and the US Department of State through the American Embassy in Beijing in 2010. This account of its origins traces back in both the US and China to earlier days of diplomacy and educational exchange. This study maps the origins of "cultural diplomacy" through developments in twentieth-century US programs of international contact. Those programs, initially developed and funded by the private philanthropic community in the United States, later moved to national government status although nongovernmental groups (NGOs, private foundations, universities) continued to play a part in overseas diplomatic efforts. A brief mention of earlier US cultural diplomacy efforts and an account of their near-defeat by the US Senate in the late 1990s will frame the role of China's Confucius Institutes of the early 2000s as a spur to new efforts at cultural interaction between the two countries. The building of American Culture Centers, such as the SCU-ASU for example, can be seen at least partly as an American response to the development of Confucius Institutes worldwide. The US Senate's role in urging this tactic, ironically, reversed that body's earlier dismissal of cultural diplomacy as a tool in the American global toolkit (Committee, 2011).

## 1. Introduction and Definitions



American cultural diplomacy has taken many forms over the years. The term "public diplomacy" describes communications between the people of countries rather than intergovernmental relationships, even thought government is often the initiator (Wang, 2008: 259). "Cultural diplomacy" uses exchanges of people and of ideas; "the cultural exchange programs are internationalist, concerned with promoting long-term mutual understanding between peoples" (Ninkovich, 1996: 3-4) while the informational role of government in foreign policy is more nationalistic and politically motivated, identified more specifically as information as propaganda. That said, however, from the time that the US Government began to engage in cultural and informational activities overseas, the two types have frequently been used for similar purposes: political aims in foreign policy. Thus any examination of cultural policy in the US (and more generally, the use of cultural diplomacy by any country) needs a two-part approach. The first is to analyze what the cultural activity is intended to accomplish and the second is to be mindful of how that accomplishment will play into the political uses of diplomacy.

## 2. The History of US Cultural Diplomacy in the Twentieth Century

In the United States, the Carnegie Endowment for International Peace (Edmunds, 1919: 62-86) formalized the notion of cultural diplomacy beginning in 1910. As Frank Ninkovich acknowledges, the privately-funded Carnegie Endowment set the pattern for programs that followed. As he said,

> It established what was to become the standard repertory of cultural relations: exchanges of professors and students, exchanges of publications, stimulation of translations and the book trade, the teaching of English, exchanges of leaders from every walk of life—all of these were to become the stock-in-trade of future governmental programs.
>
> (Ninkovich, 1981: 13)





In this period, however, in a coupling of Gilded Age wealth and Progressive Era ideology, cultural activities were the responsibility of the private sector rather than the national or federal government (Hart, 2013: 53). The Rockefeller Foundation and its related foundations entered the field in 1913 (Ninkovich, 1984: 799-820). The John Simon Guggenheim Foundation followed quickly ("The Advisory Board of the Guggenheim Memorial Foundation", 1930: 554-555). Scholarly and professional organizations took on roles in the development of cultural diplomacy: the Institute of International Education (IIE) in 1919 (Duggan, 1921: 136-137), the American Council of Learned Societies in 1920 (Lane, 2009: 236-237), the American Library Association in the late nineteen-teens and early twenties (Yu, 1998: 389-406). Much of this early activity grew out of hopes for the establishment of the League of Nations at the end of World War I. When the push for international organization failed, the groups involved took on elements of cultural diplomacy that, under other circumstances, might have been planned and pursued on the international level as a part of the League's work.

Public diplomacy as a tool of foreign policy has a long history and by the 1920s, European powers such as France and Great Britain added forms of cultural diplomacy to their national arsenals. As the Nazi threat developed in Europe during the 1930s, the US government turned to forms of cultural diplomacy to compete directly with European cultural hegemony particularly in the Americas. They also strove to overcome a domestic sense of "cultural cringe" and to claim a space in the world of arts and music for American efforts. Axis influence in South America worried President Roosevelt and many policy officials, so Roosevelt established the Office of the Coordinator of Inter-American Affairs outside of the US Department of State bureaucracy and appointed Nelson Rockefeller to head it (Hart, 2013: 39-40). Early programs sent Aaron Copland the composer, the Yale Glee Club and other musicians, writers and artists to tour South America as exhibits of American cultural development to counter the long tradition of European cultural impact (Ninkovich & Hart: 30-37). Rockefeller insisted on including technical activities with the cultural programs and in that sense, combined for the first time economics, modernization, development and culture into one government effort.



During the war, cultural and technical work continued in South America and in China. In 1942, the State Department renewed on a governmental level the tradition of educational exchange with China by establishing a cultural exchange program (Ninkovich, 1980: 471-498). According to Hart in *Empire of Ideas*, Americans, influenced by missionary accounts from the $19^{th}$ century and writers and publishers like Pearl Buck and Henry Luce, believed the Chinese to be "a hearty, industrious people," with an "ancient" and "noble" culture (Hart, 2013: 52-53). Establishing programs with China thus built on both tradition and opportunity. Without characterizing it as such, the Department of State attempted to extend South and Latin America's "Good Neighbor Policy" to their ally across the Pacific.

The Chinese program began with fanfare in 1942 but wartime prevented much activity. By 1946, China had "received the first of the Fulbright exchange scholars" (Hart, 2013: 54) and finally began to realize that the various modernization projects that World War II had made were too difficult to carry out. But as Hart notes, even this program with its wartime limits had an impact. As he writes,

> ...the ultimate significance of the China program probably lies more in its symbolism than its accomplishments. During its short tenure...the "cultural experiment" in China managed to encapsulate most of the major themes of 20th-century US foreign policy: the fascination with China as the great untapped resource of the future; the desire to use culture and ideology as a means of expanding US hegemony without incurring the costs of traditional territorial imperialism; and, ultimately, the attempt to counteract the appeal of revolutionary communism through winning hearts and minds.
>
> (Hart, 2013: 55)



The Chinese program came to an abrupt end in 1949. The United States cut all ties to the Peoples' Republic of China as a result of the Chinese revolution. The next three decades saw no formal cultural exchanges between the US and China.

## 3. The United States Information Agency, 1953-1999

After the war, President Eisenhower made cultural diplomacy efforts a permanent part of American foreign relations by establishing the United States Information Agency (USIA) in 1953. For the first time, there was a separate government agency, closely allied with but not connected to the Department of State, to carry out cultural diplomacy. As Nicholas Cull found, the agency's mandate included:

> The short-wave radio station Voice of America (VOA), wartime [American] cultural centers and libraries, documentary and television film units, Marshall Plan information offices, the *Amerika Hauser* created for the reeducation of Germany, embassy press specialists, magazines, speakers, and exhibition programs...It also included analysts charged with monitoring world opinion and feeding advice in the making of US foreign policy.
>
> (Cull, 2012: 2)

USIA practiced both an "information" track that represented US political goals in the world of the Cold War and a "cultural" route that used soft diplomacy and people-to-people interactions to shape understanding and presumably build relationships between countries around the world and the United States (Snow, 2008: 215).

Although the new federal agency played no formal role in Chinese-American exchanges during this period of separation, it worked in an atmosphere in Washington among students of China that by the early 1960s was considering informal Sino-American contacts. Wang Dong points out that in the early 1960s President John F. Kennedy called for some relaxation of strained cultural ties and he was joined by other State Department officials and leaders of prominent American foundations who had previously been active in educational activities in China (Wang, 2013: 206). Scholarly groups such as the Joint Committee on Contemporary China of the American Council of Learned Societies and the Social Science Research Council and the National Academy of Sciences united in the period 1963-1966 to explore ways of reopening the door to intellectual and educational exchange with their Chinese counterparts (Bullock, 2005: 49-51). American Studies programs developed. As Zhu Yongtao recounted:



> In answer to Chairman Mao Zedong's call for an expansion of foreign studies, some research-oriented institutions and university-based teaching-research centers were established in 1964 with emphasis on American

history, international relations, American economy, and American literature. Among them were the American History Research Office in the Institute of World History under the Chinese Academy of Social Sciences (CASS), the American Economic Research Office in the Institute of World Politics and Economy of the CASS, the American History Research Centers in the Departments of History at Nankai University and Wuhan University, the Research Group of Modern and Contemporary British and American Foreign Relations at Nanjing University, and the Institute of Modern American Literature at Shandong University. These institutions helped to organize Chinese scholars into initial American Studies programs.

(Zhu, 1987: 4)

When US President Richard Nixon visited China in 1972, discussions concerning such Sino-American scholarly exchanges began. By 1978, the US and China signed an exchange agreement. Ten years later, the Hopkins-Nanjing Center for Chinese and American Studies opened at Nanjing University (Wheeler, 2013: 8-13). The entire sequence of events preceded and then followed on China's educational reopening in the 1970s.

For the US government, the two terms of Ronald Reagan brought more power to the United States Information Agency. Reagan appointed his friend, Charles Wick, as USIA's director and instructed the agency to use educational exchanges and other forms of cultural diplomacy to utilize "sponsored educational and cultural exchanges as an opportunity to directly challenge the persuasive appeal of the Soviet Union's 'Evil Empire'" (Snow, 2008: 215). But after 1989 when the Berlin Wall fell and the Soviet Union began to collapse, as Snow details, "The Clinton Administration bowed to Congressional critics of USIA and budget hawks looking for 'peace dividends' following the collapse of the Soviet Union. USIA went from being a separate Cabinet agency to a division in the State Department headed by an Under Secretary of State who oversees the Bureaus of Educational and Cultural Affairs, International Information Programs and Public Affairs" (Committee, 2011: 4). The only parts of the agency to survive as independent units were the various broadcasting services.

USIA disappeared in 1999; the events of September 11th, 2001 pressed the legislative branch of the American government to fund more of the unit's cultural diplomatic activities. But those undertakings remained in an office in the Department of State and were quite different from pre-Reagan era efforts. As Snow details,

> The purpose of public diplomacy and strategic communication activities as presented by the [Strategic Communication and Public Diplomacy Policy Coordinating Committee of the Department of State (PCC 2007)] states, "The US government includes a renewed commitment to international exchange of persons that helps to serve the needs of the US government in the following four areas:
>
> · underscore our commitment to freedom, human rights, and the dignity and equality of every human being;
>
> · reach out to those who share our ideals;
>
> · support those who struggle for freedom and democracy; and
>
> · counter those who espouse ideologies of hate and oppression."
>
> The PPC outlines a partnership model of engagement: "With our partners, we seek to isolate and marginalize violent extremists who threaten the freedom and peace sought by civilized people of every nation, culture and faith (p. 3). To that end, exchanges are designed to identify individuals who can impact wider segments of society, including exchangees who can document their activities through old and new media technologies, such as Web chats, documentaries, YouTube, and news media programs."
>
> (Snow, 2007: 218-219)

In other words, the intellectual and personal criteria used to evaluate students and faculty exchanges in the past were, by 2007, framed by more overt governmental purposes.

## 4. Chinese Developments

In 2004, China began establishing Confucius Institutes overseas, the purpose of which was to "strengthen educational cooperation, promote the development of Chinese language education and increase mutual understanding." Established in Seoul, Republic of Korea, "the first of these institutes appeared in November 2004, and although the initial plan was to establish 100, by the end of 2007 there were already 210 Confucius Institutes in place globally" (Starr, 2004: 65). By 2009, there were more than 300. In 2014, in the United States alone, the numbers are 97 for the Institutes located mostly on American university campuses and 357 Confucius Classrooms, Chinese language and culture programs are established in middle and secondary schools across the US ( http://english.hanban.org/node_10971.htm). Those units, in turn, were patterned after the older German cultural institutes, the Goethe Institutes; and French version, the Alliances Françaises or Italy's Dante Alighieri Society (Louie, 2011: 78), except that those institutions were established as entities in the community while the Confucius Institutes are embedded in university departments and campuses (Sahlins, 2013: 5).

The first Confucius Institute to open in the US was in 2004 at the University of Maryland-College Park. The ASU Institute opened in 2007 (Louie, 2011: 78). A report on educational exchange between the US and China to the Senate Foreign Relations committee in 2011 complained that China had about 70 Institutes in the US but China had allowed only 5 American centers to be opened in China. To get around these restrictions, the report noted, the Bush administration had allowed and funded the Department of State to help universities with already established programs to set up American centers in China. The report's authors pointed out, as well, that more funding would be needed to keep up with the spread of Confucius Institutes (Committee, 2011: 5). The Minority Staff Report of the Senate Foreign Relations urged the American government to take on this challenge. The first instance involved Arizona State University. As the report described it,

As part of her re-invigoration and re-examination of US PD efforts, Under Secretary for Public Diplomacy and Public Affairs Judith McHale created a $2 million Innovation Fund from which Embassies worldwide can compete for one-time grants. As part of this, the US Embassy in Beijing submitted a winning proposal that is assisting Arizona State University with $100,000 in financial and material support to open a Center for American Culture in Sichuan University in Chengdu—in essence an expansion of ASU's prior relationship with Chengdu. ASU is adding $150,000 for in-kind services, and Sichuan is providing the space as well as a Chinese co-director, graduate student assistants, and lodging and meals for American scholars from ASU. The Center offers free Internet connectivity (students normally have to pay), regular movie showings, visiting speakers, English conversation, and collaboration between ASU and Sichuan students as well as faculty. Plans for a full-time ASU professor on the ground for a semester or a year will require additional funding. While Internet access will have to be in accordance with Chinese law, the Center stocks several thousand volumes and several dozen periodicals from around the world. As innovative as the ASU-Sichuan partnership may be, such a one-off success hardly suggests a coherent strategy to increase the number of US PD platforms, official or otherwise. Nonetheless, the role of American universities as projectors of "soft power" should not be underestimated, and the State Department should be encouraged to provide similar funding for other such US university projects in China to serve as a dual-track PD effort.

(Ibid.: 9-10)



In response to the new funding, ASU President Michael M. Crow stated,

Building on the effective collaboration between Sichuan University and Arizona State University through the Confucius Institute, the SCU-ASU

Center for American Culture will provide opportunities for students at Sichuan University to interact with faculty and students from Arizona State University to advance an understanding of American culture, history, literature, media, music and art. Chinese students will study the underpinnings of American culture and history at the Center for American Culture just as American students acquire competence in Chinese language and culture through their intensive study at the Confucius Institute.

(Crow, 2013)

It is not yet clear whether the ASU-SCU American Cultural Center will provide the language and culture education that Confucius Institutes do. The more recent development of the ACCEX network, funded by the US Department of State, built on the Sichuan experience and now includes nineteen American Cultural Centers at Chinese Universities. These programs collectively have the following mission:

The mission of these ACCs is to educate the next generation of citizens and leaders about American culture, history, values and beliefs. The ACCs create programs, outreach activities, exhibits, lectures, and performances that foster a deeper appreciation for American society and values by thoughtful exploration of the nuances and complexities of American life.

(http://www.accexnetwork.org/ Accessed 4/17/14)

Though these American efforts in China may be new, the stated impulses behind their origins clearly link back to earlier efforts at cultural diplomacy on the part of the United States. The philanthropic foundations which first focused on education in China in the nineteen-teens and -twenties would recognize the intent and, to some extent, the models in the contemporary situation. It is ironic that it took the development of the Chinese Confucius Institutes to spur the United States to once again promote its soft power in China.

Acknowledgement

*Thanks to Dr. Kathryn Mohrman, co-director of the ASU-SCU Center for American Culture and Ms. Fannie Tam of the ASU Confucius Center for help and advice.*

## Bibliography:

Bullock, Mary Brown. Mission Accomplished: The Influence of the CSCPRC on Educational Relations with China[M]// Cheng Li, ed. *Bridging Minds across the Pacific: US-China Educational Exchanges, 1978-2003*. Lanham, MD: Lexington Books, 2005: 49-51.

Committee on Foreign Relations. US Senate Minority Staff Report. Another US Deficit– China and America–Public Diplomacy in the Age of the Internet[R]. 112th Cong, First Session, Feb. 15, 2011, (S. Prt. 112-15) (Committee Print (R) Minority).

Cull, Nicholas J. *The Decline and Fall of the United States Information Agency: American Public Diplomacy, 1989-2001*[M]. New York: Palgrave Macmillan, 2012: 2.

Duggan, Stephen J. The Institute of International Education, Advocate of Peace through Justice[J]. 1921, 83(4): 136-137.



Edmunds, Charles K. Modern Education in China[J]. *The Journal of International Relations*, 1919, 10(1): 62-86.

Hart, Justin. *Empire of Ideas: The Origins of Public Diplomacy and the Transformation of US Foreign Policy*[M]. New York: Oxford University Press, 2013: 53.

http://cac.asu.edu/about/about-the-center Accessed 6/23/13.

http://english.hanban.org/node_10971.htm, accessed 4/17/14.

http://www.accexnetwork.org/ Accessed 4/17/14.

Lane, Joe. American Council of Learned Societies[J]. *PS: Political Science and Politics*, 2009, 42(1): 236-237.

Louie, Kam. Confucius the Chameleon: Dubious Envoy for "Brand China"[M]// *China after Thirty Years of Reform: Critical Reflections* (Boundary 2, Vol. 38, No. 1), 2011: 78.

Ninkovich, Frank. US Information Policy and Cultural Diplomacy No. 308 Fall 1996. New York: HEADLINE SERIES, Foreign Policy Association: 3-4.

—. The Rockefeller Foundation, China, and Cultural Change[J]. *The Journal of American History*,

1984, 70(4): 799-820. Accessed: 15/04/2014.

—. *The Diplomacy of Ideas: US Foreign Policy and Cultural Relations, 1938-1950*[M]. Cambridge: Cambridge University Press, 1981: 13.

—. Cultural Relations and American China Policy, 1942-1945[J]. *Pacific Historical Review*, 1980, 49(3): 471-498.

Sahlins, Marshall. China U: Confucius Institutes Censor Political Discussions and Restrain the Free Exchange of Ideas. Why, then, do America universities sponsor them?[J] *The Nation*, November 18, 2013: 5.

Starr, Don. Chinese Language Education in Europe: The Confucius Institutes[J]. *European Journal of Education*, 2009, 44(1): 65.

Snow, Nancy. International Exchanges and the US Image[M]//*Annals of the American Academy of Political and Social Sciences*, Vol. 616 , Public Diplomacy in a Changing World, 2008: 215.

The Advisory Board of the Guggenheim Memorial Foundation[J]. *Science, New Series*, 1930, 71(1848): 554-555. Accessed: 17/04/2014 12:03.

The perception that one's own culture is inferior to that of another group or country[EB/OL]. Dictionary.com. http://dictionary.reference.com/browse/cultural+cringe. Accessed: 6/23/2013.

Wang, Dong. *The United States and China: A History from the Eighteenth Century to the Present*[M]. Lanham, MD: Rowman&Littlefield, 2013: 206.

Wang, Yiwei. Public Diplomacy and the Rise of Chinese Soft Power[M]//*Annals of the American Academy of Political and Social Science*, Vol. 616, Public Diplomacy in a Changing World, 2008: 259.

Wheeler, Norton. *The Role of American NGOs in China's Modernization: Invited Influence*[M]. Oxford: Routledge, 2013: 8-13.

Yu, Priscilla C., Davis, Donald G. Jr. Arthur E. Bostwick and Chinese Library Development: A Chapter in International Cooperation[J] *Libraries&Culture*, 1998, 33(4): 389-406.

Zhu, Yongtao. American Studies in China[J] *American Studies International*, 1987, 25(2): 4.

# 四川大学-亚利桑那州立大学美国文化中心：美国文化外交政策背景

简奈尔·瓦伦-芬得利

（亚利桑那州立大学历史、哲学及宗教研究学院，美国坦佩，85287-5503）

**摘　要：**四川大学-亚利桑那州立大学美国文化中心于2010年在伙伴学校与美国国防部的资助下通过美国驻北京大使馆开始运行。其起源可以追溯到中美两国早前的外交与教育交流。通过20世纪美国国际交往项目的发展，这项研究指出了“文化外交”的起源。这些项目最初是由美国私人慈善发展并资助的，随后变为国家政府的项目，与此同时，非政府组织（非政府组织、私人基金会、大学）继续为海外外交努力着。而孔子学院的建立也促进两个国家的文化交流。美国文化中心，例如四川大学-亚利桑那州立大学美国文化中心，部分程度上可以看作是美国对孔子学院在全世界的发展的回应。



**关键词：**四川大学-亚利桑那州立大学美国文化中心；文化外交；孔子学院

# 美国文化外交的政治目标与非政治策略
## ——以国际访问者项目为例[1]

杨 光

（四川大学外国语学院，四川成都 610064）

**摘 要：** 国际访问者项目是由美国政府财政支持并且长期开展的大规模教育文化交流项目，它反映文化外交传播“自由、民主、平等”这一长期目标，同时也折射出现实主义国际政治思想对实现短期政策目标的考量。在比较基于媒体的信息项目和基于人员交流的教育文化项目所达成效果的差别基础上，美国以非政府组织参与实施国际访问者项目的方式，淡化了政府干预文化事务的色彩，降低了政治宣传的负面作用，以非政治策略提高了文化外交效率。国际访问者项目是美国文化外交的缩影。

**关键词：** 文化外交；国际访问者项目；政治目标；非政治策略



当今世界，文化外交与政治外交、经济外交和军事外交一道，在外交舞台上扮演着重要角色，文化成为能够“通过劝导他人或他国追随或认同我方的价值规范和制度安排，进而产生我方所意想的行为”（Keohane & Nye, 1996: 86）的软实力。在利用文化软实力实现国家利益的文化外交实践中，美国政府实施了包括国际访问者项目（International Visitor Leadership Program）[2]、富布

1 本文已发表于《太平洋学报》2014年第22卷第6期，第32-39页。此次收录，编者对文章略有修改。

2 该项目源自1940年开始的南美洲人员交流项目。1949年被称为外国领导者项目（Foreign Leader Program，简称FLP），1965年更名为国际访问者项目（International Visitor Program，简称IVP），2004年更名为国际访问领导者项目（IVLP）。为保持行文一致，本文统称国际访问者项目。

赖特项目（Fulbright Program）和汉弗莱项目（Humphrey Program）等在内的一系列文化外交项目，其中历史最悠久的国际访问者项目已经开展七十余年（早于始于1946年的富布赖特项目）。国际访问者项目在着眼推广自由、民主、平等这一美国信条的同时，也注重实现不同历史时期的短期政策目标，并采取了行之有效的策略。研究国际访问者项目所体现的美国文化外交思想，了解美国使用文化软实力达成政策目标的有效策略，在实践层面对我国开展文化外交具有借鉴意义。

## 1. 美国文化外交的长期目标与短期考量

罗斯福时期负责南美事务的助理国务卿萨姆纳·韦尔斯（Sumner Welles）曾经问道："一项真正的文化关系项目是否能够被用于执行一个国家的外交政策？"（Espinosa，1976：195）按照现实主义国际政治理论观点，国家利益是判断、指导政治行为的唯一永存的标准，外交政策必须以国家利益来界定（汉斯·摩根索，1990：15）。因此，要回答韦尔斯的问题，关键看文化关系是否服务于国家利益。塞缪尔·亨廷顿认为，国家利益通常包括两个方面，一是安全和物质利益，二是道德和伦理上的关注。就美国而言，美国的国家利益观念深受宗教使命感和国家使命感影响，捍卫和促进自由民主普世价值观成为国家利益的重要组成部分。美国著名学者路易斯·哈茨在他的《美国自由主义传统》一书中指出，美国从其建国之初就已是一个自由主义社会，在这样一个社会里，自由主义传统已是世界上最强大的牢固传统之一（路易斯·哈茨，2003：1-2）。独立战争的历史表明，美国人对丧失已经获得的自由和财富的担心，远甚于追求尚未得到的利益所带来的喜悦。美国人相信，维护自由民主制度是国家安全的重要内容，美国只有通过在全世界传播自由民主制度，建立基于民主制度的国际体系，才能够保证美国安全，促进世界繁荣。美国学者布鲁斯·詹特尔森也指出："美国对外关系从来没有仅仅局限于传统的政治、战略和经济利益，从共和国初期开始，在世界范围内促进民主价值观和理想就成为国家目标的一部分，同时也规定了美国在世界事务中应该扮演的特殊角色。"（Jentleson & Paterson, XXII）



基于此，美国政府对韦尔斯的问题给予了肯定的回答，因为对自由民主制度的推崇，使对自由理想的传播与民主共同体的扩大成为美国外交政策的重要目标，文化关系的建立以及文化项目的开展与美国实现国家利益的总体目标一致。在自由主义思想影响下，在实现国家利益目标的驱动下，美国积极推进包括人员交流在内的各种教育文化交流，以文化关系影响其他国家接受美国价值观，以期实现美国政策目标。美国前总统杜鲁门认为，美国开展的文化交流项目要“确保各国人民获得一幅完整清晰的美国生活画卷，同时了解美国政府的目标和政策”（Scott-Smith，2008：33）。美国负责教育与文化事务的前助理国务卿海琳娜·费伊（Helena Finn）也撰文指出，美国政策制定者懂得与外国观众接触和战胜自己的意识形态敌人之间的联系，文化外交对美国的国家安全利益至关重要，文化外交是美国军火库中最有力的武器之一（Finn，2003：15）。因此，美国政府鼓励通过文化交往来推进相互理解，美国教育和文化项目所寻求的就是通过使其他国家的民众充分了解美国文化生活的多样性，从而获得对美国社会文化的更好包容，进而实现美国推广自由民主这一根本政治目标。

国际访问者项目是以文化外交推广美国价值观、实现美国外交政策的有效工具。国际访问者项目每年邀请有潜力成为领袖的各国人士访问美国，让他们亲身接触美国社会，深入了解优越的美国文化带来的社会发展成果，然后通过他们进一步向本国国民传递美国的自由民主思想。截至2013年，已有累计超过20万名来自各国的社会精英通过该项目访问美国，其中330位项目成员成为国家或政府首脑。这330位首脑，包括英国前首相撒切尔夫人和前首相布莱尔、法国前总统萨科奇、澳大利亚前总理吉拉德以及台湾地区现任领导人马英九等知名领导人，另有超过1 500名项目成员成为世界各国政府内阁或议会成员[1]。美国这一文化交流项目造就了一大批各国政府的“知美派”甚或“亲美派”，为各国理解和支持美国政策创造了宽松的外部环境。可以说，美国凭借自己在文化领域强大的软实力，借助国际访问者项目，在一定程度上成功地影响了别的国家认同甚至追随美国的价值规范和制度安排，劝导他国按照美国的目标行动，从而间接实现控制他国政策、实现美国外交政策的目的。美国国务院也

1　见美国国务院网站，About IVLP[EB/OL], http://eca.state.gov/ivlp/about-ivlp, 2013年10月19日。

认为该项目是“支持美国实现外交政策目标最有效的文化教育活动”（Scott-Smith，2008：33，22）。

美国文化外交项目在着眼实现推广自由民主这一长期目标的同时，也非常注重短期现实利益，关注对短期政策目标的达成。现实主义国际关系学派认为，外交政策最根本的动力是对权力和利益的追求，而美国最重要的国家利益包括四个方面：第一是安全利益，第二是意识形态利益，第三是保护和促进商业，第四是维护有利的世界权利均势（王立新，2007：185）。纵观美国文化外交史，文化外交表现出对不同历史时期国际形势的精确估算和为此做出的灵活反应，文化外交对所追求的短期目标的不断调整始终围绕美国现实客观利益，在这一点上，国际访问者项目是一个良好例证。

首先，国际访问者项目是美国维护不同历史时期国家安全的文化利器。20世纪30年代，德国纳粹加强对南美洲的经济和文化渗透，美国后院面临威胁。为此，美国国务院于1938年正式成立文化关系司，通过向南美洲国家推介美国文化，达到抵御德国文化入侵的目的。文化关系司的成立是美国正式开始文化外交的标志。随着形势的发展，美国又成立了美洲间国家事务协调办公室（CIAA），以人员交流、报纸、电台等多种方式解释美国外交政策。1940年开始的国际访问者项目，正是针对德国威胁而采取的文化外交应对举措之一。是年，三十余位有社会影响力的南美洲人士应邀访问美国，美国寄希望于国际访问者项目“在海外建立一种公众舆论的氛围，以使美国的行动和政策能够得到正确解读”（Scott-Smith，2008：34）。“9·11”之后，布什政府意识到文化外交对促进阿拉伯世界对美国了解的重要性，于2003年成立国务院文化外交咨询委员会，负责制定文化外交政策和增加文化外交项目的运用，大力加强对包括中东和北非穆斯林地区的文化宣传，以树立更好的国际形象。在此过程中，为数众多的来自中东和其他地区伊斯兰国家的社会精英人士作为国际访问者被邀请访问美国。

其次，国际访问者项目是美国维护意识形态领域利益的重要棋子。第二次世界大战结束以后，由于欧洲在战后不断发展的经济、在国际组织中不断增强的话语权，以及对第三世界国家持续增加的影响力，争取西欧各国对美国文化和社会制度的认同，建立具有共同价值观的大西洋共同体以对抗来自东欧国家的威胁，关乎美国国家利益。根据对1954年国际访问者项目的统计，来自西欧的访问者总人数是645人，而同一年来自非洲的是93人，亚洲82人，拉丁美洲35人（Scott-Smith，2008：40），西欧成为第二次世界大战以后地缘政治的中心。通过国际访问者项目，来自欧洲各国的人士加深了对美国自由民主制度的认同。从这个意义上看，国际访问者项目对维护与美国在意识形态领域持共同价值观的国家的关系，发挥了巨大作用。在同一时期，美国加强对德国和日本的民主化改造，使德国和日本接受美国核心价值观。在这一过程中，包括国际访问者项目在内的教育文化交流项目对促进德国和日本社会了解并接受美国价值观发挥了不可替代的重要作用。

第三，国际访问者项目是维护世界权利均势的文化武器。冷战期间，随着美苏两极对立格局的形成，文化外交的目标之一是维持两大政治集团的文化均势。以美国为首的北大西洋公约组织和以前苏联为首的华沙条约组织，除了在政治、军事和经济领域全面对抗，在文化外交领域也针锋相对，力图向对方展示己方制度的巨大优越性。据统计，1955年有363个来自西欧国家的代表团应邀访问前苏联。1956年，仅法国比利牛斯地区的一个政府部门就有42人访问东欧国家（“Priority Educational Exchange Projects”）[1]。美国显然无法接受不均衡的文化交流。为保持文化均势，1958年美国与前苏联签署文化交流协议，强化文化外交。之后，文化外交的范围被扩大到南斯拉夫、波兰和罗马尼亚等国家，来自东欧的国际访问者也应美国国务院邀请访问美国。冷战期间，国际访问者项目成为美国与前苏联在文化教育领域争夺文化均势的重要手段。从以上事例不难看出，以国际访问者项目为代表的教育文化交流项目，成为美国政府除政治、经济和军事外又一实现国家利益的有力武器。不同历史时期国际访问者项目所针对的各种短期目标，是美国文化外交注重现实国家利益的最好证明。

## 2. 信息项目还是教育文化项目?

美国在开展文化外交的方式上历来有信息项目和教育文化项目之分，两类

1 Bureau of Educational and Cultural Affairs, “Priority Educational Exchange Projects”, 25 January 1956, Group IV Box 153 Folder 17.

项目由于指导思想不同和所针对目标存在差异，其发展也经历了不同的历史轨迹。信息项目主要指基于图书、报刊和电台等各类媒体的文化宣传项目，以信息单向传播为主，例如美国之音和欧洲自由电台。第二次世界大战后，信息项目主要由美国新闻署（USIA）负责运作，受现实主义国际关系思想影响，其着眼点是对外宣传美国外交政策，关注对短期外交目标的实现。教育文化项目以美国和目标国之间人员双向交流为主，着眼长期效果和持续影响力的实现，国际访问者项目和富布赖特项目均属此类。这类项目由美国国务院教育与文化事务局（CU）负责，教育文化类项目主要受美国前总统威尔逊理想主义思想影响，富布赖特参议员是力主教育文化双向交流的代表人物。

美国对在文化外交中使用信息项目一直存有争议。信息项目的使用始于第一次世界大战期间，为了说服民众支持参加第一次世界大战，美国政府成立公共信息委员会（Committee of Public Information），以讲座、展览、海报以及报纸杂志等方式宣传政府政策。美国参战后，公共信息委员会也对外开展宣传，向其他国家阐明美国的外交政策，信息项目从此被用于文化外交。然而，在自由主义传统作为主要意识形态的美国，广大民众没有政府与文化事务密切联系的意识，人们对政府控制文化事务并用于政治目的相当敌视（Ninkovich，1996：5）。美国政府对此心知肚明，在给公共信息委员会命名时使用“信息”（Information）一词而非常小心地回避了“宣传”（Propaganda）字眼的出现，因为“宣传”一词具有政府操控舆论的内涵，会对相关活动带来负面效果。尽管如此，公共信息委员会各种活动的“宣传”性质并未改变。

第一次世界大战的结束，没有如公共信息委员会所宣称的那样给世界带去威尔逊倡导的自由与和平。战后成立国际联盟努力的失败以及参战各国为争夺利益而尔虞我诈的种种劣行，使美国民众普遍产生被欺骗的感觉，这加深了美国人认为宣传就是“有目的的谎言”的看法，甚至连公共信息委员会主席乔治·克里尔（George Creel）后来在1930年参加一个学生团体的演讲时也不得不怀着矛盾的心情承认，委员会过去的宣传欺骗了学生父母那一代人，希望学生们不会再被欺骗（Arndt，2005：28）。鉴于公共信息委员会开展的各种宣传活动的效果和产生的负面影响，在第一次世界大战结束后，国会于1919年解散了委员会，终止了委员会的各项活动。

公共信息委员会的解散并不意味美国信息项目的终止。由于信息项目凸现民族主义传统，主题多关注政治，往往是针对单一目标的短期行为（胡文涛，2005：39），在美国宣传外交政策中仍然起着不可或缺的作用。第二次世界大战期间，美国成立战时信息处（Office of War Information），专门负责对轴心国宣传美国政策目标；冷战期间，美国于1953年成立美国新闻署（United States Information Agency），利用包括美国之音在内的信息项目与以苏联为首的东欧国家开展文化对抗。学界也对美国文化外交不断深入分析研究，1965年，美国塔夫茨大学教授爱德蒙德·古里恩（Edmund Gullion）首次提出现代意义上的“公共外交”概念，并特别指出“公共外交的核心是信息（Information）和理念（Idea）的跨国界流通”（檀有志，2011：31）。至此，信息项目与教育文化项目作为文化外交的重要实施手段得以获得学理上的确认。但是，随着前苏联解体，冷战结束，克林顿政府于1999年撤销了负责信息项目的美国新闻署，许多信息项目随之停止，信息项目的开展遭遇重大挫折。

与信息项目相比，以人员交流为主的美国教育文化交流项目一直由教育与文化事务局负责。美国新闻署撤销以后，该局重新划归美国国务院，继续实施包括国际访问者项目和富布赖特项目等在内的交流项目。教育文化项目在设计之初就特别强调通过教育交流增进国与国相互理解的长期价值。美国在1936年布宜诺斯艾利斯泛美和平大会上提出，美洲国家和人民间的相互理解应该在“美洲国家学者、教师和学生的交流中得到提升”（“Report of the Delegations of the United States of America to the Inter-American Conference for the Maintenance of Peace, Buenos Aires, Argentina, December 1-23”, 1936:167）。罗斯福总统也认为，“相互理解，以及由此达成对双方观点的赞赏，是邻国之间相互尊重的重要特性”（Arndt，2005：53）。在文化外交的执行理念上，美国制定了三条准则：①（文化活动）要避免宣传色彩的痕迹；②远离情报收集工作；③对一些本已脆弱濒危的外国文化的影响要最小化（Arndt，2005：xi-xii）。美国政府机构对直接参与文化外交也很谨慎，以避免被公众误读为政府操控文化活动。为了降低政府卷入文化事务的程度，淡化文化项目的政治色彩，国务院负责美洲事务的助理国务卿萨姆纳·韦尔斯提出了著名的“百分之五原则”：在所有文化外交活动中，由政府直接承担的活动数量不超过总数的百分之五，其余百分之九十五的活动要交给民间机构来完成（Arndt，2005：60）。国务院在1938年宣布成立文化关系司时也明确指出，“由国务院资助的文化交流项目将依赖私营部门作为主要合作伙伴开展”（Espinosa，1976：96）。1948年美国国会通过信息与教育交流法案（斯密斯-蒙特法案），明确授权国务卿在文化外交活动中“最大限度地利用私营机构的服务和设施”（“United States Information and Educational Exchange Act”）[1]。国会在1961年通过的富布赖特-海斯法案更是明文写道：“外国政府、国际组织、个人、协会、公司及其团体被鼓励最大程度地以总统授权可以接受的方式提供资金、财产以及服务以执行本法案。”（Johnson & Colligan，1965：336）至此，以政府为主导，以人员交流为主要内容，以非政府机构负责项目运作的美国教育文化交流模式得以正式确立。

国际访问者项目见证了美国教育文化项目的开端和发展，践行了美国文化外交思想。1940年12月，第一批35名南美各国在艺术和教育领域具有影响的人士应邀访问美国，从此拉开了国际访问者项目的帷幕，并延续至今。按照美国国务院教育与文化事务局的观点，国际访问者项目的目的是“在其他国家发展一批有影响的人士，通过他们对美国的观察和在美国的亲身经历，向他们所在国国民展现基于准确理解基础上的美国和美国人民”（Scott-Smith，2008：35）。罗斯福时期的美国国务卿科德尔·赫尔（Cordell Hull）进一步诠释了美国政府开展包括国际访问者项目在内的教育文化交流活动的根本目的：“通过建立基于大众友谊和相互理解的公众舆论，进而从各国内部控制各国政府。”（Arndt，2005：57）赫尔在20世纪30年代参与并领导了对美国文化外交方针的设计，他的话语明确表明了文化外交服务于国家利益这一基本政治属性。



## 3．国际访问者项目的非政治策略

国际访问者项目历经世界政治形势风云变幻，至今已运行七十余年，从项目开始时每年数百名国际访问者，到目前每年将近五千人，规模不断扩大，影

1 “United States Information and Educational Exchange Act”, PL. 402, Series 15: Subject Files 1953-2000, Box 48, USIA General Records, RG 306, NA.

响力与日俱增。国际访问者项目得到美国政府首肯，与其采取的成功策略和由此取得的成效密切相关。在国际访问者项目中，除受邀访美的人员由美国驻各国大使馆负责选拔和推荐以外，访问者到达美国后的一切活动都交由包括国际教育协会（IIE）和梅里迪恩国际中心（MIC）在内的7个非政府组织安排。以“非政治”的方式运作高度政治化的项目，是美国文化外交策略的独特之处。

首先，国际访问者在美国的所有参观访问由非政府组织安排，政府与文化项目保持一定距离，使受项目邀请的访问者从心理上感到远离政治宣传和政府操控。访问者有足够的时间自由旅行并接触真实的美国社会，从而使他们能够更加客观地看待美国社会制度并感悟美国价值观。国际访问者项目的访问行程公开、透明，有效提高了文化交流的真实性，达到了美国政府期望的文化交流效果。

其次，项目具体运作交给非政府组织后，政府的工作负担大大减轻，体现了自由主义传统下美国“小政府，大社会”的格局。美国驻各地大使馆和领事馆专注于选拔合适的国际访问者人选，与他们建立并保持联系。这些社会精英通常成为美国在当地的重要联络对象，从而构建起一张受美国意识形态支配的关系网络。需要特别指出的是，即便在冷战期间美国与前苏联在各领域激烈对抗的过程中，美国政府成立美国新闻署负责对外宣传的背景下，包括国际访问者项目在内的人员交流项目也一直由教育与文化事务局负责，教育文化项目与以“宣传”为主要目的的信息项目被严格区分开，进一步减弱了“宣传”的性质，提高了项目的实际效率。

第三，非政府组织在美国各地构建了专业网络，提高了国际访问者项目的运作效率。从1954年开始，美国国务院国际教育交流服务局（IES）不再负责国际访问者项目，国际访问者在美国访问期间的行程安排由三家非政府组织负责。其中，政府事务协会主要负责政治、新闻媒体和经济领域的访问安排；美国教育理事会主要负责教育与文化事务、社会福利以及青年活动等领域的访问安排；国际劳工事务办公室则负责安排国际访问者了解美国工会事务。随着国际访问者规模的不断扩大，国务院为避免个别非政府组织对项目的垄断，对签约承办项目的非政府组织不断调整。按照目前的架构，国际访问者项目由国际教育协会和梅里迪恩国际中心等七家机构负责组织实施。这七家机构与国际访问者全国协会（NCIV）在美国各城市的分支机构，共同构建了一张专业、高效的网络，使国际访问者项目得以顺利运转。

除了上述非政府组织，福特基金会、洛克菲勒基金会以及卡耐基基金会等非政府组织也积极参与美国文化外交。虽然是非政府组织，但上述基金会与政府保持着千丝万缕的联系，基金会的不少管理者来自政府机构，政府机构也有来自基金会的高层管理人员，例如马歇尔计划行政领导保罗·霍夫曼在退职后就长期担任福特基金会主席（韩铁，2004：40）。因此，基金会的文化项目无论形式、内容还是目标都与美国政府的文化项目保持高度一致。受益于机构的中立性质，基金会可以像一枚“楔子”，相对容易地进入一些国家的敏感领域，而政府机构则得以紧随其后。福特基金会也与国务院的合作机构国际教育协会（IIE）签订合同，开展类似国际访问者项目的教育合作计划，通过影响商业、媒体、政府部门和研究机构的社会精英人士，促进亚洲和非洲民主价值观的形成，从而推动目标社会的自由民主进程。

除了由政府主导、非政府组织运作这一非政治策略，国际访问者项目始终聚焦各国社会精英阶层，通过对精准目标的访问邀请，实现项目效益的最大化。文化霸权理论创始者葛兰西早在20世纪20年代就指出，获得文化领导权是获取政治领导权的前提，而要获得文化领导权，最重要的就是“从‘意识形态上’竭力同化并征服传统的知识分子。这种同化和征服的工作做得越快，越有成效，则该集团在精心造就自己有组织的知识分子的工作中就越成功”（戴维·麦克莱伦，2004：203）。葛兰西所谓的知识分子，就是社会精英，也是国际访问者项目的重点目标人群。洛克菲勒基金会对社会精英所发挥具体作用进行专门研究的结果表明，广大民众更认同来自社会精英的信息，通过他们传播信息比直接通过媒体传播信息具有更好的效果（Scott-Smith，2008：59）。社会学家梅耶也认为，现代社会主要是由有意识的个人行为所组织，如果能够找到“正确”的个人，就能操纵整个社会（Scott-Smith，2008：63）。



国际访问者项目正是通过找出目标国家的“正确”个人，向他们介绍美国社会制度和价值观，并通过他们实现对目标群体的影响，从而达成美国的政策目标。第二次世界大战之后对纳粹德国的民主化改造方式之一，就是利用教育文化交流，强化对社会精英灌输自由民主价值观，进而实现德国重新进入自由民主社会的成功案例。据统计，仅1950年就有1 288位德国社会精英应邀访问美国，深入了解美国的民主社会制度，从而在德国民众心中解构过去希特勒的强权政治。正因如此，美国驻德国军事管理当局前主任鲁修斯·克莱认为教育文化交流项目是“（德国）重建的根基所在”（Clay，1950：301）。

在针对社会精英所开展的文化外交活动效果调查中，美国也发现教育交流活动的作用更好地体现在对精英人士既有观点的强化，而不是改变他们原有观点。美国学者科泽尔认为，美国文化外交的兴趣“主要放在那些基本上友好的国家，而不是认为这种（友好）关系理所当然，转而去追求那些怀有敌意的目标”（Ketzel，1955：55）。根据这些研究结果，美国政府在确定受邀请访问美国的人士中，特别关注那些对美国持正面态度，且过去没有到访过美国的人士，加强他们对美国的深入了解，强化他们对美国的良好印象，进而通过他们在更大的范围实现美国的影响力。

最后，国际访问者项目的经费使用策略，也凸现美国政府精明之处。文化交流项目的长期运作，离不开强有力的经费保障。受项目邀请访问美国的人均经费从初期的2 000美元上升到2012年的10 000至12 000美元，其中包括国际旅费和在美国国内四至五个城市之间访问的交通费、住宿费、餐费以及非政府机构的管理费用。若计算每年4 000至5 000名国际访问者的庞大数量，国务院每年的相应支出也是一笔不小的数字。但是，从项目经费的使用来看，资金主要用于为访问者购买美国各家航空公司的国际国内机票，支付访问者在美国国内宾馆住宿以及餐饮等开销，实际上把美国纳税人交给政府的钱，用于提振美国国内相关行业消费，具有促进美国经济发展和增加就业机会的效果。如此，在资金几乎全部用于美国国内，没有“损失”的情况下，国际访问者项目使大量来自其他国家的社会精英深度了解了美国社会制度，培养了一大批“知美派”甚或“亲美派”，无论从哪个角度看，着实是一笔非常合算的交易。

## 4. 结语

从1938年文化关系司成立以来，美国开展文化外交已经超过70年，形成了相对完善的机制，具有明确的目标和有效的策略，文化外交成为实现美国外交政策的重要工具。近年，随着孔子学院等中国教育文化交流项目的不断推进，中国文化的海外传播为世界各国进一步了解中国文化起到了良好的促进作用。中国文化外交在和谐世界理念指导下，可以借鉴美国文化外交的成功之处，确立自己的战略目标，同时积极鼓励非政府机构参与中国文化与世界文化交流，进而形成中国文化外交大战略，为中国文化走向世界服务，为实现中国国家外交战略服务。

## 参考文献：

哈茨，路易斯. 美国的自由主义传统[M]. 张敏谦，译. 北京：中国社会科学出版社，2003.

韩铁. 福特基金会与美国的中国学[M]. 北京：中国社会科学出版社，2004.

胡文涛. 美国文化外交及其在中国的运用[M]. 北京：世界知识出版社，2005.

麦克莱伦，戴维. 马克思以后的马克思主义[M]. 李智，译. 北京：中国人民大学出版社，2004.

摩根索，汉斯. 国家间政治——寻求权利与和平的斗争[M]. 徐昕，等，译. 北京：中国人民公安大学出版社，1990.

檀有志. 美国对华公共外交战略[M]. 北京：时事出版社，2011.

王立新. 意识形态与美国外交政策[M]. 北京：北京大学出版社，2007.

Arndt, Richard. *The First Resort of Kings: American Cultural Diplomacy in the Twentieth Century*[M]. Dulles: Potomac Books, 2005.



Bureau of Educational and Cultural Affairs. Priority Educational Exchange Projects[G]. 25 January 1956, Group IV Box 153 Folder 17.

Bureau of Educational and Cultural Affairs. *Report of the Delegations of the United States of America to the Inter-American Conference for the Maintenance of Peace, Buenos Aires, Argentina, December 1-23*[R]. Washington, D.C., 1936: 167.

Clay, Lucius. *Decision in Germany*[M]. New York: Doubleday, 1950.

Espinosa, J. Manuel. *Inter-American Beginnings of US Cultural Diplomacy*[M]. Washington: Department of State Publication, 1976.

Finn, Helena. The Case for Cultural Diplomacy[J]. *Foreign Affairs*, 2003, 82(6): 15.

Jentleson, Paterson. *Encyclopedia of US Foreign Relations,* (Vol. 1, XXII)[M].

Johnson, W., Colligan, F. *The Fulbright Program: A History*[M]. Chicago: University of Chicago Press, 1965.

Keohane, Robert, Joseph Nye. Power and Interdependence in the Information Age[J]. *Foreign Affairs*, Sept./Oct., 1998: 86.

Ketzel, C. Exchange of Persons and American Foreign Policy: The Foreign Leader Program of the Depart of State[D]. University of California, 1955.

Ninkovich, Frank. *US Information Policy and Cultural Diplomacy*[M]. New York: Foreign Policy Association, 1996.

Scott-Smith, Giles. *Networks of Empire: The US State Department's Foreign Leader Program in the Netherlands, France, and Britain 1950-1970*[M]. Brussels: Peter Lang, 2008.

United States Information and Educational Exchange Act, PL. 402, Series 15: Subject Files 1953-2000, Box 48, USIA General Records, RG 306, NA.

# American Cultural Diplomacy in International Visitor Leadership Program: Political Goals and Non-political Strategy

Yang Guang

(College of Foreign Languages and Cultures, Sichuan University, Chengdu, China, 610064)

**Abstract:** International Visitor Leadership Program (IVLP) is an educational and cultural program conducted by US government. Its liberalism orientation declares its emphasis on the spread of freedom and democracy. It is also a reflection of the American concern of realistic goals under the influence of realistic international relation theory. IVLP use of non-governmental organizations in implementing the program weakens the involvement of government in cultural affairs and reduces the negative aspects of political propaganda. The non-political strategy raises the efficiency of IVLP.

**Key Words:** Cultural Diplomacy; IVLP; Political Goals; Non-political Strategy

# 西南边疆在明清史研究中的地位

## ——美国现代学术视野下的中国西南边疆史研究[1]

邹立波[1]　李沛容[2]

（1 四川大学中国藏学研究所，四川成都 610029；2 四川大学历史文化学院，四川成都　610029）

**摘　要**：20世纪90年代是美国学界研究中国明清时期西南边疆史的分水岭。受西方人类学界对中国西南少数民族研究及西方中国学研究"边疆"范式的激发和推动，西南边疆史研究日益演变为美国学界中国史研究中不容忽视的重要领域，并涌现出一批颇具学术影响力的著作。基于反思与批判以往"汉族中心观"和"汉化"研究范式的共同学术目标，美国学界强调边疆的地方性视野，并引入早期殖民帝国、族群认同等概念和理论，对晚期中华帝国与边疆复杂关系的研究颇富创见和启发的同时，又将两者置于另一类二元对立的框架内。但是西南边疆史无疑能够对国内外学术界重新理解和修正晚期中华帝国历史及其与边疆的关系有所帮助。

**关键词**：中国西南边疆史；美国；明清



自19世纪后期特纳从美国文明发展的本土视角提出著名的"边疆假说"以来，边疆史观逐步演变为长期影响美国学界认知人类历史发展进程的独特研究路径而倍受青睐。到20世纪60年代，曾经一度沉寂的边疆史观，再度受到美国学界的关注与重视。一些学者试图将之引入同其他国家或地区的边疆比较史研究中。这一学术趋向，很快与同一时期欧美传统"汉学"向"中国研究"的学

1　基金项目：四川大学美国文化研究中心项目"美国'新清史'与藏学研究"阶段性成果（ASC201213）；四川大学"985工程"三期"区域历史与民族创新基地"阶段性成果。本文已发表于《思想战线》2013年第39卷第6期，第149-156页。此次收录，编者对文章略有修改。

术范式转型相结合。拉铁摩尔对亚洲内陆边疆早期研究的学术价值得到学界的重新认识和发掘，进而深刻影响到美国史学界对明清史，尤其是清朝历史属性的界定，引发对传统中国学研究视角的反思和批判。近年来，在不断综合吸纳后现代理论基础上，越来越多的美国明清史学者呼吁应破除以往的“汉族中心”史观，高度重视边疆史研究，乃至将边疆史提升至清史研究的核心地位。从边疆视角反观明清史的学术氛围下，多数学者将研究领域集中在关系中国历史发展进程最为深切的亚洲内陆边疆，以全球视角的比较史眼光，力图重新书写明清史。

但是从20世纪90年代起，部分美国年轻学人开始将学术眼光投射到遥远的中国西南边疆。明清时期西南边疆更为复杂和多元的历史，促使他们在美国学界掀起一场从另一类“边疆”审视明清史的学术热潮。一批颇具学术含量的论著相继问世。时至今日，这场方兴未艾的研究思潮已引起国内学界的初步关注[1]。不过，这股思潮毕竟同美国学界有关中国边疆史研究的整体学术脉络紧密相连，既具有共同性，也有自身的独特之处。在现今以“新清史”为代表的史学观念冲击下，国内学界如何回应和批判美国学界对明清时期边疆历史的解构式研究，深入借鉴其有益的研究方法，实现中西学术界的深层次交流，对美国现代学术视野下明清时期西南边疆史研究做进一步研讨，是极有必要的。本文选择了近年出版的几部代表性专著，结合相关论著，在回顾美国学界有关西南边疆史研究学术脉络的前提下，研判某些重要命题和假说的内在逻辑，以此探讨西南边疆在明清史研究中的学术地位。





## 1．从《中国向热带行进》到《亚洲边陲》

与20世纪上半叶西方传统“汉学”对亚洲内陆边疆相对成熟的研究相比，西方学界对同一时期中国西南边疆的认识，主要是通过探险家、传教士、外交

1　目前国内有关美国西南边疆史研究论著的综合性专论文章，仅见陆韧的《现代西方学术视野中的中国西南边疆史研究（代序）》（昆明：云南大学出版社，2007年）。陆文对国内学界了解西方现代学术视野中的中国西南边疆史研究的思路具有重要的引介意义，但是该文偏重于云南部分，对一些重要的学术问题也缺乏足够的重视。另有部分学术著作书评，散见于《历史人类学刊》《台湾人类学刊》等刊物中。

官等的游历性描述获得。像约瑟夫·洛克、伯希和那样对纳西历史文化、中国南方和印度支那（Indochina）关系有较为深入研究的学者，在当时的西方学术界可谓凤毛麟角。西南边疆史研究更是如此。长期以来，基于政治地缘关系，西方学界极为重视亚洲内陆边疆的研究，视其为现代早期"欧亚大陆的十字路口"，赋予其世界史的意义。故而亚洲内陆边疆的研究光环将中国其他边疆地区的研究重重遮掩起来（Perdue，2005：9-10）。直到20世纪50年代，美国学界才从现代学术研究层面对中国西南边疆史有所涉及。早期中国西南边疆史的研究，首先是同汉文明在整个中国南方扩张进程联系起来的。1954年，维恩斯（Herold. J. Wiens）出版了《中国向热带行进：历史与文化地理视角下与南中国非汉人群攸关的汉文化、移民与政治控制向南渗透的研究》[1]一书。作为耶鲁大学国外区域研究系列丛书之一，该书主要依据中文文献，大量吸收西方和中国学者的研究成果，特别是沃尔夫拉姆·埃伯哈德（Wolfram Eberhard）有关中国边疆原始人群（primitive people）的德文著作，兼重历史与现实，既梳理了公元前250年至晚近汉人移民向南方扩张、征服，和汉文化融合南方族群的长时段历史过程，也概述了中国南方族群结构、分布和社会组织的面貌。尽管该书内容结构显得相当粗略，且人名、地名的对译存在不规范和错讹之处，因毕竟是首部阐述中国南方边疆的英文著作，遂引起美国学界一定的关注。时人期望以此书为开端，能够对当时西方知之甚少的傣、缅等南方边疆族群及汉人在南方边疆活动历史的研究有所拓展和深入（Eberhard, 1995: 324-325; Hanks, 1995: 1322-1323; Hinton, 1995: 565-566）。但事与愿违，在此后的二十余年间，美国学界对西南边疆史研究的实质性推进并不大。史密斯（Knet C. Smith）的《清代政策与中国西南的发展：鄂尔泰总督任期的1726-1731年》等少数博士学位论文预示着美国学界将目光转向西南边疆史专题性研究的趋向，



1 Herold J.Wiens, *China's March toward the Tropics( a Discussion of the Southward Penetration of China's Culture, People, and Political Control in Relation to the Non-Han-Chinese Peoples of South China and in the Perspective of Historical and Cultural Geography)*,The Shoe String Press, Inc., 1954.为行文方便，下文简称为《中国向热带行进》。该书再版后，标题改为《汉人在南中国的扩张》，但内容结构并无变动。参见Herold J. Wiens, *Han Chinese Expansion in South China*, The Shoe String Press, Inc., 1967。

但影响却十分有限[1]。同发表的少量学术文章一样，此类论文仍然被限定在传统的清史研究范畴内，以清朝治边政策为探讨主题，偏重史实的论述。

西南边疆史研究真正在美国学界实现研究范式的转变，成为中国边疆史研究的重要组成部分则始于20世纪90年代。而其转变同西方学术界整个研究范式和理论方法的巨大转型背景息息相关，其直接推动力量主要源自西方人类学界对中国西南少数民族的研究，及西方中国研究“边疆范式”的确立。从20世纪80年代起，为探讨身份认同的意义和性质，深入反思族性问题，检视弗雷德里克·巴斯（Fredrik Barth）族群认同理论在多族群共居区域的应用，西方人类学界在中国内地开放后不久，即将学术视野从中国东南沿海延伸到文化、族群多样的中国西南边疆地区。在西南边疆复杂多样的族群与文化现象不断吸引西方学者学术目光的同时，部分美国学者在切身的长期田野调查体验后，开始对20世纪50年代以来中国学界的民族史研究范式提出严厉的批判。关注西南边疆的美国学者愈加不满中国学者以往将少数民族边缘化，“任意”从“汉族中心”史观解释少数民族历史，以此强调中国多民族大一统历史的做法。在后殖民主义理论的影响下，去“汉族中心”观，立足于本土历史视角，重构西南边疆史变得愈加必要（Harrel，1995：63–91）。另一方面，自社会人类学家施坚雅（G. W. Skinner）提出著名的区域体系理论以来，西方学者日益认识到中国内部区域间存在的显著差异性。到20世纪90年代，中国内部非均质化、非单一化的观点已是西方学界的共识。与宏观层面的整体性研究同样重要，区域性视角俨然成为推动中国历史各领域研究深入的有力工具。作为中国内部区域研究的重要组成，曾经被忽视的边疆的学术价值再度被发掘，加之此时恰值当今





1　据“ProQuest 学位论文全文库”粗略统计，20世纪90年代以前，与明清时期西南边疆史直接相关的学位论文仅有4篇，参见Knet. C. Smith，“Ch’ing Policy and the Development of Southwest China: Aspects of Ortai’s Governor-generalship,1726-1731,” Yale University, Ph.D.,1970; William R. Johnson, “China’s 1911 Revolution in the Provinces of Yunan and Kweichow,” University of Washington, Ph.D.,1962; Robert Darrah Jenks, “The Miao Rebellion, 1854-1872: Insurgency and Social Disorder in Kweichow during the Taiping Era,” Harvard University, Ph.D.,1985. 值得一提的是，美籍华裔学者李中清（James Lee）的博士学位论文《中国西南的经济：政治结构域经济发展》及发表的一系列相关文章，在当时的中国西南边疆研究领域独树一帜，成为美国学界研究中国西南边疆移民、经济人口问题的典范之作和必备的参考论著。

影响颇大的美国“新清史”出现在美国学界，提倡研究清史应“去汉化”，突出满族自身历史的独立性和亚洲内陆边疆在清朝历史上的重要意义，有关亚洲内陆边疆的著作遂纷纷面世，拉铁摩尔的研究论著一再出现在西方学者研究中国史的必备参考书目中。边疆由此被看作是可资期待的必需的研究领域。而对于从事中国研究的学者而言，“意识到边疆的存在和清晰区分边疆的需要，是历史学家研究工作的必要前提之一”（Cosmo & Wyatt, 2003: 3-4; 姚大力，2007）。

于是，在此两股学术思潮的助推和激发下，从20世纪90年代初起，美国学界对中国西南边疆史的研究越加丰富和多元化，日益发展为中国边疆史研究中不容忽视的重要领域。这主要表现在两个方面：一是研究群体的逐步形成，相关专题性学术会议的召开，以及同中国边疆史、明清史研究领域的长期密切互动。美国学界从事明清时期西南边疆研究的主力群体基本是20世纪90年代博士毕业的中青年学者。其大多已在美国各高校任教，并继续长期活跃于西南边疆史研究领域。自由开放、求新务实的宽松学术环境，为这批学者同其他中国研究领域学者的合作和交流提供了极好的平台。各类边疆史或明清史会议或论坛上，常见西南边疆史研究学者的身影。如1996年5月在美国达特茅斯学院举行的“族群认同与中国边疆研讨会”（Conference on Ethnic Identity and the China Frontier），齐集现今美国学界明清史研究的主要代表性学者，包括西南边疆在内的中国南部边疆史研究引起与会者的极大关注，改变了美国学界对中国南部边疆地区汉人与其他民族间差异性的具体认知。会后结集出版的《帝国在边缘：现代早期中国的文化、族群与边疆》的一半篇幅是探讨中国南方边疆（Crossley, Siu & Sutton, 2006）[1]，亚洲内陆边疆研究占主导性优势的研究格局已被逐步改变；二是具有影响力的研究著述相继出版，逐渐在美国学界形成较为浓厚的有关明清时期西南边疆史研究的学术氛围。仅根据“ProQuest 学位论文全文库”的粗略统计，从1993年到2013年7月，与明清时期西南边疆研究直接相关的学位论文近30篇，这与此前美国高校在读博（硕）士对中国西南边疆史极少问津的状态形成鲜明反差。更为重要的是，一批颇具学术影响力的著作



1 有关此书书评，可参见赵世瑜《书评：Empire at the Margins》，《历史人类学学刊》2006年第4卷第2期；赵世瑜《在历史中发现族群，于草野间审视朝廷》，《神州交流》2006年第3卷第3期。

大多是由此类学位论文修改完成的。从2001年起，美国学界相关的代表性著作中关于云南的有三种，贵州、广西的各两种，四川的一种，地跨云贵川者一种[1]。多数著作研究时段偏重清代，区域性、时代性特征十分鲜明，讨论议题颇为广泛，但又带有某些共性。此处仅略述近年来较具代表性，且与本文论旨相关的四部著作。

现任教于伊利诺斯州立大学的霍斯特勒（Laura Hosteler）的《清代殖民事业：早期近代中国的人种志与地图学》于2001年出版后，在美国学术界引发激烈的评议和争论，仅英文书评就多达12篇。该书力图挑战近代"东方"与"西方"二元对立的研究模式，将清朝前期对地图和人种志的使用方式，放在同近代早期欧洲各国相比较的全球视野下，阐明清朝同近代欧洲各国一样积极参与早期近代世界的形成，经历过"殖民扩张"的过程。为剖析清朝人种志的性质，作者选择贵州作为考察案例，用一半多的笔墨分析贵州苗图册与同时期欧洲人种志的异同。但是该书结构内容、观点分析等方面均存在诸多重大缺陷（Hosteler，2001）。为此，各方英文书评提出一系列质问，如近代早期中国与欧洲地图学对比的可行性和可靠性，两者在人种志方面是否存在清晰的联系，地图学、人种志为何在清代民间影响不大，为什么清朝人种志事业主要出现在西南边疆，19世纪中期以后清朝为什么不再关注此类边疆信息的搜集，以及引证的文献资料过于单薄，等等。尽管如此，美国学界还是对作者将17、18世纪的清朝从隔离、孤立的状态中转移至全球扩张性帝国比较视野下的大胆尝试赞誉有加。

受"新清史"影响，鉴于清朝"征服王朝"的独特性和边疆治理的复杂性，美国学界往往普遍关注清代边疆史研究。在此背景下，两部以明代广西、贵州边疆研究为主题的著作显得尤为引人注目。就职于加拿大大不列颠哥伦比亚大学的单国钺的《中国国家之建构：明代边境的族群性与扩张》一书，是根据其普林斯顿大学博士学位论文《边疆的部落化：明代中国南方的野蛮人、移

1　除文中引出的著作外，还包括Dai, Yingcong, *The Sichuan Frontier and Tibet: Imperial Strategy in the Early Qing*, University of Washington Press,2009;Bello, David Anthony, *Opium and the Limits of Empire: Drugs Prohibition in the Chinese Interior,1729-1850*, Harvard University Press,2005;Jennifer Took, *A Native Chieftaincy in Southwest China: Franchising a Tai Chieftaincy under the Tusi System of Late Imperial China, Brill Leiden*, Boston, 2005.

民与国家》修改而成。除结构和内容上的调整外，两者最大的不同在于作者舍弃了学位论文中使用的部落化（Tribalizing）概念。这一概念原本用以表明，明代边境族群在现实政治与社会的活动已超越现代意义上的国家与族群性范畴。全书利用大量的汉文文献，阐述明代是如何通过军屯政策、土司制度等在广西治与乱的纷繁历史图景中实践政治边界的，统治者又是如何对边境族群进行“民”与“蛮”、“生蛮”与“熟蛮”的辨识与分类，从而指出近代中国民族国家的建构根源可以追溯至明代（Shin, 2006, 1999）[1]。弗吉尼亚联合大学的赫曼（John E. Herman）的《云雾之间：中国在贵州的拓殖1200–1700》，是首部使用彝文材料研究贵州西北部边疆的英文著作。全书目的在于检视500年间，元明清三代是如何在西南边疆征服、拓殖与控制当地主权，当地土著又是如何回应中国在西南边疆的拓殖活动的。作者力图兼纳拓殖的中华帝国与贵州彝族统治精英的双重视角，其观点主张虽存有争议，且材料运用上略有欠缺，但对元明时期土司与帝国关系的变化、帝国“儒家教化使命”（Confucian civilizing mission）观念的实践、明朝拓殖对土著社会结构的影响、汉人移民的作用等问题，却均有独到的精湛见解（Herman, 2007）[2]。



不过，与明代相比，清代西南边疆的族群、政治与文化面貌的确在世人面前展现出一幅纷然杂陈的动态图景，显示出清代西南边疆史研究的独特魅力，这在威斯利学院（Wellesley College）纪若诚的《亚洲边陲：清代云南边疆的变迁》一书中得到极好的诠释。该书是第一部探讨18至19世纪清朝与东南亚跨境区域社会变迁的英文专著，也是以作者耶鲁大学博士学位论文《清朝的难言之隐：云南边疆的本土社群与帝国》修改而成。全书篇幅不大，却是研究清代模糊性边境区域社会的开拓性著作。为揭示18至19世纪中期，云南沿中缅边境半月形地带的傣贵族、汉移民、清帝国官员等多边政治势力，在政治经济文化网络中错综复杂的种种会遇关系，作者运用和发挥了特纳的“边疆学说”和理查德·怀特的“中间地带”（Middle Ground）理论，将边疆地带的本土社会

1　有关《中国国家之建构》的书评，参见唐立宗《书评：The making of the Chinese State》，《历史人类学刊》（香港）2007年第5卷第1期。

2　有关书评，参见何汉威《书评：Amid the Clouds and Mist》，《中国文化研究所学报》2008年第48期；Jodi L.Weinsten, “Review: Amid the Clouds and Mist,” *The Journal of Asian Studies*, Vol.67, No.4, 2008, pp.1420-1422.

置于中心位置，以比较的视角，阐释中华帝国晚期的边疆是如何被形塑和改变的，以此显示出边疆自身具有的发展动力[1]。

## 2．从“汉化”到“殖民化”

纵观美国学者近半个多世纪对中国西南边疆史研究的学术历程，可以看出，从《中国向热带行进》到《亚洲边陲》研究议题和构思的显著变化。这种变化既展现出美国学界将西南边疆史从整个单一的中国边疆编年史框架中分离出来，综合利用多学科研究方法，以之作为崭新研究领域的学术建构过程[2]，也暗含着20世纪90年代以来，在多元化研究理念和范式指导下，美国学者试图超越和推翻传统中国学研究，特别是边疆史的众多基本命题和重要概念，系统解构明清边疆史的学术目的。各类西南边疆史著作在研究区域、视角和论题意旨、时段等方面虽各有侧重，却同“新清史”的某些研究命题和假说有着千丝万缕的联系，共同构成一套具有自身内在逻辑的论证体系。

当前从事中国西南边疆史研究的美国学者一个共同研究目标，即反驳和批判以往的“汉族中心”观和“汉化”研究范式。五十余年前，维恩斯依据汉文文献，在《中国向热带行进》中论证了中国南部边疆的土著社会如何被淹没在汉族移民的洪流中，如何被优越的汉文化征服而“汉化”。这一观点曾经在美国学界长期流行。当时的学者普遍接受“汉文明（Chinese Civilization）的形塑是通过不同社会单元及不同文化的整合，由诸多文明交融而成”的假说。但是到20世纪90年代，“汉族中心”观已经难以在美国学界立足（Eberhard,

1　有关书评，参见Yingcong Dai, “Review: Asian Borderlans, Pacific Affairs”, Vol.79, No.3, 2006, pp.531-532; Mark C. Elliott, “Asian Boderlands: The Transformation of Qing China’s Yunnan Frontier by C.Patterson Giersch”, *The Journal of Asian Studies*, Vol.67, No.1, 2008, pp. 268-270; 陈玫妏：《书评：Asian Borderlands》，《台湾人类学刊》2009年第7卷第2期；袁剑：《清朝场域的西南印象》，《书品》2009年第5期。

2　研究明清时期西南边疆史的美国学者的研究领域、方法各有侧重，观点和主张也有所不同，根本无法将其归结为一个新兴的研究流派，但是这些学者普遍借用了中国“西南”的地域概念，并以之作为研究的主要对象，而与内陆亚洲边疆的研究区别开来。有关中西学者对“西南”地域概念的认知，可参见Bin Yang, *Between Winds and Clouds: the Making of Yunnan (Second Century BCE to Twentieth Century CE)*, Columbia University Press, 2008。

1995：324）。对“汉族中心”观的质疑，首先是从中国历史上异族王朝被“汉化”的问题开始的。早在1949年，德裔美国学者魏特夫（Karl Wittfogel）就已提出“征服王朝”（Dynasties of conquest）的概念，以此否认异族王朝最终不可避免都要被“汉化”的误识。不过，“汉化”观彻底被打破是在美国“新清史”思潮兴起后（Karl，1949：3-25）。“新清史”学者极力强调清朝统治中的满洲因素，将清朝主体认知的立足点从“汉化”转移到满洲本身。讨论主体的转变，得到美国研究中国西南边疆史学者的普遍赞同和回应。维恩斯的观点成为研究的起点和被批驳的主要对象，向热带行进的历史甚至被斥责为“霸权式历史”（Hegemonizing history）。如同“新清史”学者们受到柯文“中国中心观”倡导的“地方性策略”的启发一样（Herman，2007:6）[1]，他们强烈不满“汉族中心”观视角下过分简化明清时期西南边疆政治和社会复杂性的书写模式，而在一定程度上借鉴了“新清史”的研究范式，沿着“地方性策略”的逻辑来思考问题：既然研究中国近代史的学者应当摒弃“西方中心”的偏见和干扰，从“置于中国历史环境中的中国问题着手研究”，那么研究清史的学者应“寻求跳脱‘大汉族中心主义’的局限，发现非汉他者的观点，并将之整合进对整个国家与社会日益增加的了解中”（柯文，2002:170）[2]；那么，当研究中国边疆时，如果学者过分依赖汉文文献和遵循单向的“汉化”涵化视角，就会将文化偏见带入研究中，使研究陷入“汉”与“非汉”、“中国”与“非中国”的二元对立论述框架中，无法准确完整地理解和认识多元复杂的边疆社会，因而应当将边疆土著及其社会作为研究的重心，并重视移民的作用。以“边疆”为考察中心是多数研究西南边疆史学者试图转换研究视角，努力实现的研究方向。例如艾特维尔（David G. Atwill）在《中国伊斯兰聚居地：中国西南的伊斯兰教、族群性与潘泰起义1856-1873》一书中阐述的那样：



1　夏明方：《一部没有“近代”的中国近代史——从“柯文三论”看“中国中心观”的内在逻辑及其困境》，《近代史研究》2007年第1期；李爱勇：《新清史与“中华帝国”问题——又一次冲击与反应？》，《史学月刊》2012年第4期。

2　欧立德：《满文档案与新清史》，《故宫博物院学术季刊》（台北）2006年第24卷第2期。

> 只有当我们转换为地方性视野后，我们才能清晰地认识到云南问题的症结所在。这一问题并非只是同遥远的帝国中心的利益有关，而是对区域和地方重要性的权衡。一旦我们认识这一路径，即跳出二元论的框架体系，我们就能开始真正理解云南人的行为。
>
> （Atwill，2005：14）

抛弃“汉族中心”观和“汉化”概念并强调边疆的地方性视野，促使学者们质疑“汉族中心观”影响下汉文文献记载的可靠性，开始寻求新的边疆阐释材料和方法，来摆脱以往侧重明清政权治边政策探讨的局限。单国钺注意到明代广西边疆族群构成、类别的内涵在特定政治与文化时空下的演变，帝国的政治利益、移民的经济需求和文化精英的想象如何影响着边疆族群的划分和分类，以及边疆扩张与帝国建构之间的内在关联，意在拒绝将汉与非汉作为解读中国历史的基础；赫曼（John E. Herman）力图使帝国与边疆土著的两种声音，同时汇响在明代贵州的边疆社会场景中。而他指出，为维护汉人的边疆统治，明朝的边疆“儒家教化”运作模式，极大限制了边疆非汉族群接受汉文化的进程，则显示出边疆被纳入帝国的过程要远比想象的复杂。纪若诚对清代云南半月形地带的研究，具有土著社群与跨境相结合的视角，引入“边疆学说”和“中间地带”理论的同时，借鉴舍菲尔德（Shepherd）对清代台湾的研究成果（1993），考察了土著社群及其风俗如何使得清朝的边疆制度变得富有弹性。在复杂的政治经济联络网中，统治成本迫使清朝限制汉人移民的活动，以缓和移民与土著族群的紧张关系。

这些新的观点无疑颠覆了以往的许多传统认知，这得益于族性及族群认同等概念和理论的启示和运用。不过，在一系列推陈出新的边疆研究方法和理论中，现代早期殖民帝国研究取向的冲击和影响最大。这一概念是“新清史”倡导的“早期殖民主义”与“前现代帝国论”的结合，一经提出便引起美国学界的广泛讨论。为此，1998年《国际历史评论》（*The International History Review*）杂志以“满洲殖民主义”为题专刊刊载相关评论性和研究文章，将“殖民主义”的理论运用到对清代蒙古、西藏等内陆亚洲边疆的研究中，自此揭开美国学界研究明清时期边疆史“泛帝国论”的序幕。通过对比清朝与现代早期西方国家，他们将晚期中华帝国纳入早期现代世界体系的研究范畴内，重新定位清朝征服、统治边疆行为的性质，认为同近代欧洲在海外的殖民扩张有诸多相似之处，清朝在边疆地区的行为具有殖民化的特征（Perdue, 1998: 255-262; 刘凤云，2013）。很快，研究明清时期西南边疆史的美国学者相当普遍地援引了“现代早期殖民帝国”的概念，并推及至明代的边疆史探讨中。如纪若诚将其视作是消减对汉化概念和汉文化中心主义依赖，“寻求更高级、更进一步的分析范畴的路标”，直言清朝为“殖民帝国”（Giersch, 2011: 71-72）[1]。单国钺则直截了当地宣称，“中国向南方的扩张历史毫无疑问是一部殖民化、文化移植的历史”。赫曼亦将土木堡之变后明朝在中国西南边疆从事的活动称为“一项庞大的殖民工程”（Shin，2006：5）。最为显著的例子是霍斯特勒（Laura Hosteler）的《清代殖民事业》，该书单薄且粗略的论述遭到评论者非议的同时，却受到欧立德、罗友枝、米华健等美国“新清史”学者的一致好评，被认为是富有“原创性的”“深思熟虑的”著作，正是源于霍斯特勒将17至18世纪的清朝“放在‘现代早期’和‘殖民主义’的世界史中来探讨”，以全球视野的比较史框架理解中国的历史发展，拒绝以往的中国例外论和孤立论，由此提出“殖民化”（Colonization）、“同化”（Assimilation）、“象征化”（Representation）等一系列中心议题（John E, 2007：9）。时至今日，“殖民主义”的字眼已经充斥于美国有关明清时期西南边疆史研究的各类著述中（主要是19世纪以前），并蔓延至民国时期的相关研究论著内，俨然已是美国学界认可的“普适性”概念（Eliot，2003：547-554）。



从某种程度上来说，“殖民”概念的应用是美国“新清史”学者在涉及中国边疆、族群和“征服王朝”等问题时，受后殖民理论影响，过分强调“去汉化”“去中心化”的后设之见，而西南边疆史研究对“殖民”概念的采纳则是其翻版。为破除汉化和汉族中心观，边疆成为再理解和重构中国历史的重心。这一点可以从“新清史”重新肯定内陆亚洲边疆研究价值及其延伸看出。在“新清史”学者看来，内陆亚洲边疆是同汉人居住的“中国”相平行的重要组成部分，而不能简单地视作是“中国”的一部分，因而“清朝”是否能以“中

1 译文参见沈海梅译《“混杂的人群”：中国西南近代早期边疆的社会变迁（1700-1800）》，载陆韧主编《现代西方学术视野中的中国西南边疆史研究》，昆明：云南大学出版社，2007年，第143-144页。

国”称之，是值得商榷的。从世界史的比较眼光，美国学者引入“现代早期”（Early Modern）概念，通过对比清朝边疆政策同其他现代早期帝国的异同，提出“清朝是否是殖民帝国”的问题，实则隐含着对中国近代兴起的民族主义观念下的中国大一统认识的根本否定（欧立德，2006）。如此，“殖民”的话语就不只是简单的“去汉化”，而是关系到“去中国”和作为民族国家的现代中国对边疆统治合法性的问题。这些主张被急于摆脱汉化观的西南边疆史研究的美国学者所继承，霍斯特勒的研究就是极佳的样板。纪若诚在《亚洲边陲》一书的开端也开宗明义地声称，本书的写作目的在于打破两种观点：一是汉化观，二是过去认为中国历史上的政治文化扩张是平和、进步的统一进程，最终铸就现今多民族国家的认识（C. Patterson Giersch，2006：14）。

应当说，“殖民”一词在西方早期的中国边疆研究中并不陌生。拉铁摩尔在其《汉人在满洲里的殖民》一文中便使用了这一词语（Lattimore, 1962）。尽管此“殖民”内涵与后殖民理论影响下的“殖民”话语已不可同日而语，尤其是严重缺乏被征服者的声音，但从中我们仍然隐约地看到西方学术发展脉络背景下两者的某些内在关联。这使我们不禁怀疑以“殖民化”取代“汉化”是否可取？是否又落入另一个学术陷阱中？研究西南边疆史的美国学者试图从多维角度突破汉与非汉的二元式研究框架，但他们过于强调边疆的声音以实现“去汉化”的目的，对边疆同晚期中华帝国的对抗性冲突给予更多的关注，渲染“清朝的残酷和汉人的经济掠夺破坏了帝国部分（边疆）区域的土著社会”。在他们的笔下，边疆非汉族群的频繁叛乱和暴力事件常充斥于明代的广西、贵州和清代云南的边疆地区。一幅幅动荡的边疆社会场景的确符合边疆被“殖民化”的界定（C. Patterson Giersch，2006：217）。然而，他们往往低估甚至忽视了明清时期边疆非汉族群的能动性，及其同中华帝国之间的长期依存关系。何汉威就曾批评赫曼道：“明代贵州汉、彝关系，或不宜纯从冲突着眼。如果说清代边政，因时空不同而异，明代情况亦然，不应以偏概全。”（2008）实际上，两者张弛有度的关系和非汉族群对帝国各种资源的反利用，或许能从边疆地区土司历史的深入研究中得到意想不到的学术收获。晚期中华帝国处理边疆事务有时也是相当被动的，有意或无意地被边疆地区的各种势力所左右和利用。过度的阐释晚期中华帝国在边疆扩张过程中同非汉族群的对抗，反而无形中将两者置于另一类二元对立的框架之内，而无法更为全面地展现出边疆社会错综复杂的关系。因而与其将帝国与边疆对立起来，毋宁说两者是多元互竞的关系。在这一点上，纪若诚对清代云南半月形边疆社会兼顾政治文化融合与“冲撞”的研究，应能够提供给我们和美国学界更多的启示，以便超越“汉族中心”观和“殖民”话语的框架束缚。

另一方面，“殖民”话语在将晚期中华帝国同边疆之间的横向互动关系硬性切割开来的同时，以西方现代民族国家的理念嫁接到对传统帝国的理解上，直接忽视和否定了中国政治与文化发展的历史延续性。试想，倘若以此种逻辑来认识中国历史，我们就无法意识到“和欧洲不同，中国的政治疆域和文化空间是从中心向边疆弥漫开来”（葛兆光，2005）的特殊性，也就难以溯源中华早期文明发展的历史，阐释汉族民间文化的包容性和柔韧性，以及西南边疆地区多族群共生、共存的独特文化现象了。这或许同布拉姆（Susan Blum）提示的，现今西方学术界过于关注中国边疆地区的非汉族群文化，忽略对汉族形成问题的深入分析有一定关联（2002：1287-1310）。

不可否认，美国学界对明清时期中国西南边疆史多视角、多维度的研究，为我们重新审视和研究晚期中华帝国与边疆的复杂关系开辟了一片新的学术天地。尽管美国学界至今依然无法完全摆脱阿达斯（Michel Adas）所言“持续地以西方中心观书写和概念化全球历史”（1998：371-388）的隐忧，研究西南边疆史的学者们仍以多族群文献资料为基础，摒弃单一的中心视角，从多层面对“族群”概念、全球视野的比较史观、“边疆学说”及“中间地带”等理论与假说进行了富有创见的尝试性运用。这些已然令我们无法继续在传统的中国西南民族史研究领域故步自封，而对此无动于衷了。幸运的是，目前国内学界一些有识之士已意识到并且大声疾呼对美国边疆研究范式的重视和借鉴，乃至提倡“‘从中国边疆社会发现历史’，从边疆社会解构长期在中原汉族中心观支配下的正统历史叙事”（张世明，2011；许建英，2011；袁剑，2010；章永俊，2006）。在现代学术研究的语境下，我们很难完全抛开西方学术话语，因为这样做，就等于失去了对话的可能。如何扬长避短，将传统的民族史研究同西方的边疆研究范式相结合，成为未来实现中国西南民族研究转型和再发展、迎接西方学术挑战与对话的关键。中国西南民族史研究有着数十年传统实证研究的学术根基，这是一笔宝贵的财富。时至今日，传统实证研究仍具有持久的不可或缺的重要学术价值。立足于实证研究，突出边疆的重要性，充分发掘各类非汉文献资料，以边疆反观中国历史，改变过去从汉文化立场溯源式的研究范式，关注边疆非汉族群的“主观归属意识之状况及其历史变迁”（姚大力，2007），并将之引入到更为广阔的历史场景中加以阐释，已变得日趋迫切。但是这并不是说要如美国学者那样过分夸大边疆在中国历史上的意义，以“边疆”为中心，将帝国与边疆对立起来，进而将“中国”历史解构。而是应既着眼于，又要跳出中心与边缘的阐释框架，重点探讨帝国与边疆多元势力“同时在场”的互动机制，及其对边疆社会、晚期中华帝国的建构带来的种种影响。

对此，西南边疆史研究或许能够为重新理解晚期中华帝国与边疆的关系，甚至清代历史带来一番新的气象。与内陆亚洲边疆不同，中国的南方边疆，尤其是明清时期的西南边疆并未对晚期中华帝国的王朝更替产生决定性影响，却始终处于拉铁摩尔界定的“南方式非有限扩张”（陈君静，1998）范围之内。故而有学者指出，中原文明实则面临着“南”与“北”两个边疆的碰撞与交融（黄达远，2011）。不过，农耕文明的同质性使西南边疆与晚期中华帝国的关系，在很大程度上不同于游牧的内陆亚洲边疆与帝国的联系。晚期中华帝国向西南边疆的扩张是持续的、不间断的，两者的关系既有连续性，也存在着断裂，这从赫曼对元明时期贵州土司制度的异同即可得到印证。更为重要的是，西南边疆族群地理的多样性，使晚期中华帝国面对的是一个不同于内陆亚洲边疆的边疆。西南边疆众多族群也不似内陆亚洲边疆各族群那样与满清存有密切关联。因而晚期中华帝国与西南边疆的关系要复杂得多，纪若诚的研究即证实了这一点（Dodgen，2002：366）。即便是帝国各阶层对于西南边疆及其族群的认知也有其自身的逻辑体系，这又可从单国钺对明代广西边疆的研究中看出。因此，要完整地全面认识晚期中华帝国的边疆史，就需要从南北两大边疆的深入研究及其比较中得出，仅侧重内陆亚洲边疆，显然是有失偏颇的。当部分美国学者从内陆亚洲边疆反观清朝历史，来印证“新清史”的各种观点时，西南边疆史的研究或可对我们重新理解和修正晚期中华帝国历史及其与边疆的关系有所帮助，这应是西南边疆史在明清史研究中的重要学术价值。

## 参考文献：

陈君静. 拉铁摩尔和他的中国问题研究[J]. 华东师范大学学报：哲学社会科学版，1998（2）.

葛兆光. 重建关于“中国”的历史论述：从民族国家中拯救历史，还是在历史中理解民族国家[J]. 二十一世纪，2005（8）.

何汉威. 书评：Amid the Clouds and Mist[J]. 中国文化研究所学报，2008（48）.

黄达远. 边疆、民族与国家：对拉铁摩尔“中国边疆观”的思考[J]. 中国边疆史地研究，2011（4）.

柯文. 在中国发现历史：中国中心观在美国的兴起[M]. 林同奇，译. 北京：中华书局，2002: 170.

刘凤云. 理论与方法的推陈出新：清史研究三十年[J]. 史学月刊，2013（1）.

欧立德. 满文档案与新清史[J]. 故宫博物院学术季刊（台北），2006，24（2）.

许建英. 拉铁摩尔对中国新疆的考察与研究[J]. 中国边疆史地研究，2011（4）.

姚大力. 西方中国研究的“边疆范式”：一篇书目式述评[N]. 文汇报，2007-05-25.

袁剑. 旧疆新命：西南少数族群的“再发现”——兼读《从“异域”到“旧疆”：宋至清贵州西北部地区的制度、开发与认同》[M]//何明主编. 西南边疆民族研究：第8辑，昆明：云南大学出版社，2010.



张世明. 拉铁摩尔及其相互边疆理论[J]. 史林，2011（6）.

章永俊. 欧文·拉铁摩尔的中国边疆史研究[J]. 史学史研究，2006（2）.

Adas, Michel. Imperialism and Colonialism in Comparative Perspective[J]. *The International History Review*, 1998, 20(2): 371-388.

Atwill, David G. *The Chinese Sultanate: Islam, Ethnicity, and the Panthay Rebellion in Southwest China*, 1856-1873[M]. Redwood: Stanford University Press, 2005:14.

Blum, Susan D. Margins and Centers: A Decade of publishing on China's Ethnic Minorities[J]. *The Journal of Asian Studies*, 2002, 61(4): 1287-1310.

Cosmo, Nicolo Di, Don J. Wyatt. *Political Frontiers Ethnic Boundaries, and Human Geographies in Chinese History*[M]. London and New York: Taylor & Francis Group, 2003: 3-4.

Crossley, Pamela Kyle, Helen F. Siu, Donald S. Sutton. *Empire at the Margins: Culture, Ethnicity and Frontier in Early Modern China*[M]. Oakland: University of California Press, 2006.

Dodgen, Randall. Review: Qing Colonial Enterprise[J]. *The British Journal for the History of Science*, 2002, 35(3):366.

Elliot, Mark C. Review: Qing Colonial Enterprise[J]. *Journal of the Economic and Social History of the Orient*, 2003, 46(4): 547-549.

Giersch, C. Pat. A Motley Throng: Social Change on Southwest China's Early Modern Frontier, 1700-1880[J]. *The Journal of Asian Studies*, 2001, 60(1): 71-72.

Giersch, C.Patterson. *Asian Borderlands: The Transformation of Qing China's Yunnan Frontier*[M]. Cambridge, MA: Harvard University Press, 2006: 14, 217.

Giersch, C.Patterson. Qing China's Reluctant Subjects: Indigenous Communities and Empire along the Yunan Frontier[D]. Yale University, Ph.D., 1998.

Hanks, L.M. Review: China's March toward the Tropics by Herold J.Wiens[J]. *American Anthropologist*, New Series, 1955, 57(6): 1322-1323.

Harrell, Stevan. The History of the History of the Yi[M]// *Cultural Encounters on China's Ethnic Frontiers*. Seattle: University of Washington Press, 1995: 63-91.

Herman, John E. *Amid the Clouds and Mist: China's Colonization of Guizhou,1200-1700* [M]. Cambridge, MA: Harvard University Press, 2007: 6, 9.

Hinton, Harold C. Review: China's March toward the Tropics by Herold J.Wiens[J]. *The Far Eastern Quarterly*, 1955, 14(4): 565-566.

Hosteler, Laura. *Qing Colonial Enterprise: Ethnography and Cartography in Early Modern China*[M]. Chicago: The University of Chicago Press, 2001.

Lamar, Howard and Leonard Thompson. *The Frontier in History: North America and Southern Africa Compared*[M]. New Haven: Yale University Press, 1981.

Owen Lattimore. *Chinese Colonization in Manchuria, Studies in Frontier History: Collected Papers1928-1958*[M]. Oxford: Oxford University Press, 1962.

Perdue, Peter C. *China Marches West: The Qing Conquest of Central Eurasia*[M]. Cambridge, MA: Harvard University Press, 2005: 9-10.

Perdue, Peter C. Comparing Empires: Manchu Colonialism[J]. *The International History Review*, 1998, 20(2): 255-262.

Shepherd, John Robert. *Statecraft and Political Economy on the Taiwan Frontier*[M]. Redwood: Stanford University Press, 1993.

Shin, Leo K. *The Making of the Chinese State: Ethnicity and Expansion on the Ming Borderlands*[M]. Cambridge: Cambridge University Press, 2006: 5.

Shin, Leo K. Tribalizing the Frontier: Barbarians, Settlers, and the State in Ming South China[D]. Princeton University, Ph.D., 1999.

W. Eberhard. Review: China's March toward the Tropics by Herold J.Wiens[J]. *Pacific Historical*

*Review,* 1955, 24(3): 324-325.

Wittfogel, Karl, Feng Chia-sheng. *History of Chinese Society: Liao(907-1125)*[M]. Philadelphia, American Philosophical Society(distributed by the Macmillan Co., New York), 1949: 3-25a

# The Status of the Southwest Borderland in Studies on Ming and Qing Dynasties: A Study on the History of Southwest Borderland in China Under the Modern American Academic Perspective

Zou Libo[1] Li Peirong[2]

(1 China Tibetan Studies Institute, Sichuan University, Chengdu, China, 610029; 2 College of History and Tourism, Sichuan University, Chengdu, China, 610029)

**Abstract:** The 1990s is the watershed of American study on the history of southwest borderland in Ming and Qing dynasties of China. Influenced by the researches of western anthropology on southwest minorities of China as well as inspired and promoted by the "frontier" paradigm of western studies on China, the history of southwest borderland has evolved as an important field in American studies on China with a batch of influential academic works. Based on the same academic goal to reflect and criticize the old "concept of Han center" or "localization", American studies emphasized the localized view of the borderland and also introduced the concept and the theory of the early imperial and ethnic identities. They inspired the researches on the complex relations between the late imperial China and the borderland, meanwhile, they put both into another frame of binary position. The history of southwest borderland certainly could help the academic fields both at home and abroad to understand and revise the relation between the history of late imperial China and its borderland.

**Key Words:** The History of Southwest Borderland of China; America; Ming and Qing Dynasties

# “文化碰撞”、墨西哥人北迁与心灵边界[1]

卡洛斯·G. 维勒兹-艾巴那兹

(亚利桑那州立大学边疆研究所，美国坦佩　85287-5503)

**摘　要：**本文讨论了从西班牙统治期前到西班牙殖民期，中美洲边缘地带与大西南地区之间的文化“介入”。北迁中直接、间接的人口、文化流动过程见证了各族裔的有力“碰撞”，以及他们或融合或抵抗或消亡的结局。边境背景下的墨西哥人通过南北贸易交流实现了文化上的相互借鉴与融合，进入劳动力流通阶段。墨西哥人民及其劳动力被打造成了廉价商品，19世纪末和20世纪他们受到排挤，被驱逐，抵抗、反叛、迁移、创造、发明，陆续成为墨西哥人的文化回应。不同团体之间的“碰撞”、反抗使得心灵与空间的边界越来越少。但是旧的边界缩小的同时，新的心灵边界也正在建立。



**关键词：**“文化碰撞”；墨西哥人北迁；心灵边界

关于这个话题，我多年来一直从事相关研究，并将研究结果集结成册。每日看着裹了橘黄色的阳光划过一排排仙人掌，每晚呼吸着沙尘的气息，就这样在亚利桑那州生活了将近半个世纪的我，想来也有资格聊聊居住于“新墨西哥西南部”（Greater Mexican Southwest）的墨西哥人民，那里便是人们熟知的美国西南地区，希望读者能有所收获。

我出生在墨美边境上。我的出生地是亚利桑那州而不是索诺拉州（墨西哥），这不过是个巧合。现如今，每天有数以千计的家庭见证这样的偶然。

于我们这一代而言，亚利桑那州也好，索诺拉州也罢，出生地并不重要，

1　本文出自亚利桑那州立大学卡洛斯·维勒兹-艾巴那兹（Carlos G. Velez-ibznez）教授的著作《边疆视野》（*Border Visions*，亚利桑那州大学出版社，1996年）的《前言》和最后一章，编者对内容进行了编译。

因为这是父母的选择，他们决定你的国籍。于父母那一代而言，两地相差无几。他们出生前43年，这里原本都属于索诺拉州，人们的生活夹杂着货车故事，上演着与阿帕奇族人无休止的割地斗争。在我们眼中，索诺拉州人乐于走亲访友，而亚利桑那州让人际关系变得生疏。正因为此，父母将索诺拉州视为文化充电器，频繁地往返于两地间。我也就顺理成章地出生在从马格达莱纳（索诺拉州）至图森（亚利桑那州）的返程路上——处于两镇中点的诺加利斯（亚利桑那州）。负责接生的圣·约瑟夫医院就几乎挨着墨美边境北侧的防护栏。

成长过程中，到索诺拉州的一次次旅程让我领略历史，学会思考，感受为生存而斗争的勇气。记得一次回索诺拉时，唐·梅利顿讲述了他40年前饱受亚基战争[1]折磨的往事。战乱中，他小腿肌腱断裂。恢复后只能踮脚走路的他，犹如醉酒的芭蕾舞者在寻找平衡。尽管如此，精心搭配的呢帽和刀痕裤，外加长款大衣和领带，这般考究的着装为他重拾体面。

50年后的今天，一段段回索之旅成为我弥足珍贵的回忆。与此同时，我也在探究边境南北的墨西哥人为何格格不入的问题。许多次往返途中，我看着出生地不远处的边境防护网，常误以为它只有一侧。其实，这道护栏为人们划下的界限也仅是单方面的：边境以北排挤边境以南；然而，边境以南毫无此意。这让我对这一现象的潜在原因更加困惑、好奇，也质疑自己对这个区域的假设。

从西班牙殖民边陲、大西南地区到墨西哥大西北部，乃至中美洲北部，人们给这片土地贴过各类标签。而我认为，它代表着美国西南地区和墨西哥北部。本文的内容虽不能面面俱到，但也试图拼凑出这里的历史版图，去了解那些意识形态异于美国的墨西哥移民：他们如何在美国西南部营造自己的文化，旁观者又是如何在隔阂中看待或排斥他们的。第一道隔阂便是由使用了政治而非文化的视角审视这一地区的墨西哥群体而造成的。国家在确保公民权益的同时，忽略了人民解决生计问题时借以支撑的“文化”（cultural）世界。因此，要了解西南区墨西哥群体及其形成的文化体系，需要从他们在社会、工作

1　亚基战争（Yaqui Wars）：1533年至1929年间，新西班牙以及后来的墨西哥共和国与美洲土著亚基人之间爆发的一系列战争。

中的角色入手，剖析其自食其力的方式，劳动力变成商品的来由，以及根本思想、价值观重于公民权的原因。在国家及各州的影响下，地方文化与国家文化相互冲突，又相互融合。

第二道隔阂起因于人类文化是“纯洁的”（pristine）这一误解。毋庸置疑，任何种族的文化都不会孤立存在，不同文化会不可避免地相互“碰撞”（bump）。从古至今，为了生存，人类迁移，然后碰见彼此。迁移故事如何发展是理解区域、地方文化身份的关键。有时候，过程是沉重的，“受到碰撞”（bumped）的群体会因为疾病、饥荒、战争失去同伴。有时候，某些阶层间的抑制、调节、整合会挖掘并重塑当地居民的社会关系。还有些时候，一方占上风会引发掌权者更替及文化更新。地域、语言或文化不同的群体发生碰撞，其结局可能是同化或异化。

美国西南地区的“碰撞”（bumping）史起于16世纪，早于欧洲移民。西班牙统治期前，北迁碰撞经历了占领、贸易及劳动力流动阶段（Reff：1990，80），这些现象一直延续至今。

我从考古学、历史学、人口统计学、人种学、族裔志等角度描述并分析人口与思想从中美洲边缘至美国西南部的不断北迁的过程。至少从欧洲统治期前开始，北迁中直接、间接的人口、文化流动过程见证了各族裔的有力“碰撞”，以及他们融合、抵抗或消亡的结局。此次北迁研究旨在挖掘“文化空间与地域”（cultural space and place），从而将在排斥与妥协中经过剧烈“碰撞”的本土美国人、西班牙人、墨西哥人汇聚在同一舞台上，展示新的文化、阶层和群体。

北美洲人民迁入西南地区，通过边境商业往来，将墨西哥人民及其劳动力打造为廉价商品，尽管他们为区域经济发展提供了不可或缺的知识与技能。身份的文化外延，使人们通过身份定义自己，以及所处的社会、经济、政治关系。而墨西哥人由此获得不可忽视的“商品”（commodity）身份。在资本主义经济体系中，劳动力、物质和工艺是可交易的，部分人群也被附加上可买卖的属性，待遇无异于其他一次性材料或二手产品。

随着美国资本主义渗透美国西南部及墨西哥西北地区，“墨西哥”也逐渐成为“廉价劳动力”（cheap labor）的代名词。整体来看，美墨历史进程不曾摆脱“商品身份”（commodity identity）。这一身份很大程度上对外界认识墨西哥人民，以及墨西哥人民认识自己造成影响。

尽管如此，边境往来持续不断，朝气蓬勃的墨西哥社区逐渐成长起来。当时盛行“城区化”（barrioization），墨西哥人被压缩进了以墨西哥人为主体的社区，而这些社区又归属于更大范围的白人区域。接下来的主要工作，便是建立诸如公益协会、工会及文化社团等政治性或文化性组织，以便墨西哥人在寻找文化空间与地域的过程中，对抗商业化的经济及政治进程。同时，也正是由于这些进程，墨西哥人在某些方面的问题显得尤为突出。如在贫穷、犯罪、疾病、战争等方面，墨西哥人所占的比例极高，我称之为“痛苦分配”（the distribution of sadness）。

伴随伤痛，墨西哥人继续寻找文化空间与地域。许多文学、艺术作品以这般“苦楚”（sadness）与寻觅为创作主题。人们将壁画视为艺术形式的巅峰，它不仅再现寻觅历程，而且延伸至后续发展问题。因为，即使墨西哥人世代更迭，文化寻觅之路从未中断。

墨西哥人不许自己以“商品身份”（commodity identity）得过且过。与商业化无关，他们编织的文化体系经过时间的打磨，经过反复尝试，逐渐具有适应性，且富有创造力，最终沉淀为墨西哥“文化身份”（cultural identity），为后人打造益于身心健康的社会搭建了平台。这一文化体系包含边境身份认同，越境家庭，居民群，“父权制”（patriarchy）变革，儿童养育方式，互惠与信任，以及以沟通和多样性为原则、基于彼此深厚关系而成立的政治、经济、社会组织。显然，身份表现方式以多维度、全息为特点。

很久以前，墨西哥人离开故土，踏上西南土地，正是这段久远的历史让往昔与今朝交错，并与思想、活动、创造、争端相伴相生。从西班牙统治期前到西班牙殖民期，中美洲边缘地带与大西南地区之间的文化“介入”（interruption）是本文讨论的核心问题。正因为墨西哥核心地带在机构、文化、经济、政治方面的影响，大西南地区文化论题才不可孤立看待。虚拟政治界限更无从定义当下墨西哥人及该区域的历史和文化马赛克。这一群体不再是由疆界而定的移民，而是文化发展、适应、排斥、接纳过程中的主体。

我的父亲就生长在边境区域，受两个国家、两种文化的浸润。他的幸福感染我，他的痛苦感化我，他是启发我最多的人。本文的观点一部分来自于我的父亲。他认为政治界限使文化支离破碎，所以两国需要先实现政治和平。

这说明各地人民的生存权利是不可剥夺的，并且凡有适应能力，有一技之长，追求优质生活的人都值得尊重。这些人正是经济、自然变化多端的边境生活需要的。然而，适应边境生活也需要忍耐事事的不确定性，否则会于己不利。边境背景下的文化群体天生适应力强，有创造力，敢于推陈出新。另外，这些墨西哥人在与他国人互动的同时，尽管以自身、家庭利益为重，他们也在寻找、创建慰藉自己的空间与地域。墨西哥人长于包容，文化界限与因战争、条约立下的政治界限不同，它不过是随时可以渗透的一层隔膜。我父亲持有这样的观点，我也不例外。

某种程度上，我试图提供一种环境和方法来理解美国西南部的墨西哥人这一文化族群。术语和范畴都不重要，除非它们对墨西哥人来说有所指代或是为他们所有。同时，这次探索对我来说让我对出现的关于心灵边界和地区边界的词语既抱有友好态度，也充满敌意，更有沟通和协商的意愿。

对许多墨西哥人来说，也包括我在内，边界是生活中最重要的概念，因为我们的身份和边界的产生息息相关。几乎每隔十年，边界就产生一次。1836年德克萨斯州起义[1]，德州人的边界产生了；1847年墨西哥战争[2]，加州人和新墨西哥人的边界产生了；1858年的加兹登购地[3]再一次让索诺拉雷州人的边界产生了。边界就如一种永久的产物，政府有权力决定墨西哥人何时或是否被准许“跨过”边界，持有某种带有特权的标签，比如“绿卡”，或者达到最高层次，成为“自然归属”（naturalized）公民。“自然归属”这个词尤有讽刺意义，因为只有植物和动物才会生来自然就属于某个地域。

墨西哥人通过各种“藩篱”（fenses）向北张望，而非墨西哥人通过这些“藩篱”向南张望，“藩篱”对于美国和墨西哥建立的边界变得不可或缺。这样的边界不仅造成了空间上的隔阂，同时也造成了两地居民文化与历史观念上



1　德克萨斯起义（Texas Rebellion）：从美国移居到德克萨斯的人民不满墨西哥政府的集权主义统治，最终，移民和政府之间的冲突导致1835年德克萨斯起义的爆发，1836年4月德克萨斯宣布独立。

2　墨西哥战争（Mexican War）：美国与墨西哥之间于1846年至1848年爆发墨西哥战争，美国通过这场战争夺取了大片土地，包括今天的加利福尼亚、内华达、犹他等州。

3　加兹登购地（Gadsden Purchase）：1853年，美国驻墨西哥公使J. 加兹登受总统F. 皮尔斯之命，以购买方式兼并墨西哥领土的事件。向墨西哥购买的领土成为今天的亚利桑那州的南部以及新墨西哥州的西南部。

的阻碍。经济不景气时，墨西哥人就被驱逐，那些留下的也被嫌弃。已经归属的墨西哥人甚至拒绝与非归属墨西哥人之间产生关联。经济兴旺时，墨西哥人则大受欢迎。这种接受与驱逐的过程让许多人把墨西哥人当作可以买卖的商品，就像汽车，如无用处，便可遗弃。

实际上，人口、思想和发明由南向北的迁徙运动比玉米、南瓜和大豆（也可能是辣椒）从南方向北方的引进要早得多。霍霍坎文化[1]里程碑式的发展，比如寺庙、球场，是南方迁徙的直接结果。通过灌溉获得的农产品种类在公元900年快速增长，比起单一作物的缓慢发展，从某种程度上说，这更是南北方相互借鉴、相互融合的结果。

在消长变化的贸易交流中，中美洲的边缘地带在前欧洲和史前时期就已形成。大卡萨斯、普韦布洛、霍霍卡姆、索诺兰、查奇威德斯和萨卡特卡斯[2]之间不同时期的贸易交流证明，蚀刻壳、黑曜石、绿松石、兽皮、鹦鹉、绯红金刚鹦鹉以及其他手工艺品在东西南北之间流通。这些物品的流通表明，至少从公元300年到16世纪，有序的政治、经济和社会系统之间存在着交易。

这个时期的贸易几乎从未被战争打断过，此外，相邻地域的人群使用多种语言进行交流。而且，这些人群的符号系统和意识形态也被囊括在对该时期的影响之中。基瓦以及伴随该地区的羽蛇神神话[3]、卡齐纳教派[4]、墓葬制度便直接来源于南部地区和各人群之间的交流。

当把商品人口的概念结合到“美国化”程序中时，只用英语、移民突击检查、双倍工资结构、劳动力束缚，19世纪90年代，20世纪30年代、50年代、70年代、80年代由经济原因诱发的大屠杀，以及90年代的歇斯底里使得极端排外

1 霍霍坎文化（Hohokam）：公元前300年至公元1 400年间的北美印第安人文化，主要位于今美国亚利桑那州中部和南部地区，主要分布于基拉河及盐河的半干旱区域。

2 大卡萨斯、普韦布洛、霍霍卡姆、索诺兰、查奇威德斯、萨卡特卡斯均为美洲印第安部落。

3 羽蛇神神话（Quetzalcoatl myths）：羽蛇神是一个在中部美洲文明中普遍信奉的神祇，一般被描绘为一条长满羽毛的蛇的形象。根据传说，羽蛇神主宰晨星，发明了书籍、历法，而且给人类带来了玉米。它是玛雅人心目中带来雨季，与播种、收获、五谷丰登有关的神祇。

4 卡齐纳教派（Katsina cults）：美国西南部叫作普埃布罗族的印第安部落信仰卡齐纳神灵。卡齐纳有三种不同的守护神——超自然体、宗教仪式上戴着面具扮演卡齐纳的舞者和用来送给孩子的卡齐纳形象的娃娃。

的边界出现了。一些美国墨西哥人开始认为应该否定传统，而且，美国公民身份是文化可接受性的标记，这也是唯一避免边界综合征的方法。此外，像“大流散”（diaspora）[1]这种描述人类悲剧的流行术语，本用于非裔美国人和犹太人，却误用于墨西哥人。墨西哥人不是从南方而是从北方被驱逐的，和“大流散”这个概念相反。

然而，不论过去还是现在，许多墨西哥人都患上了“边界综合征”或被驱逐，抵抗、反叛、迁移、创造、发明，陆续成为墨西哥人的文化回应方式。从19世纪开始，他们就有了加州、新墨西哥、亚利桑那州/索诺拉和德州的文化英雄，以及20年代、30年代、40年代的互助组织——工会。墨西哥人不会放任自己毫无作为，令自己持续受到限制、挫败、迫害，他们发起的“奇卡诺运动”（Chicano Convulsive Transition Movement）[2]至今仍在持续。

这样的冲突也出现在墨西哥家庭的同化上。墨西哥族群以“跨界”模式生存，频繁来往和多方关系带来了密集的人口与众多的后代。所有人都被女性主导的规律性活动“粘连”在一起。在这些活动中，大量知识得以展现和交流，墨西哥人不断创造、适应、遗弃、润色从劳动力衍生而来的且源自家庭的信息。所有这些冲突、关系、问题和活动造就了个人、家庭、邻里和地区的历史生命。



彰显于这场反对压迫的斗争中的是，墨西哥人展现了他们状态的各个方面，展现了生存和文化的多种维度，这种表达在那些表现生活地域与空间的文学作品和壁画中便可找到。在创造文化多维度时，不论是文学作品还是壁画，都否定边界综合征是一种疾病。要说有什么不同的话，边界是可以被跨越、破坏和对抗的，而心灵边界、文化边界、边缘身份通常在文学作品中被分解和重构，被称之为痛苦的儿时记忆和辛酸孤独的内心独白。多数情况下，文学作品

1 大流散（diaspora）：特指历史上大规模的非自愿的人口驱散，如犹太人的流散、非洲跨大西洋奴隶贸易、中国南部或印度的苦力贸易、斯巴达人统治下长达一个世纪的对麦西尼亚人的流放等。

2 奇卡诺运动（Chicano Convulsive Transition Movement）：开始于20世纪60年代末的美国墨西哥人争取民族自由平等权利的社会运动，它是继美国黑人民权运动后的又一个美国少数族裔集团的民权运动。“奇卡诺运动”的一个直接结果是唤醒了美籍墨西哥人的民族意识，并将处于“边缘地带”的墨西哥文化推向美国文化的中心。

出自综合而非二元的斗争。有时候，整个领域的双模感知和反差被拆开重塑为可以改变形状和方式的全息影片。这种影片大胆地将性别、种族、文化、阶级斗争与理查德·罗德里格斯[1]书中的“公开”世界与“私人”世界的边界做对比。

然而，这种对比是部分不一致的，也显示了墨西哥族群的多样化特点。像文学作品一样，在最不平等的社会经济环境下进行的关于地域和空间的斗争中，壁画产生了。这些画没有边界，因为它们与墨西哥人以及他们的无边界文化有着即刻的一致性。如果说壁画确实表现出了非凡的“人类学”洞察力，那是因为美国墨西哥文化大多是基于团体和工薪阶层的，这种文化在动态中十分包容。除一些不足之外，比如日渐衰退但至今仍存在的父权制和信仰压制，美国墨西哥文化就像一场可移动的盛会，盛会上男性和女性相互结合而非互相抵制，相互包容而非相互驱逐，创新而非复制那些同于自己或异于自己的观点、关系与表达方式。壁画捕捉到了这种共同性、易接受性、多样性及相互性。除了这些动态关系，为数较多且更加庞大的经济政治过程对美国墨西哥人并不友善。政治从属、文化压迫、语言磨蚀、教育误导、社会阶层分化、心理创伤及工作带来的伤亡同样也是西南部一些地区和团体延续至今的社会历史经历。

有人指出，这些情况并非全部，未曾有过对“撞进来”（bumped）的人群的完全统治。从这个观点来看，随着选择性文化形式伴随着选择性传统的出现，接踵而至的便是对立性文化，即对特定事件、行为及未知历史联系的解构性“重构”（desconstructed “reconstruction”）。然而，这种观点把过多的权力放在了统治群体上，而忽略了被统治的群体的能力；它没有注意到的是，某种程度上统治“开小差”了，产生了缝隙，这样被统治者便有机会创造与其背道而驰的选择和历史。这种观点从被统治者手中夺走了行事权（agency），并且欺骗说这样做可以让被统治者在道德上高人一等。因此，行事权只存在于“统治”（dominating）过程的裂缝中，而有意识的、有组织和动员能力的文化创造者却没有这样的权力。

19世纪的文化英雄、二三十年代的罢工者和社会动员者、铁路和矿产业的

1 理查德·罗德里格斯（Richard Rodriguez）：1944年生，美国作家，著有作品《记忆的渴望：理查德·罗德里格斯的教育》（*Hunger of Memory: The Education of Richard Rodriguez*, 1982）。

女工、参加抗议的大学生，以及文学和壁画作者，是没有可以行使行事权的裂缝的。没有文化就没有政治，而没有文化的政治仅仅是一次练习（exercise）罢了。对于这些“被统治”的人群来说，文化才是斗争和创新的基础。

那么，是什么提供了动力，让文化基础得以持续，让抵抗力、行事权和集体性得以形成？答案是不言而喻的。正是人口从南部的不断迁徙，以及对价值、行为、关系、线性联系和矛盾的补充、强调、替代和再生产，为其提供了动力。如上文所述，这种运动比当下的文化制造要古老得多，且一直持续着，过程中伴随着不同团体之间的“冲撞”、反抗、不断的战争与合作、冲突与联姻、“美国化”与镇压、群体的压缩与政治动员和回应，以及家庭、文化地域与空间的产生。没有边界的墨西哥人完成了上述所有进程，不论出身何处，他们互相联合，跨越了经验与文化交流的网。这种不同群体的联合将会增加而非减少，随之，心灵与空间的边界也会越来越少。

加州州长派遣国民警卫队到边界地区“力挽狂澜”（to stem the tide），即使这样做会将财政赤字由2 500万美元增加到3 000万。这么一来，新的边界就开始形成，新的心灵边界也出现在报纸上。新闻图片里天空乌云密布，一名边界巡逻警官正在押送一名戴着手铐的年轻墨西哥人。图片上面写着这样的标题：“坚守防线：边界巡警与牛仔和墨西哥人的死亡游戏”（《旧金山记事报》，1993年11月7日）。同样，在1993年9月19日的“封锁行动”（Operation Blockade）中，为了封锁住埃尔帕索-华雷斯边界[1]，大量军力用于对边界进行军事化监视。



从美国大众角度来看，1990年的一次民意调查让新边界逐渐显现。该调查显示，超过60%的美国人认为所有西班牙裔都是“不爱国的”（unpatriotic），同时，72%的人认为他们依赖于社会提供的福利。同样，超过50%的人认为他们愚笨、懒散，具有暴力倾向。当这样的边界“分散”（distributed）在墨西哥年轻人当中时，对他们的心理、文化的影响是悲剧性的。像雨果·萨拉查（Hugo Salazar）这样颇有天赋的艺术家，同时也是一名少年犯，至今仍有情感上的边界：“人都有一死。只是时间的问题罢了：一次

1　埃尔帕索-华雷斯边界：埃尔帕索-华雷斯是墨西哥和美国两国边境上的大城市区域，以墨西哥奇瓦瓦州的华雷斯和美国德克萨斯州的埃尔帕索两大城市为中心。

犯罪，或一次事故。不重要了……轮到你时，怎么都躲不过的。这也是我不惧怕死亡的原因。我17岁，但有些孩子死于更加年幼之时，那又如何呢？不过是上帝将他们带走而已。”（《旧金山考察者报》，1994年5月8日）

在文化创造与文化压迫的辩证关系中，新的边界产生了。文化身份动摇了，新的版本也产生了，他们在实际政治关系行为中表达自己，有时不平衡地自我摧毁，也有时解脱似地寻求自主。新的边界刺激人们寻找独立空间与生存平台，人类情感也变得待价而沽，像雨果一样，他们戴着沮丧的面具寻找躲避之处。

另一方面，新的边界也有另一种用处。像塔玛拉·艾尔瓦拉多（Tamara Alvarado）、费利佩·巴拉甘（Felipe Barragan）、朱莉亚·冈萨雷斯·卢娜（Julia Gonzalez Luna）、埃尔韦拉·普列托（Elvira Prieto）和伊娃·席尔瓦（Eva Silva）这样的大学生，他们遵循恺撒·查维斯[1]一贯的传统，于1994年5月在斯坦福大学参加了绝食抗议，抗议一位墨西哥管理员遭到的不公正待遇。成百上千的美国墨西哥学生加入了此次绝食抗议。这些墨西哥学生在成长过程中就经常遭受饥饿，那为什么他们还要进行绝食抗议呢？朱莉娅·冈萨雷斯·卢娜简单回答道：“我内心的感受非常真实……那种感觉很复杂，一两句话说不清楚……我不得不面对的事实是，我之所以不被接受，是因为我的长相和说话方式不同。”

虽然雨果来自加州的墨西哥贫民区，朱莉亚来自斯坦福大学，但他们的文化身份问题却来源相同：他人与自我的心灵边界。他们两人的不同之处在于雨果的生存地域和空间是自己造成的，而朱莉亚却是与生俱来的。

他们都是我们的孩子。

1　恺撒·查维斯（Cesar Chavex, 1927-1993）：美国最著名的拉丁裔美国民权运动家、劳工运动者、联合农场工人联盟领袖。他倡导的激进但非暴力策略从道义上为农场工人的斗争赢得了全国性的支持。20世纪70年代，激进但非暴力策略使得联合农场工人联盟影响力显著扩大。

# Cultural Bumping, Mexicans' Northward Migration and Borders of Mind

Carlos G. Velez-ibznez

(School of Transborder Studies, Arizona State University, Tempe, USA, 85287-5503)

**Abstract:** This essay explores the cultural interruption between the border area of Central America and the big southeast region from before Spanish reign to Spanish colonial period. The population and cultural movement during the northward migration, direct and indirect, witnessed culture bumping, blending, resisting or extincting among different ethnics. The north-south trade of the Mexicans around the border promoted cultural communication and fusion. In the stage of labor movement, the Mexican people and their labor were made cheap commodity; in the late 19th century and 20th century, Mexican people were removed and expelled. They, however, made their cultural response with resistance, rebellion, migration, creation and invention. The bumping and resistance among different groups narrowed the mind boundary as well as space boundary. While the old mind boundary was shrinking, the new one was establishing.

**Key Words:** Cultural Bumping; Mexicans' Northward Migration; Borders of Mind

# 中美文学作品中知识分子形象的对比研究
## ——以《赫索格》和《围城》为例

段丽斌

（四川师范大学基础教学学院，四川成都　610068）

**摘　要：**纵观人类发展史，文明的进步和科技的发展必然会带来社会结构和生活方式的转变，知识具有无穷的力量。但是，掌握知识的精英即知识分子，在社会中的地位常常是起起落落，容易被边缘化。本文关注在当前社会转型期不断被边缘化的知识分子的境遇和他们的历史使命，首先简述中美两国知识界悠久的人文传统，然后以美国犹太作家索尔·贝娄的代表作《赫索格》和钱钟书的《围城》中的主人公为例，对中美文学作品中知识分子的形象做了对比研究，分析他们社会环境、性格特征、人生观、爱情观以及遭遇等各方面的异同，探讨在物质文明高度发达，传统的价值观和人文精神却日渐衰落的社会转型期，知识分子如何既坚守自己的信仰，又适应社会发展趋势，并继续引领人们建设美好的精神家园。

**关键词：**知识分子形象；《赫索格》；《围城》；方鸿渐

中美两国知识界都具有悠久的人文传统。中国的知识分子在古代社会以“先天下之忧而忧，后天下之乐而乐”的具有忧患意识的士大夫们为代表。从五四运动开始，在民族危机和文化危机的双重挤压下，知识分子不得不尝试抛弃传统文化中的糟粕，学习西方先进的技术和民主政治，但转变的道路是蜿蜒曲折的。自文艺复兴以来，西方知识分子逐渐形成了一个独立的社会阶层，他们善于对自己的文明体系内部进行反思和批判，涌现出了以巴尔扎克、托尔斯泰等为代表的批判现实主义文学，真实反映了日趋复杂的社会矛盾，批判现实的罪恶。在批判现实主义文学之后出现了以贝克特等为代表的现代主义文学，以反传统的写作风格，反映了在第二次世界大战以后动荡不安的社会环境中现代人面临的信仰缺失、道德沦丧的精神危机。

本文以美国犹太作家索尔·贝娄的代表作《赫索格》和钱钟书的《围城》中的主人公为例，对中美文学作品中知识分子的形象做了对比研究。首先笔者对两部小说的主人公即倒霉的知识分子的不幸婚姻进行了对比分析，其次分析了两位主人公在社会转型期遭遇的强烈的文化冲突反映出现代人普遍面临的精神危机。两部小说都是典型的知识分子小说，既描绘主人公个体的经历和遭遇，也探讨了知识分子关心的政治、哲学、文学、性别歧视、失业等社会问题。

## 1．倒霉的知识分子

《赫索格》是美国第二次世界大战后著名的心理现实主义犹太作家索尔·贝娄的代表作，最初发表于1964年。《围城》是我国“五四”新文化运动之后涌现出的重要的白话长篇小说之一，也是我国学贯中西的大家钱钟书先生的代表作之一，1947年在上海出版。



前者主要讲述犹太裔大学历史学教授赫索格苦心经营的第二次婚姻破裂后面临的精神崩溃的危机。他试图通过未寄出的一封封信件和古往今来的先贤、哲人，及在世与过世的亲友进行假想式的对话，以及对社会、政治、经济、军事、环境、浪漫主义、基督教、存在主义等所做的深刻的精神探索，来摆脱他的精神危机。索尔·贝娄以既嘲讽又幽默的笔调，描绘了崇尚理性和人道主义的高级知识分子赫索格在现实社会中处处碰壁的倒霉蛋形象（Bellow，1976：11）。

后者主要讲述刚从欧洲游学归来，并带回了一张花钱购买的某德国大学哲学博士文凭的半吊子知识分子方鸿渐在事业和爱情上遭遇的种种挫折。表面上玩世不恭的方鸿渐，其实是个既有独立见解，又缺乏斗争精神的自相矛盾的知识青年。他在父亲因循守旧的封建礼教的熏陶下长大，继承了孝顺父母、男尊女卑等儒家传统文化。但是在欧洲游学四年，他的思想和行为都留下了西化的痕迹。表现在工作上他不趋炎附势，不拉帮结派，流露出知识分子的洒脱和孤傲，因而得不到上司的赏识，先后从事了三份工作，结果都被辞退。在爱情上他开始追求至真至美的爱，但因为他优柔寡断、性格软弱而遭人误会、诽谤，和最爱的人失之交臂；后来方鸿渐追求平平淡淡的幸福，但因为信仰封建礼教的家人从中作梗，他的内心深处也是个相信男尊女卑的大男子主义者，不可避免地和受过高等教育的、信仰女权主义的现代知识女青年孙小姐发生了许多冲突，最后婚姻宣告失败（钱钟书，2013：153）。

在小说《赫索格》中几乎导致赫索格精神崩溃的是，马德琳竟然抛弃他这样的历史学教授和大善人，而嫁给他最好的朋友，他的模仿者，瘸子格斯贝奇。其实，他们的婚姻一开始就注定要失败，因为赫索格迎娶比自己小20岁的马德琳为妻，他的内心深处不是因为真爱，而是因为想要扮演一个救世主的角色，把不会做家务的、患有购物狂病症的、不会收拾屋子的、喜怒无常的，但是年轻、漂亮、聪明、自信的美国现代女性逐渐改造成一个温柔善良的、对丈夫言听计从的传统的犹太人理想中的模范妻子。另一方面，深受当时美国社会女权主义运动影响的马德琳，追求独立、自由，希望和丈夫建立平等、互相尊重、互爱互助的亲密关系。因此，他们之间的冲突是传统的犹太文化和自由民主的现代文化的冲突。

犹太民族男尊女卑的观念来源于希伯来《圣经》中相关的几个故事。这些故事表明：上帝要求妇女对丈夫绝对“忠贞”。唯有满足于丈夫的利益，服从于丈夫的信仰，方可称得上一位合格的犹太妇女。以《创世纪》里记载的两个故事为例。在第一个故事里，撒加不能生孩子，她对她的丈夫亚伯拉罕说：“耶和华使我不能生育，求你和我的使女同房，或者我可以因她得到孩子。”在第二个故事里，另一个不能生育的妻子拉结“把她的使女皮拉给丈夫为妾，雅各便与她同房”（《圣经》，2006：10）。

谙熟犹太传统文化的历史学教授赫索格便试图以此为模板来改造马德琳，希望已经疏离了犹太文化传统、融入了现代美国主流文化的年轻一代犹太妇女的代表马德琳能够改过自新，重拾犹太传统文化，扮演一个唯丈夫马首是瞻、没有独立人格的贤妻良母。

在《围城》中，方鸿渐本来在国内学中文，但又迫于准老丈人和父亲的压力而出国留学。他在国外本来没有学到什么自己感兴趣的东西，也没有为了一纸文凭而强迫自己学习，但回国前为了满足准老丈人和父亲的要求，光宗耀祖，匆忙购买了一张假文凭。到上海后他原本住在原老丈人家里，在老丈人的银行里工作，但因为拒绝迎娶有权有势的苏文纨小姐，和原老丈人一家决裂。本来他真心喜欢唐晓芙小姐，为她神魂颠倒，但是当唐小姐因为误会坚决拒绝了她的求爱之后，他就再没有勇气去执着地追求他的真爱了。后来到了内地的三间大学教书，因为不同意迎娶外文系系主任刘东方的妹妹刘小姐，被早就看他不顺眼的三间大学校长以莫须有的罪名辞退了。在三间大学娶了同事孙柔嘉小姐，并一起回到上海，结果小家庭一开始就摩擦不断，两人经常怄气吵架，最后分道扬镳。方鸿渐在报馆的工作也因为战乱做不下去了。在遭遇事业和爱情的变故后，他又准备奔赴重庆，投靠他的好朋友赵辛楣（钱钟书，2013：180）。

方鸿渐和太太孙柔嘉之间的冲突是典型的儒家文化和“五四”新文化的冲突。众所周知，以血缘为纽带的家庭是中国社会结构的基础，是最重要的社会细胞。而儒家文化作为中国传统文化的主流，特别强调伦理秩序的建构，并确立了一整套伦理准则。两者相结合，形成了绵延数千年的家庭伦理规范：“父慈、子孝、兄友、弟恭”，长幼有序，各居其位，各司其职。在家庭内部，妇女的地位是卑贱的、从属的。为了保证男性的绝对优势，封建卫道士们为女性制定了一系列伦理道德规范。“三从四德”是其最本质、最核心的内容。“三从”是指“未嫁从父，既嫁从夫，夫死从子”（李学勤，1999：955-973），“四德”是关于妇女在家庭道德方面的四项具体要求，始见于《周礼》。此外，中国传统意义上的好妻子都是可以为了丈夫的后继烟火而主动为其纳妾的，不论自己有无嫡亲子嗣，为丈夫物色另外的妻子是身为一名好妻子的义务，更严格一点说，如果妻子对丈夫的另外的配偶心存妒念，都是不被允许的，更成了“休妻”的罪状（王纯菲，2006：23-29）。



方老先生和方老太太首先不满意鸿渐的婚姻自己做主，自己操办，没有媒妁之言，也没有遵守必要的礼数。其次，他们认为孙柔嘉的职责是当好家庭主妇，而不是出去工作。另一方面，孙小姐也讨厌方家人经常让他们小夫妻回去参加各种旧式的家庭活动，如祭祀、亲戚聚会等。

在传统文化和现代文化的碰撞中，传统文化只有自我改造，摒弃不合时宜的糟粕，推陈出新，才能适应时代的发展，和现代文化相融合。因此，在《赫索格》中，当马德琳拒绝救赎，不愿成为依附于赫索格的传统的贤妻良母时，他们的婚姻便出现了严重的分歧。而当坚持传统犹太家庭观念的赫索格对马德琳的各种苛刻要求和挥霍浪费难以忍受时，当女权主义的代表马德琳厌倦了赫索格和他奇怪的性爱方式时，这场婚姻的解体便是合理的、必然的结局。在《围城》中，方鸿渐和孙小姐刚开始的摩擦源于他们对各自家庭的维护，每次吵架之后都是方鸿渐道歉，两人和好如初。后来，当方鸿渐报馆的工作丢掉，回到家孙柔嘉还像往常一样用言语伤害他作为男子汉和一家之主的尊严时，他忍无可忍第一次打了她，两人就都负气决定离婚。正如小说中当方鸿渐看到卖原始笨拙的没人要的玩具的一个老人时所发的感叹，他作为坚守传统儒家文化的知识分子在“五四”新文化运动中必然要处处碰壁，和具有现代女权主义思想的孙柔嘉的婚姻关系肯定存在很多矛盾。当矛盾激化到一定程度，他们的婚姻也自然解体了。方鸿渐和孙柔嘉最初是怀着对美好婚姻生活的无比向往而结合的，但结婚之后才发现他们之间有那么多问题，离婚也是他们两人信仰各异，不能相互理解，年轻气盛，相互伤害的必然结局。这个故事情节暗合了小说的主题“围城”，即围城外的人想进去，围城内的人想出来，这是很多人婚姻生活的真实写照。

## 2．知识分子小说

《赫索格》一出版便引起了轰动。“不计其数的读者给索尔·贝娄写信说这正是他们的生活，正是他们所面临的生存困境。”（Atlas，2002：343）的确，索尔·贝娄的成功，在于他揭示了在高度丰裕的物质生活背后，现代西方人普遍面临的心灵危机——传统的道德价值观丧失殆尽，高尚的精神追求难以实现。小说中赫索格是一位睿智、受过良好教育、思想深邃、信仰人道主义和传统价值观的高级知识分子，但是却难以在躁动不安的、拜金主义的、腐朽堕落的现代社会里找到一席之地。他感到迷惘、愤懑，无所适从。

纵观美国历史，第二次世界大战以后，美国经济空前繁荣，但随之而来的是连续不断的政治、军事和社会问题，如麦卡锡主义、越南战争、民权运动和反主流文化思潮。典型的社会问题，如犯罪、性别歧视、种族异化和失业等，至今仍然令美国人民和美国政府一筹莫展。置身于这种非人性的、充满竞争的社会里，思想高尚的犹太知识分子赫索格孤独地、艰难地寻找着人生的意义。

他在未发出的信中写道："生命正在变成交易的过程。对我来说，这似乎是对生命意义所做的最糟糕的阐释。"（Bellow，1976：11）

当赫索格回忆到给律师辛金打电话，想要咨询雇一位私家侦探去调查妻子玛德琳及格斯贝奇的婚外情问题时，"作者借辛金之口揭露了当代美国的种种社会问题：在现在的这种纳税体制下，那些大企业大公司已经造就了一批新贵族。汽车、飞机、旅馆套间——额外的福利。餐馆、戏院等，还有好的私立学校也都把价钱提高了，超出了收入较低的人的支付水平。就连妓院也涨价了"（程锡麟，2012：45-52）。

在他婚姻破裂四处流浪之时，赫索格来到了曼哈顿的一个法庭。在这里他吃惊地见识了更多非人性的、道德沦丧的案例。"这些案件包括两件抢劫案、一件性侵犯案及一对同居的穷苦青年杀害自己三岁孩子的凶杀案。对这些案件的描述本身就是对美国社会问题的直接反映。"（程锡麟，2012：45-52）

犹太哲学家迈蒙尼德的人生境界说指出犹太民族是注重精神追求的民族，而且终极目标是皈依上帝，和上帝合一，以便实现人生的永恒。这种精神重于物质的理念，当然和拜金主义有着不可调和的矛盾。赫索格从社会环境和个人的不幸遭遇深刻地领悟到现代西方社会物欲横流，人们精神空虚，人道主义正在走向衰落。为了从宗教上、道德上救赎马德琳，赫索格力劝她不要皈依天主教，并在她自残后细心照料她，甘愿放弃在芝加哥诱人的学术职位以便和她一起到偏远的乡村享受宁静而浪漫的田园生活。但是，马德琳却以怨报德，羞辱他，欺骗他，最后还无情地抛弃了他。另外一个令赫索格几乎精神分裂的人物是他曾经的好友格斯贝奇。仁慈的赫索格允许他住在自己的家里，并为他找到一份很好的工作。结果，格斯贝奇这个十足的伪君子假装是赫索格的崇拜者和忠实的朋友。他一边和马德琳通奸，一边建议赫索格如何去挽救他的婚姻。



在这种冷漠的、物欲横流的社会里，赫索格很难实现他的犹太式的理想生活：心灵美好的丈夫，超凡脱俗的妻子，可爱的孩子，和品德高尚的朋友。在被马德琳抛弃之后，赫索格迷失了自我，不得不通过写信来剖析自己的灵魂，争取找到摆脱严重的心灵危机的途径。在赫索格的头脑中，形形色色的现代实用主义的价值观和传统的道德价值观在对抗着，两个"自我"——现实的"本我"和理想的"超我"在斗争着，这使他头痛欲裂。徒劳地进行了一番精神探索后，赫索格不得不暂时向现实社会妥协。

《围城》反映了在抗战胜利之后的中国，种种社会危机依然存在并且日益加深，中国传统的政治与文化秩序难以为继，但是几代中国知识分子追求的科学、民主、自由的西方先进文化并没有在中国大地生根发芽，整个社会转型期呈现出混乱的、畸形的、信仰缺失的、腐朽没落的殖民地文化特征。

方鸿渐的性格及命运映射出社会转型期知识分子面临的困境和普遍的生存状态。从表面上看，方鸿渐已是一个十足西化的人物，离中国传统文化的距离较远，对某些虚荣的殖民文化心理，对官僚政客和小市民都怀着本能的憎恶。但我们不难看出，由于没有救国救世的理想和追求，方鸿渐的人生是得过且过、随波逐流的人生。他读过四书五经，受到中国传统文化的熏陶，但是没有下过苦功，只能算作半吊子文人。后来由于种种原因，在欧洲学习中国文学，使他从未走入西方文化的核心和精髓之中，没有对抗于专制的民主思想、人道主义的救世精神、宗教信仰的终极关怀等，于是便有了他回国时在船上与鲍小姐逢场作戏苟且的一幕，也有了他在家乡那番让人捧腹作呕的演讲，有了他一幕幕碰壁的洋相和悲剧（张清华，1995：187）。

《围城》这部小说以同样诙谐幽默的方式，生动形象地描述了方鸿渐周围各种人物喜剧性的性格和命运，也是一部知识分子小说、讽刺小说，对现代人，尤其是现代知识分子自私狭隘、争权夺利、尔虞我诈、腐朽堕落的阴暗面进行了巧妙的讽刺和揭露，“反映了20世纪半殖民地半封建社会的中国土壤上滋生出来的知识分子的灵魂空虚和精神病态，简直构成了一幅高层知识分子的群丑图”（王延雄，2000：61）。

例如，钱钟书在介绍三闾大学的校长时，调侃道：“三闾大学校长高松年是位老科学家。这‘老’字的位置非常为难，可以形容科学，也可以形容科学家。不幸的是，科学家跟科学大不相同，科学家像酒，愈老愈可贵，而科学像女人，老了便不值钱。”（钱钟书，2013：226）接着，作者对中国大学的为官之道进行了精辟的幽默的解释。

又譬如，“在苏小姐的交际圈中，曹元朗、董斜川、褚慎明，这些不中不西、不伦不类的文化怪胎们，或者以诗人自诩，或者以哲人自居，妄自以为深得中西文化的精华妙处；他们或者满口西文洋话，或者言必称古典诗祖，董斜川开口自夸作诗‘一开笔就做的同光体’，而褚慎明则自吹曾解答过英国哲学家罗素的疑难问题，这样的一些愚妄之徒居然能够凑聚一起谈吐生色，真是一场文化的杂耍嬉戏”（张清华，1995：187）。

作者对三闾大学的教授以及教授的太太们都分别进行了调侃加讽刺的描绘，喜剧性地反映了他们虚伪、自私、贪婪、堕落的畸形人格和时代通病。例如，作者描绘了韩学愈老师和方鸿渐买了同样的假文凭，害怕被对方揭穿的窘态。为了让俄国太太有机会担任学校的英语教师，韩学愈谎称他的太太是地道的美国人。作者还描绘了训导长李梅亭表面上传统守旧，禁止师生赌博，但如果请他一起赌牌，他就什么都不说了。他禁止单身男女老师有过分亲密的关系，但是在和方鸿渐等一同来三闾大学的路上，他还费尽心思去嫖“土娼”。

在索尔·贝娄的这部代表作里，赫索格的沉思不仅是为了摆脱他个人的心灵危机，同时也映射出“贝娄本人对于当代文化富于人性的分析和精妙的见解”（贝娄，诺贝尔文学奖颁奖词）不仅具有犹太性，也具有世界性。

《围城》的第一章在讲述方鸿渐在上海的经历时，还借主人公之口探讨了一系列知识分子关心的政治、哲学、文学、教育等人文学科的话题，具体包括中国文学和西方文学的比较、哲学、逻辑学、风俗习惯、法律、教育制度，以及外语和女权主义等。作者的知识面相当广泛，也许是中国现代社会最伟大的“学者型小说家”，即那些“创作长篇小说不仅为了讲故事，也是为了满足他们自己表现一下丰富的知识和文学素养”的小说家。



到目前为止，《围城》第二版已经印刷了23次，并被翻译成英语、德语、法语等多国文字，受到文学评论家和国内外读者的青睐，并被搬上银幕。它的成功在于小说的主人公方鸿渐不是一个形象光辉的知识分子，但他代表的是一个20世纪三四十年代普普通通的、受过良好教育的中国现代知识分子。他生活在兵荒马乱的战争年代，新旧思想和各种观念激烈冲突的社会转型期，被他无法完全理解的各种力量所围困，无法掌控自己的事业和爱情的令人同情的倒霉蛋（Ch’ien，2011：xxiv）。

综上所述，两部小说都以幽默讽刺的方式，成功地塑造了一位信奉人道主义却在事业和爱情上屡遭挫折的倒霉知识分子形象。两部小说都从有良知的知识分子的角度，探讨了在物欲横流、传统文化和传统价值观受到强烈冲击的现代社会，人们普遍面临的孤独异化、道德沦丧、信仰缺失、无所适从的精神危机，以及他们苦苦探索、四处碰壁之后不得不暂时向命运妥协或远走他乡的无奈之举。

## 参考文献:


贝娄. 被授予诺贝尔文学奖时的颁奖词.

程锡麟. 书信、记忆与空间——重读《赫索格》[J].外国文学，2012，5: 45-52.

李学勤. 礼记・丧服小记第十五[M]// 十三经注疏. 北京：北京大学出版社，1999: 955-973.

钱钟书. 围城[M]. 北京：人民文学出版社，2013: 153, 180, 226.

圣经：创世纪16. 中国基督教协会，2006, 10.

王纯菲. 女神与女从[J]. 南开大学学报：哲学社会科学版，2006, 6: 23-29.

王延雄. 《围城》中知识分子生存困境分析[J]. 延安教育学院学报，2000, 18(1): 61.

张清华. 启蒙神话的坍塌和殖民文化的反讽——《围城》主题与文化策略新论[J]. 中国现代文学研究丛刊，1995, 4: 193-194, 187.

Atlas, James. *Bellow: A Biography*[M]. New York: Random House, 2002: 343.

Bellow, Saul. *Herzog*[M]. New York: Penguin Books, 1976: 11.

Ch'ien, Chung-shu. *Fortress Besieged*[M]. Trans., Jeanne Kelly, Nathan K.Mao. Beijing: Foreign Language Teaching and Research Press, 2011: xxiv.

# A Comparative Study on the Intellectual Images in Chinese and American Literature: Take the Novels *Herzog* and *Fortress Besieged* as Examples

Duan Libin

(College of Fundamental Education, Sichuan Normal University, Chengdu, China, 610068)

**Abstract:** When we examine the history of human development, it is evident that progress in civilization and technology always brings the change of social structure and living style, which shows the great power of knowledge. However, the social status of the elite and intellectuals with rich knowledge often faces ebb and flow and tends to be isolated. We are concerned about the fate and mission of the isolated intellectuals in modern transitional society. So this paper first briefly discusses the humanism tradition of Sino-US intellectuals, then based on Saul Bellow's *Herzog* and Zhongshu Qian's *Fortress Besieged*, it comparatively studies the intellectuals' images in Chinese and American literature, analyzing the similarities and differences in their social environment, character, philosophy, love affairs, and their predicament, etc., and exploring the way intellectuals stick to their beliefs, adapt to the trend of social development, and lead common people to build their beautiful spiritual world, under the condition that the society is more and more prosperous in economy but faces a sharp decline in traditional virtues and human spirits.

**Key Words:** Image of Intellectuals; *Herzog*; *Fortress Besieged*; Fang Hung-chien

# A Great Reality[1]: Willa Cather and the American Southwest

Li Li

(College of Foreign Languages and Cultures, Sichuan University, Chengdu, China, 610029)

**Abstract:** Willa Cather was a great writer of place. In this essay, four of her main works on the American Southwest will be explored. Through a close reading of certain passages, we can find that Cather's understanding of this region and the Indigenous Indian culture was not achieved in one day, instead it had been a long and dynamic process in consistent with her personal experience and the historical, political climate of her time. It was in her last Southwest novel *Death Comes for the Archbishop* that Willa Cather's geographic awareness came to its maturity.

**Key Words:** Willa Cather; the American Southwest; Indian Culture; *Death Comes for the Archbishop*; Geographic Awareness



Willa Cather was a great writer of place. Midwest Nebraska Plains, the American Northeast, the city of Quebec in 17th century, Europe in the WWI, and most importantly, the American Southwest, all get a humane portrait under her pen. Willa Cather was a deep lover of the American Southwest. Ever since her first trip to Flagstaff, Arizona, she was fascinated by its oppressive vacancy and the quiet, solemn beauty. "The great American Southwest," writes geographer Ted Jojola, "is a testament to how sustained human collective interaction has molded a landscape that is the embodiment of both human intervention and the natural ecosystem"(Casey, 1997: 257). All through her life, Cather had made

1 D.H. Lawrence: "Call it what you like, but the spirit of place is a great reality" from *The Role of Place in Literature* by Leonard Lutwack, Syracuse NY: Syracuse UP, 1984:16.

altogether 5 visits to this legendary land. Deeply moved by the harmonious unity of man and nature here, she gradually developed an ethical relationship to the American Southwest, a relationship based on love, respect, and admiration for the land and its inhabitants. In her Southwest novels, Cather caught the spirit of this place and conveyed it in the most loving and poetic way.

In this essay, four of her main works on the American Southwest will be explored. Through a close reading of certain passages, we can find that Cather's understanding of this region and the Indigenous Indian culture was not achieved in one day, instead it had been a long and dynamic process in consistent with her personal experience and the historical, political climate of her time. The American Southwest, as a representation, has been transformed, from an elusive ideal and empty symbol in Cather's earlier story "The Enchanted Bluff", into a spiritual haven in *The Song of the Lark* and *The Professor's House*, until eventually, in *Death Comes for the Archbishop*, a physical, tangible place where a great soul could live and die. It was in this book that Cather's geographical awareness (Sack, 1997: 31)[1] finally came to its maturity.



"The Enchanted Bluff" is a short story written in 1909. Six boys were having a day out beside a river, then they started to talk about the places they wanted to go to. One of them said, "My place is awful far away."

> It's down in New Mexico somewheres....There's a big red rock there that goes right up out of the sand for about nine hundred feet. The country's flat all around it, and this here rock goes up all by itself, like a monument. They call it the Enchanted Bluff down there, because no white man has ever been on top of it. The sides are smooth rock, and straight up, like a wall.
>
> (Cather, 1992: 69)

Then the boys made a deal: "Whoever gets to the Bluff first has got to

1 According to Geographer Robert David Sack, a geographical awareness helps reveal how the segments of our lives fit together. It shows how we are cultural and natural, autonomous and independent. More important, it focuses our will on our common purpose as geographic agents—transforming the earth and making it into a home.

promise to tell the rest of us exactly what he finds." In the end of the story, we are told that "Although that was twenty years ago, none of us have ever climbed the Enchanted Bluff."(72)

This is how the American Southwest was first presented in Willa Cather's works. Those country boys who talked about the bluff knew actually nothing about it. The huge cliff down somewhere in New Mexico was an ideal, a symbol of their youthful dreams. Not a place in geological sense, it was a romantically impossible destination they could never reach but forever tantalizing. This kind of representation is understandable when we realize that Willa Cather's intimate interaction with the Southwest was yet to begin in 1912, three years after "The Enchanted Bluff" was completed. Her creation of this place was a combination of imagination and sporadic reading. Grown up with various Southwest legends and romances passed by mouth, she desired and feared it at the same time.

In the year of 1912, Cather was a writer of three little known books, still far from success, still fumbling for direction. Then in that summer, she spent a few weeks in Flagstaff, Arizona, roaming around with her brother Douglass. Though shocked by the big strangeness and vacancy of the land, she fell in love with its quiet, solemn beauty immediately. In a letter to her friend Sergeant, she explained that she felt like being born again, full of energy and vitality, fearless of any problem in the road ahead (Swift & Urgo, 2002: 5). Yes, she meant that. In 1913, *O Pioneers!* was published. It was in this book that she finally found her own voice. It was in this book that she began to explore the power of place and made it a striking mark of her writing. Then in 1915, in her autobiographical novel *The Song of the Lark*, Cather transplanted her Southwest experience to her soprano Thea Kronborg.

Like her creator, when she took an excursion in Panther Canon, near Flagstaff at Arizona, Thea Kronborg was basically a failure in her career. "So far she had failed. Her two years in Chicago had not resulted in anything. She had failed with Harsanyi, and she had made no great progress with her voice...and that in the essential things she had made no advance. Her student life closed behind her, like the forest, and she doubted whether she could go back to it if she tried." (Cather, 1983: 368)

"Panther Canon had been deserted for hundreds of years." While roaming there, Thea found a small cave that was perfect for her need. It (the cave) was like "a nest in a high cliff, full of sun. All morning long the sun beat upon her cliff, while the ruins on the opposite side of the canon were in shadow." "Here she could lie for half a day undistracted, holding pleasant and incomplete conceptions in her mind—almost in her hands."(373) Then miraculously, " It seemed to Thea that a certain understanding of those old people (ancient Indians) came up to her out of the rock-shelf on which she lay; that certain feelings were transmitted to her, suggestions that were simple, insistent, and monotonous, like the beating of Indian drums."(376)

She was, like Willa Cather, having an artistic epiphany while realizing a close kinship to the ancient Indian woman who climbed the rocky trail every day carrying water up from the deep valley with a baby hanging to her back. Bathing under the warm and overwhelming sun, melted into this wide and quiet space, she felt that every particle of her body had been distilled and purified. With the strength conveyed to her by the ancient Indians, she felt like a new-born baby. Now she had the courage to return to the madding city, to get back to the stage, brave enough to face any challenge.



In August 1915, Willa Cather had a visit to Mesa Verde, Colorado. Here she found "whole cities in stone: the tangible, complex architecture of a nobly humane past, replete with technology, science, art, religion" (Swift & Urgo, 2002: 3). Then in her 1925 novel *The Professor's House*, she had Tom Outland, a cowboy and amateur archeologist in his twenties, discover a stone city on Blue Mesa, sleeping there quietly for hundreds of years:

> Far up above me, a thousand feet or so, set in a great cavern in the face of the cliff, I saw a little city of stone, asleep. It was as still as sculpture—and something like that. It all hung together, seemed to have a kind of composition...Such silence and stillness and repose—immortal repose.
>
> (Cather, 1990: 221)

A few lines down, Tom claimed,

> I knew at once that I had come upon the city of some extinct civilization, hidden away in this **inaccessible** mesa for centuries, preserved in the dry air and almost perpetual sunlight like a fly in amber, guarded by the cliffs and the river and the desert.
>
> (221)

Tom Outland, like Thea Kronborg, came to the Southwest as a troubled soul, tired of worldly struggle, wounded by the vulgar commercialism. He could only be comforted by his Blue Mesa.

> Once again I had that glorious feeling that I've never had anywhere else, the feeling of being on the mesa, **in a world above the world**. And the air, my God, what air!—Soft, tingling, gold, hot with an edge of chill on it, full of the smell of pinons—it was like breathing the sun, breathing the color of the sky.
>
> (246)



Being visitors to the American Southwest, Tom and Thea appreciated its beauty, loved this land for what it is. The fresh air that blew off the Mesa dispersed the heavy mists around them, preparing them for a more fulfilled life. But at the same time, we also notice that their Southwest, be it the Panther Canon at Arizona or Blue Mesa at Colorado, was just a mirage. To be a spiritual haven providing them with inspiration and catharsis, it must be a place isolated and inaccessible. Thea could lie hours in her undistracted "nest" in a high cliff, musing, while Tom's shelter was "a world above the world." This space is, in essence, not a place to live in, but a place to come and go, a place hostile to family and domesticity.

There is another more disturbing fact in the Southwest adventure of Thea and Tom. During their long sojourn in that area, our protagonists had no encounter with its local residents, the Indians. Instead, they cast an appreciative eye to their ancient ancestors. Thea got artistic enlightenment from the delicate shaped pottery of the Indian women who lived there thousands of years ago, while Tom paid his worship to a long extinguished tribe: "A people who had the hardihood to build there, and who lived day after day looking down upon such grandeur, who came and went by those hazardous trails, must have been, as we often told each other, a fine people."(228)

In *The Song of the Lark*, we find only one brief mention of its current inhabitants at the beginning of "The Ancient People":

> The Navajos are **not** much in the habit of giving or of asking help. Their language is **not** a communicative one, and they **never** attempt an interchange of personality in speech.
>
> (367)

Such a description of the living Indians is rather negative and problematic, rendering them actually insignificant and invisible. This, if we consider the historical and political environment then, would not be too hard to understand.



The last half of the nineteenth century was devastating for American Indians. "There has never been a greater misnomer than to call Indians the 'vanishing Americans.'"(Dan, 2009: 324) By 1900, 65% to 99% of native people had been wiped out from their ancient homes. The loss of life from war and disease may have slowed as the twentieth century got underway, but other losses continued. Two-thirds of Indian land in 1887 was in the hands of non-natives by 1934. This unrelenting encroachment and theft of Indian soil led to a loss of homeland, a loss more spiritual than financial. To be clear, early twentieth-century Indian reservations were among the most desperate places in the country, fixed in neglect and oblivion. The first inhabitants of the American Southwest, residents before the lands were territories or states, were not citizens in the eyes of the federal government until 1924. Considering this historical background, it is not strange that Cather chose ignorance, distortion and embarrassed silence on this issue.

After finishing *The Professor's House*, Cather made two final trips to the Southwest in the summer of 1925 and 1926, during which she conceived and finalized her ideas for *Death Comes for the Archbishop*. On her final two trips to the Southwest, Cather spent a great deal of time with Tony Luhan, a tribal leader of the Tiwa pueblo. He took Cather on long drives through the country and introduced her to aspects of both Native American and Mexican cultures. From Tony, Willa Cather learned many things about the country and the people that she could not have learned otherwise.

*Death Comes for the Archbishop* is a great romance about the American Southwest. Father Latour, a learned French who spread Catholicism among Indians and Mexicans in the New Mexico desert, was transformed physically and spiritually by this legendary land and its loving people. It was in this book that the spirit of place became a great reality and Cather's geographical awareness came to maturity. And it was also in this book that man and nature came to a perfect union. Here "man" refers not only to the white people represented by Father Latour, but also to the Native Americans represented by Eusabio.

Eusabio, the Archbishop's Navajo friend, is actually a reflection of Tony Luhan(Cather's Indian guide) in both appearance and spirit:

> Though he was ten years younger than Father Latour, Eusabio was one of the most influential men among the Navajo people. In Santa Fe and Albuquerque he was respected for his intelligence and authority, and admired for his fine presence...He always dressed very elegantly in velvet and buckskin rich with bead and quill embroidery, belted with silver, and wore a blanket of the finest wool and design. His arms, under the loose sleeves of his shirt, were covered with silver bracelets, and on his breast hung very old necklaces of wampum and turquoise and coral—Mediterranean coral, that had been left in the Navajo country by Coronado's captains when they passed through it on their way to discover the Hopi villages and the Grand Canyon.
>
> (Cather, 1927: 220)

It was the first time that Cather made a humane portrait of a living Indian in such vivid details. The use of words like "influential," "elegantly," "fine," and so on all indicates that Cather's understanding of Native Americans has long transcended over the stage when she could only get inspiration from ancient Indian women and the mummies in the cliff city. Now she was capable to view them in an objective and appreciative way.

> Travelling with Eusabio was like travelling with the landscape made human. He accepted chance and weather as the country did, with a sort of grave enjoyment. He talked little, ate little, slept anywhere, preserved a countenance open and warm, and like Jacinto he had unfailing good manners.
> (232)

Native American writer N. Scott Momaday once said: "To [the Indian] the sense of place is paramount. Only in reference to the earth can he persist in his true identity."(Olson, 2002: 137) Eusabio was such a true, noble man because of his pristine love for land and life itself.



Different from Thea and Tom, Father Latour left France for New Mexico not to find his spiritual haven, but to spread the blessings of God. He came to the desert as a young, ambitious priest, died there as an old, satisfied Archbishop, loved by Indians and Mexicans alike. After five decades' of interaction with this land and its people, Father Latour felt like a tree or rock of the New Mexico desert, unable to breathe in any other place. He could have spent his rest life in Paris, surrounded by his family and friends, but after a short stay in his home country, he came back to New Mexico again. This was the reason:

> Beautiful surroundings, the society of learned men, the charm of noble women, the graces of art, could not make up to him for the loss of those light-hearted mornings of the desert, for that wind that made one a boy again.
> (275)

> He did not know just when it (the air of the desert) had become so necessary to him, but he had come back to die in exile for the sake of it. Something soft and wild and free, something that whispered to the ear on the pillow, lightened the heart, softly, softly picked the lock, slid the bolts, and released the prisoned spirit of man into the wind, into the blue and gold, into the morning, into the morning!
>
> (276)

Father Latour was obviously enjoying a transcendental empathy with the American Southwest. Geographer Gary Snyder writes in the preface to *The Practice of the Wild*: "Recollecting that we once lived in places is part of our contemporary self-discovery...The 'place' gave us far-seeing eyes, the streams and breezes gave us versatile tongues and wholly ears. The land gave us a stride, and the lake a dive. The amazement gave us our kind of mind. We should be thankful for that, and take nature's stricter lessons with some grace."(Snyder, 1991: 29) Father Latour, who was good at taking messages and lessons from the wind and air of the New Mexico desert, firmly believed that this was the only place he could die with ease, peace and grace. So he did.



## 参考文献:


Casey, Edward S. *The Fate of Place: A Philosophical History*[M]. Berkeley: University of California Press, 1997: 257.

Cather, Willa. *Cather: Later Novels*[M]. New York: The Library of America, 1990: 221.

Cather, Willa. *Cather: Stories, Poems and Other Writings*[M]. New York: The Library of America, 1992: 69.

Cather, Willa. *Death Comes for the Archbishop*[M]. New York: Alfred A. Knopf, Inc., 1927: 220.

Cather, Willa. *The Song of the Lark*[M]. Boston: Houghton Mifflin Company, 1983: 368.

Dan, Shilling. Aldo Leopold Listens to the Southwest[J]. *Journal of the Southwest*, 2009, 51(3): 324.

Olson, Steve. *Mapping Human History: Discovering the Past through Our Genes*[M]. Boston: Houghton Mifflin, 2002:137.

Sack, Robert David. *Homo Geographicus: A Framework for Action, Awareness, and Moral Concern*[M]. Baltimore: Johns Hopkins University Press, 1997:31.

Snyder, Gary. *The Practice of the Wild*[M]. San Francisco: North Point Press, 1990: 29.

Swift, John N., Urgo, Joseph R. *Willa Cather and the American Southwest*[M]. Lincoln: University of Nebraska Press, 2002: 5.

Swift, John N., Urgo, Joseph R. *Willa Cather and the American Southwest*[M]. Lincoln: University of Nebraska Press, 2002: 3.

# 一个伟大的现实——威拉·凯瑟和美国的大西南

李　莉

（四川大学外国语学院，四川成都　610029）

**摘　要：**地理学家爱德华·卡西（Edward S. Casey）曾说过：“没有地域就没有人类，是特定的地理空间塑造了我们的身体和灵魂。”威拉·凯瑟的创作无疑是对这种地域意识的最好诠释。本文以威拉·凯瑟的四部“美国大西南作品”为研究对象，通过对具体篇章段落的分析解读，指出作家对大西南和这片土地上的印第安文化的理解、热爱并非一蹴而就，而是一个很漫长曲折的过程。受制于作家本人的经历和当时的历史背景及政治气候，在最后一部大西南小说《死神来迎大主教》中，作家的地域意识才臻于成熟，大西南所蕴含的精神价值才成为作品中的“伟大现实”。

**关键词：**威拉·凯瑟；美国大西南；印第安文化；《死神来迎大主教》；地域意识

# 教　育

*Education*

# From China's Southwest to America's Midwest: Ethnic Minorities and Higher Education

MaryJo Benton Lee

(Department of Sociology and Rural Studies, South Dakota State University, Brookings, USA, 57007)

**Abstract:** This paper examines ethnic minorities and their educational attainment in two settings, Yunnan Province in China's Southwest and South Dakota in America's Midwest. Issues of equity and access, as these relate to higher education in the PRC and the US, are discussed. The focus is on academic success and ethnic identity. Questions posed are "How do ethnic minority students in two cultures construct identities that help them succeed in school?" and "How can the larger social context, in which identity construction occurs, support academic achievement by ethnic minorities?" Examples are drawn from the experiences of ethnic minority students attending Yunnan Normal (Teachers) University in Kunming, PRC, and American Indian students participating in a college preparatory program at South Dakota State University. "Perceived efficacy" is introduced as a concept useful for discussing the role of preferential policies in China and the lack of affirmative action in the US.

**Key Words:** Yunnan Province; South Dakota; Ethnic Minorities; Educational Attainment; Perceived Efficacy

## 1. Introduction: Ethnic Minorities and Educational Attainment

Despite dramatic increases in postsecondary enrollments, at both American and Chinese universities, gaps still exist in who goes to college and who ultimately succeeds. American Indians face multiple challenges in gaining access to college and continue to be grossly underrepresented in higher education institutions (Swail & Perna, 2002: 15). As well, bold experiments in Chinese higher education have led to expansion but not necessarily to equity (Luo & Yang, 2013: 108).

In this paper, I write about educational access and equity, as these issues have been brought into sharp relief for me through two experiences, one in China's Southwest and the other in America's Midwest. The first experience occurred in 1997 when I had the opportunity, together with colleague Li Hong, to interview 32 successful minority nationality (*shaoshu minzu*) students attending Yunnan Normal University in Kunming, PRC (Lee, 2001; Li Lee & Luo, 2012). The second experience has extended over the past 12 years and has involved working with more than 2,000 American Indian students from across the US in a college preparatory program called Success Academy, headquartered at my home university, South Dakota State (Lee, 2013).

These experiences have challenged me to question some precious democratic ideals about equitable access to opportunity through an educational system I have been part of for more than 50 years—as a student, as a teacher, as a researcher and as an administrator. These experiences have also given me hope in the possibility of school and social change (Cochran-Smith, 2000: 157).



I begin by outlining the problem. I then set forth my theoretical orientation, drawing from works in comparative education, critical ethnography and symbolic interactionism. Next I talk about identity work by minority nationality students and about preferential policies operating in the Chinese context. I must address the "divisive and contentious" issues (Edlin, 2009: 227) surrounding affirmative action in the United States before moving on to a discussion of identity work by American Indian students. I conclude with suggestions for further study.

## 2. The Problem: A Crisis of Justice

Higher education in both the US and China is becoming increasingly essential for young people who want to have full careers and lead satisfying lives. Thus it is a "crisis of justice" (Meyer et al., 2013: 1) when large proportions of eligible young people are barred from accessing higher education. That is precisely the situation for American Indian students in South Dakota and for minority nationality students in Yunnan Province, both areas of great ethnic diversity and material poverty.

The renowned $19^{th}$-century Navajo Chief Manuelito once said, "My grandchild, education is the ladder. Tell our people to take it." (San Juan School District, 2003) Today many indigenous people see education as the way out of poverty. But the statistics regarding educational outcomes for ethnic minorities do not bode well for either Yunnan Province or for South Dakota.

### 2.1 In Yunnan Province

Yunnan has 25 of China's officially recognized minority nationality groups living within its borders. Well over one-third of Yunnan's population is ethnic minority as compared to about 9 % for China as a whole.

By the end of the Qing Dynasty (1644-1911), most of China's national minorities were mainly inhabiting the country's border regions. In Yunnan this means that much of the minority population now lives in remote areas, some mountainous, others subtropical. Poor transportation systems further contribute to low economic development in minority areas (Zhang, 2004: 72). According to Chinese government reports, about one-fourth of Yunnan Province's people live in poverty. "The poorest among the population mainly live in the ethnic and border areas and regions disadvantaged by their natural conditions," *People's Daily Online* (2002) reports.

Much emphasis has been placed by the central government on using education to develop skilled and talented individuals (*rencai*) who will in turn boost economic development (Postiglione, 1992: 322). But in Yunnan, "high levels of enrollment in primary school coexist with low levels of completion," write Yanchun Dai and Changjiang Xu (2009: 110-111). "Almost all school-age children go to school in minority communities. However, beyond the compulsory years the retention rate has decreased and the dropout rate has increased significantly." In some areas, the dropout levels are up to 13%, way beyond the 3% level set by the national government.

### 2.2 In South Dakota

South Dakota has much in common with Yunnan, relative to diversity, poverty and education. South Dakota, with a Native American population of 10.1%, ranks fourth highest among all the states in its proportion of Natives per capita (US Census Bureau, 2011). Throughout the 1800s, the federal government forcibly relocated Indian tribes from throughout the country to parcels of land called "reservations." Consequently, South Dakota is home to nine reservations, which constitute almost 20% of the state's land mass.

South Dakota is also home to the three counties with the nation's highest poverty rates: Ziebach County where the Cheyenne River Sioux Indian Reservation is located; Todd County, where the Rosebud Sioux Indian Reservation is located; and Shannon County, where the Pine Ridge (Oglala Sioux) Indian Reservation is located (Lengerich, 2012). According to the US Census (Ogunwole, 2006: 12), 38.9% of all Sioux people live in poverty, the highest percentage among all American Indian tribal groups.



Only 57.1% of all Indian children in the state graduated from high school in 2011, compared to 85.9% of all students (Rick, 2012). Of the seven states with the highest percentage of American Indian and Alaska Native students, South Dakota had the lowest high school graduation rate for Native students (30.4%) compared to non-Native students (75.6%) during 2005, the year studied (Faircloth and Tippeconnic III, 2010: 11).

### 2.3 Comparisons Between Yunnan Province and South Dakota

The focus of this paper is on the educational attainment of ethnic minorities at the college level, where the problem becomes particularly acute. In China, the minority population having a university education amounts to only about 0.4% of the total population above the age of five. The proportion of the minority population having a secondary education and higher is still less than 2% in the four southwest Provinces of Yunnan, Sichuan, Guangxi and Guizhou (Bhalla & Qiu, 2006: 49). The rates of access to university by minorities—and their academic performance once at university—remain far below the national average (Zhao & Postiglione, 2008: 135).

Closer to home for me, Native American students accounted for only 1.9% of all students who enrolled for the fall 2010 semester at South Dakota's six public universities (South Dakota Board of Regents, 2011: 12), this in a state with a 10% Native population. And, only 41% of all new American Indian students in 2002 graduated from South Dakota colleges within six years of entering; this compared to a 47% graduation rate for all new students in the 2002-2008 cohort (Alliance for Excellent Education, 2011).

## 3. This Paper's Orientation: Comparative with a Focus on Academic Success and Ethnic Identity

### 3.1 Comparative Education



"Doing comparative education," as explained by two giants in the field, Harold J. Noah and Max A. Eckstein (1998), allows us to learn from international examples. It also provides us with a yardstick with which to measure ourselves. As Noah and Eckstein write (1998):

> The variety of educational practices and their outcomes in many nations of the world may be regarded as a series of natural experiments created by different political, social, and economic circumstances. Comparative study investigates their meanings and seeks to relate them to persistent problems in understanding education.



### 3.2 Academic Success

A persistent problem in education is clearly the achievement gap that exists between minority and majority students in both the US and China. Ample research has already been done in many settings on underachievement among minority students. This paper takes a different tack by focusing on "what works." In other words, what factors might explain minority student success in situations where failure seems to be a more certain outcome?

Critical ethnographers Henry T. Trueba and Yali Zou (1994: 5-6), in their important work on successful Miao university students, remind us that continuing to document failure only demonstrates the obvious. It does not open the way to a better future for the next generation. Thus this paper begins with information from qualitative interviews with successful minority nationality students at Yunnan Normal University. The paper then moves on to examine a program called Flandreau Indian School-South Dakota State University Success Academy, which increased college attendance tenfold among the Native American students participating in it. The words of the noted American sociologist Robert Merton (1968: 490) serve as a guide: "More is learned from the single success than from the multiple failures. A single success proves it can be done. Thereafter, it is necessary only to learn what made it work."



### 3.3 Ethnic Identity

Scholarly literature, spanning two decades and multiple cultures, suggests a strong relationship between ethnic identity, academic success or the lack thereof. Since our initial fieldwork was conducted in Yunnan Province in the 1990s, research by Chinese scholars on identity, ethnicity and education has blossomed (Postiglione, 2009). This scholarship includes important books on Naxi students in a Yunnan secondary school (Yu, 2010), Tibetan students (Zhu, 2007) and Muslim Uyghur students (Chen, 2008) at inland boarding schools, and Mongolian students at university (Zhao, 2007; Zhao, 2010a). Comparative books include one by Lin Yi (2008) on the state schooling of Tibetan and Muslim students in Qinghai Province and another by Mette Halskov Hansen (1999) on the education of Dai and Naxi middle school students in Yunnan Province. Gerard A. Postiglione (2009) says that this research "represents the growing vitality of the sociological study of ethnic minority education in China."

Literature on ethnic identity and educational attainment is often situated within the sociological framework of symbolic interactionism. (It was this theoretical orientation that guided our work in Yunnan.) Symbolic interactionists believe that meanings do not reside in objects per se, but rather that meanings emerge from social processes.

Identity theory is one branch of symbolic interactionism. It suggests that a student's identity or sense of "self" (Mead, 1934) is constructed through interactions with others. Two aspects of the identity construction process, as they relate particularly to ethnicity, will be introduced briefly here. Then the remainder of the paper will provide illustrations of "identity work" (Snow & Anderson, 1987: 1348) first as performed by successful ethnic minority students in Yunnan Province and next by successful American Indian students in South Dakota.

**Social construction of a scholar self.**

The successful student builds a personal identity by combining his or her own definitions of self with those of significant others (Heiss, 1981). Significant others include those people with whom the student interacts in the family, village and school. Carolyn R. Hodges and Olga M. Welch (2003: 2) explain that in order for a minority student to succeed academically, a "scholar self" must evolve over time, as a result of a series of negotiations and reconstructions of personal identity. The successful minority student is one who can overcome "stereotype threat," that is, others' judgments that his or her minority group membership means lowered academic achievement (Steele, 1997). In other words, developing a "scholar self" means cultivating the ability to see academic achievement as possible, even in a larger structural context strewn with racial and ethnic barriers.

**Structural context.**

It is important to emphasize that identity construction at the micro level, as just described, occurs within a larger macro structural context, a context that often limits the occupational, educational and economic attainment of minorities (Ogbu, 1978, 1985, 1992). In other words, self-conceptions are influenced by social structures. As Sheldon Stryker (1989: 53) explains, "Constraints... may exist within situations with respect to the behavioral expression of given identities...One cannot be a swimmer in the absence of a pool."

## 4. Identity Work by Minority Students in Yunnan Province

We spent two and a half months during summer 1997 doing intensive interviews with 32 ethnic minority students attending Yunnan Normal University in Kunming, the capital of Yunnan Province. At the time, they were part of a tiny elite of ethnic minority students who had defied the odds and won college admittance. They had found ways to function effectively in the mainstream culture of higher education, in most cases, studying in Mandarin other than their native ones. The almost insurmountable obstacles and odds they had to overcome in order to achieve their professional goals have been well documented elsewhere (Lee, 2001). The ethnic minority students we interviewed, however, had managed to construct "scholar selves" (Hodges & Welch, 2003: 2)—in their families, in their villages and in their schools—that fostered academic success. How this happened will be explained below.



### 4.1 Identity Construction in the Family

For many poor minority families, educating their children is a double-edged sword. On the one hand, these families are becoming responsible for an ever-larger portion of school tuition and fees, as the government's share in education costs decreases (Cao, 2008: 335). On the other hand, sending their children to school means losing their labor on the land, labor that would otherwise contribute to the families' livelihood. Most of our successful student interviewees had come from poor rural families. Nevertheless, accounts like the following one by a Lahu student, were common:

> My family don't have much education. They support my study. They give me money. They don't let me do farm work. They give me time to

read. My junior middle school is not far away, 20 kilometers (about 12 miles), but my secondary normal school is 60 kilometers away (about 37 miles). I came home once a week.

While financial aid from families was key to academic success, the interviewees repeatedly emphasized that it was not nearly as important as other kinds of support. As this Bulang student reported:

> In my family, because my father didn't get (any formal) education, my mother was very strict with the children. She got her education before 1949. She was a student. My mother thinks if a person doesn't have any knowledge, he is no good. Every day she checks our homework. After every exam, she goes to the school to ask about her children. Whether the school is near or far, once a month my mother goes to the school.

Clearly the relatives of the Lahu and Bulang students were actively helping their children construct scholar selves. Trueba and Zou (1994) explain the motivation of successful minority nationality students this way:

> Their willingness to suffer pain and deprivation, to delay gratification and rewards, and to pursue a long and arduous course of intellectual development becomes an opportunity to repay family and village members their own sacrifices with the prestige and honor they generate as university students and members of a new elite.
>
> (Truba & Zon, 1994: 131)





### 4.2 Identity Construction in the Village

For the minority nationality students we interviewed, the "identity work" (Snow & Anderson, 1987: 1348) begun in the family seemed to continue on in their villages. A Jingpo student told of being "the first university student in my hometown, so my parents are very proud of me." A Lisu girl, attending middle school in the Lijiang Naxi Autonomous County, recalled the time when she learned of her acceptance to the Yunnan Institute for the Nationalities in Kunming. Her village organized a three-day celebration in her honor. She, like all the other interviewees, had her college expenses paid for by the government. People in the students' villages, like the students themselves, fully expected them to return home after college to teach. In the process they would become fundamental players in spreading China's newly implemented nine-year compulsory education plan to those areas in greatest need. As one Wa student explained:

> In my hometown we have a tradition. When children come back from other places, old people come to the family to visit. Every time I go back to my family, old people come to see me...Young people like me very much. In my village, we still don't have electricity. Only recently did we get a road. The conditions are very poor. People don't have the opportunity to go to other places. People hope I can come back, bring wonderful information to them, help them study, write Chinese characters, speak Mandarin and take part in art activities...In my hometown they have a custom. They think if a person leaves his hometown and goes to another place to work, he must help his hometown. He must help others study...The people in my hometown hope the younger generation can bring a lot of help to them...I want to go back to my hometown. Before coming to university, I worked at the primary school there and taught Wa children. After graduation I want to teach Wa children.



### 4.3 Identity Construction in the School

Some of the material hardships that stand between ethnic students and academic success have been mentioned in the previous sections. It is important to note two more obstacles that made education truly challenging for our interviewees. The first obstacle was that most of our interviewees grew up speaking their nationality languages at home. Mandarin, however, is the language of classroom instruction and of national examinations, which determine who will and will not advance to the next level of education. The second obstacle was that most of our interviewees had to leave their remote rural villages while still very young in order to attend distant boarding schools and continue on with their education. From then on, they returned home to their families only about twice a year. Teachers, like those described by this Zhuang student, functioned in the identity construction process much as parents had earlier:

> My teachers were a big influence...My primary school, middle school and secondary normal school teachers gave me special care and help. They provided an office for me to study and review my lessons. When I was sick, I went to their homes. They cared for me like their own child. They gave me medicine and food. Because I could work hard at studying, I had very good marks...My teachers liked me very much.

Teachers, like the ones just described, help students construct what Daphna Oyserman, Larry Gant and Joel Ager (1995: 1216) call "achievement-related possible selves." Students with "achievement-related possible selves" see academic success as possible, while remaining well aware of the structural limitations imposed on them because of their ethnicity. A Naxi student recalled one of his teachers, an intellectual who had suffered much persecution during the Cultural Revolution, this way:

> He taught us reading. In his lessons, I learned something about an attitude toward life and the future I will face. I learned about society and not only about the course reading. We learned more from him. From him I learned to be a true person. I learned character—to be kind, honest and optimistic if I face some difficulties in life.

### 4.4 Structural Context

The identity construction process, as just described, occurs within a larger structural context that limits the occupational, educational and economic attainment of minorities (Ogbu, 1978, 1985, 1992). However, while some social structures can be constraining, others can be enabling (Giddens, 1984). Relative to minority education in the PRC, social structures provide students with opportunities to do things, like construct scholar selves and be successful, that they would otherwise not be able to do.

In the remainder of this paper I will argue that the structural context in which student identity construction occurs differs dramatically between the PRC and the US. This, in turn, compels American educators to adopt dramatically different approaches to working with minority students and helping them prepare for college.

Numerous scholarly articles have focused on ethnic minorities and higher education in the PRC. Some address higher education issues as they relate to specific nationality groups—the Li (Netting, 1997), the Naxi (Wang, Tsung & Ki, 2012), Uyghurs (Hou, 2000), Koreans (Choi, 2010), Mongolians and Tibetans (Kormondy, 2002). Others focus on access and equity, particularly in light of China's recent market reforms, financial decentralization and economic globalization (Zhu, 2010). "Preferential policies" for ethnic minority students have received particularly close scrutiny (Wang, 2007; Jacob, Wu & Cheng, 2011; Wang, et al., 2011).



China has one of the world's largest programs of state-sponsored "preferential policies" for ethnic minorities (Sautman, 1999: 173). "Preferential policies" in China are similar to "affirmative action" in the United States. Western scholars of education, like Ruth Hayhoe (1996: 209-210), have called these policies "vigorous" and "remarkable." They have allowed record numbers of minorities to succeed in education, employment and other aspects of Chinese life.

In Yunnan Province, with its high concentration of ethnic minorities, many preferential policies have been enacted in the field of education. The successful ethnic minority students we interviewed identified the preferential policies outlined below as having been especially beneficial to them.

**Special schools and classes for ethnic students**

Many of our interviewees were from remote and poor villages where schooling was offered only through the primary level. Afterward these students could choose to move away to attend boarding schools, called "full-accommodation junior and senior middle schools," with their tuition, food and housing covered by government funds.

Another option for those students wishing to continue on with education were the "nationality sections," established in the best middle schools throughout Yunnan's most impoverished counties. The brightest minority students, from the poorest families in the most remote villages, are selected for the nationality sections. The nationality section is an extra class in the school, solely for minority students. The minority students live at the school (unlike the other students there) and have their tuition, room and board paid by the government.

**Financial support for minority education**

Neither the special schools nor the special classes for ethnic students just described could operate without substantial government funding. In Yunnan this financial support for minority education comes from all levels of government—county, prefectural, provincial and central—and goes to all levels of minority-serving schools—primary, secondary and tertiary. The ethnic students we interviewed told us of receiving stipends throughout their academic careers for everything from room and board to tuition and books. At Yunnan's secondary normal schools, at its teachers colleges and at Yunnan Normal University, the students interviewed received free tuition in exchange for agreeing to return to their home areas and work as teachers after graduation.

**Additional points on national examinations**

In China, moving from one level of school to the next (junior middle school to senior middle school and senior middle school to university) depends on national examination scores. The better the school, the higher the score required for entrance. Minority students receive additional points, which are added to the marks they actually score on the examinations. This means minority students are allowed to enter schools with lower scores than those required for the majority or Han students.

In addition, most higher education institutions in Yunnan Province offer "preliminary classes" for minority students. The "preparatory students" in these classes have finished senior middle school and have taken the college entrance examination, but have not scored high enough to be admitted to the university. At Yunnan Normal University, preparatory students spend one year taking courses like Chinese, math and physics, brushing up on their basic skills. Then the students retake the college entrance examination, and if they pass, they can immediately advance into the university.

## 5. Making Connections: Preferential Policies in China, Affirmative Action in the US and Perceived Efficacy



Numerous scholars outside of China have commented favorably on its many preferential policies that are aimed at increasing educational access for ethnic minorities. "This wide range of choice belies the stereotype of the 'totalitarian' society and indeed should give western democracies food for thought," writes Doug Daniels (1984: 23-24). Trueba and Zou (1994) weigh in with a similar opinion:

> While China has taken drastic measures and used enforcement methods disliked in Western societies to assure equality of groups since 1949 with Chairman Mao's Revolution, Western societies have maintained institutional inequalities and the mistreatment of minorities in ways that would not happen in China.
>
> (Trueba & Zou, 1994: 23)

Consider the Province of Yunnan and the state of California, two territories of roughly similar size, both with immense ethnic diversity. In the late 1990s I returned to the US from Yunnan, where minority students were benefiting from a wide array of integrated preferential policies. At the same time California was passing Proposition 227, which ended bilingual education; Proposition 187, which prevented illegal aliens from receiving social services including schooling; and Proposition 209, which terminated affirmative action (Munoz, 1999). As Evelyn Hu-DeHart (2009: 214) rightly explains, "The decline of affirmative action in the United States, which invented the idea, coincides with a growing and diverse number of nations around the world that looked to the United States for inspiration and thus adopted their own unique forms of affirmative action."

I had to try to make sense of this contradiction as I transitioned from visiting scholar at Yunnan Normal University to clinical sociologist at South Dakota State University. How would my research in Yunnan with ethnic minorities inform my work in South Dakota with American Indians? Most helpful to me was the concept of "perceived efficacy" as it was then being developed by Daphna Oyserman, Kathy Harrison and Deborah Bybee (2001: 379) at the University of Michigan. "Perceived efficacy" is the ability to believe one has the power to influence one's environment and control one's destiny. In working with minority youth, Oyserman and her colleagues found that "perceived efficacy" bolstered adolescent resilience and academic achievement, leading to persistence in school. Successful students with "perceived efficacy" recognize their connectedness to their ethnic groups, are able to see themselves succeeding as ethnic group members but also have an awareness of the structural limitations imposed upon them by ethnic group membership.

The concept of "perceived efficacy" helped me make sense of what I learned in China. At the micro level, it appears that our minority student interviewees experienced what Jacqueline P. Wiseman (1991: 5) calls "definitional careers." That is, their relatives, neighbors and teachers all provided them with definitions of themselves as successful scholars, over and over again throughout the course of their young lives. At the same time at the macro level, the students were moving through an educational system with numerous preferential policies in place. Social structures—such as special schools for ethnic students, financial aid for minority education and additional points on national examinations—help make academic success possible for national minorities. In short, micro level interactions and macro level supports engendered in the minority students we interviewed the perceived efficacy they needed to persevere and succeed in school.

## 6. Success Academy for American Indians in South Dakota

The Flandreau Indian School-South Dakota State University Success Academy was started in 2000 by a small group of committed educators from two neighboring institutions on South Dakota's eastern border. The concept of perceived efficacy certainly guided me as I worked with others back home in South Dakota to create what ultimately became a nationally recognized college preparatory program for American Indian high school students. Besides being one of the program's co-founders, I also worked as Success Academy coordinator throughout its 12-year history.



In the absence of vigorous policies of affirmative action, like those that exist in China, I believe it is imperative for American educators to create programs that engender perceived efficacy in their participants. At the micro level, each and every aspect of the Success Academy program was designed to strengthen the identities of the American Indian students it served. At the macro level, structural supports were built into the program to ensure that all participants were provided with the "social and cultural capital" (St. John, Hu & Fisher, 2011) needed to break through the barriers standing between Indian students and college access.

As seen from the Chinese examples presented earlier, the construction of a scholar self must start early. Students began Success Academy during their first year at the Flandreau Indian School, a time when adolescents start making critical decisions about life after graduation. (FIS is an off-reservation federal Indian boarding school, serving students in grades 9 through 12 from more than 40 tribes throughout the US.)

Again, as discussed previously in the Chinese context, effective identity work must be intensive. In this regard, working with boarding school students, who return home only twice a year, was a great asset. All Flandreau Indian School freshmen and sophomores participated in the hands-on career workshops presented by more than 300 faculty and staff at South Dakota State University. This meant that all FIS students started their junior year having spent 10 days on a college campus, SDSU, located just 25 miles away from their high school.

### 6.1 Success Academy Freshmen and Sophomores and Their Identity Work

All 100 FIS freshmen came to SDSU for six visits, and all 100 FIS sophomores came to SDSU for four visits, each academic year. Many of these younger students initially had no inkling that they could attend college, having come from families and communities where individuals with higher education were in short supply. Much identity work needed to occur in order for these students to picture themselves first as scholars, attending college, and later as professionals, pursuing careers.

Tribal leaders speak passionately about the need for their youth to "complete the circle" (Garrod & Larimore, 1997), that is, to acquire education, return home and serve their people. Yet often American Indian youth do not have a clear idea of the many vocational opportunities open to them or of the education needed to prepare for these opportunities. From the start, Success Academy's emphasis was on college preparation for career areas identified by tribal leaders as being of critical need in reservation communities. Success Academy workshop titles ranged from "Wokunze: Life Pathways in Nursing" to "Education: Wiconi Waste." Workshops were held on Friday afternoons in SDSU labs and classrooms.

Workshops were designed to be experiential, or put another way, to be "hands-on." For example, in the Pharmacy workshop students donned white coats and used mortars and pestles to fill capsules with "medicine" (in this case, talcum powder). They worked under the direction of students, like Tasha

Standing Soldier, who graduated from SDSU with a Doctor of Pharmacy degree. Success Academy allowed students to "try on" different professional identities such as that of "Native American pharmacist" or "American Indian engineer." The message was clear: the students did not need to leave their identities parked outside the university gates in order to succeed. Success Academy affirmed the American Indian identities that the students brought with them into the program.

Involving role models who students recognize as coming from similar backgrounds as themselves (Tierney, 2000: 229) was another important aspect of Success Academy, and one that aided in the construction of American Indian scholar identities. During the Journalism workshop, Professor Doris Giago, an enrolled member of the Oglala Sioux Tribe, greeted students in the Lakota/Dakota Conference Room and explained to them the need for more Indian reporters and editors. Students gathered around a circular red table, the color of sacred pipestone. The table surrounded a four-foot-wide drum made from a hollowed-out cottonwood trunk. Meeting here and at similar places on campus suggested to students that their Native identities were celebrated throughout SDSU.



Workshop subjects as well honored the identities of the American Indian participants. The College of Engineering workshop gave students a chance to try out different geospatial technologies, and, in the process, view imagery of the Grand Canyon. Since a sizeable number of FIS students are Havasupai and live inside the Grand Canyon with their families when not at school, this session was particularly engaging. During an ethnobotany workshop, hosted by the College of Agriculture and Biological Sciences, students learned about plant species of special significance to indigenous peoples, where to find these plants in their native habitats, and how the plants look when harvested. It is important for students to see their culture reflected in the curriculum (Nichols&Nichols, 1998: 40).

"One important way to enhance a feeling of belonging at college is to celebrate American Indian ethnicity on campus," Terry E. Huffman (1999: 174) notes. Sharing food has always been an important part of Native American celebrations. Great emphasis was placed on the Success Academy dinners that followed the afternoon workshops. Always first to arrive were the members of the SDSU Native American Club, who served as hosts for all these dinners. Over the years, as students have graduated from FIS and have enrolled at SDSU, the Club has grown to include former Success Academy scholars. These scholars are a key part of the identity work that occurs throughout the program, because they provide role models of success for the younger FIS students aspiring to attend college. They show that achievement is possible for all Flandreau Indian School graduates.

After the evening meals, Native American Club members and Success Academy students stayed on campus and attended co-curricular events. "An organizational culture that truly celebrates diverse groups will have myriad activities, symbols, and events that speak to diversity," William G. Tierney (1992: 159) explains. "Indian ways of life and values will be celebrated and affirmed." At a midsized public university like South Dakota State, with more than 12,500 students, there are many Friday evening events from which to choose. Whenever possible, Success Academy organizers chose to have students attend campus activities that celebrated Indian identity. These included a hoop dancing performance by Sisseton-Wahpeton Sioux tribal member Jackie Bird, an art exhibition by Lakota artist Arthur Amiotte and SDSU's annual wacipi (pow wow) held in the Frost Arena.



### 6.2 Structural Supports for Success Academy Juniors and Seniors

It is important to repeat that the micro level identity work just described occurs within a larger macro structural context. Self-conceptions are influenced by social structures. As identity theorist Stryker (1989: 53) remarks, "One cannot be a swimmer in the absence of a pool." Preferential policies, when they exist, provide the structure or "pool" in which ethnic minority students can construct identities and be successful. In the absence of preferential policies, such as those that exist in China, college preparatory programs in the US simply must fill the void. FIS-SDSU Success Academy did this by supplying social and cultural capital to students who come from families without access to the material and temporal resources needed to assist with school careers (Lareau, 1989).

This philosophy was expressed in the Memorandum of Understanding that laid the official groundwork for the FIS-SDSU partnership. In the MOU South Dakota State University committed itself to "providing, through its various programs and services, educational opportunities for the students at the Flandreau Indian School," and the Flandreau Indian School promised cooperation "in building and nurturing this partnership (that) will be crucial to narrowing the educational achievement gap that has long existed between major society students and Native American students" (South Dakota State University-Flandreau Indian School, 2000: 1-2).

**Social capital**

In attempting to narrow the achievement gap for Flandreau Indian School students, Success Academy provided access to "social capital" or "social networks." Hugh Mehan et al. (1996) describe "social networks" as:



> ...well placed adults who either directly or indirectly provide institutional resources and opportunities...(Their) power is derived from the ability to situate youth within resource-rich social networks by actively manipulating the social and institutional forces that determine who shall "make it" and who shall not. From the point of view of the student then, gaining access to educational opportunities and life choices essentially entails gaining access to social networks.
>
> (Hugh Mehan, et al., 1996: 214)

As juniors, Success Academy scholars met and formed social networks with:

· American Indian professionals and scholars from across the country, individuals who had to merge what they called the "academic and moccasined pathways" in pursuit of degrees;

· "Academic parents," retired SDSU faculty members who worked one-on-one with the FIS students and discussed with them their plans for higher education; and

· Student affairs staff, from offices throughout the university, who were key resources for students as they moved from high school into college.

**Cultural capital**

"Cultural capital," as first defined by Pierre Bourdieu (1977, 1986) is a resource inherited by children of high-status families and passed on via the system of formal schooling. In Bourdieu's view society is divided between the educational "haves" and the educational "have-nots." Those fortunate enough to have been born into power and privilege use those resources to sustain their positions, to the detriment of those less fortunate.

Cultural capital is "the knowledge that elites value yet schools do not teach" (McDonough, 1997: 9). Over the years, Success Academy became a state-sponsored source (Mehan, et al., 1996: 216) of cultural capital in the following ways:



· College-educated parents routinely help their children fill out college applications and apply for financial aid. SDSU staffers provided this kind of hands-on assistance for Success Academy seniors.

· Success Academy provided an ACT prep course for its seniors, something that is often not available to low-income students. Success Academy also purchased ACT prep books and on-line tutorials for the seniors' use.

· Success Academy scholars did college campus visits with their "academic parents," since as boarding school students, they were geographically far separated from their true families, who might otherwise have accompanied them. The scholars talked with faculty in the academic disciplines in which they intended to major.

Success Academy seniors also were able to take two three-credit courses at South Dakota State University during their final year of high school. This experience, which would otherwise have been financially out of reach, was made possible by generous external grants from federal and private sources.

By taking the courses, Success Academy seniors accrued cultural capital and reaped four significant benefits. First, they experienced the demands of college-level work while still in high school, and they were ultimately better prepared for higher education than most of their peers. Second, they learned that they had "what it takes" to be successful in college. Third, they earned six credits before starting college. And, most importantly, they realized that college was exciting and thus worth doing.

## 7. Conclusion: the Need for More Comparative Work

This paper has examined ethnic minorities and their educational attainment in two settings, Yunnan Province in China's Southwest and South Dakota in America's Midwest. Issues of equity and access, as these relate to higher education in the PRC and the US, have been discussed. The focus, however, has been on academic success and ethnic identity. Questions posed were "How do ethnic minority students in two cultures construct identities that help them succeed in school?" and "How can the larger social context, in which identity construction occurs, support academic achievement by ethnic minorities?". Examples were drawn from the experiences of ethnic minority students attending Yunnan Normal University in Kunming, and American Indian students participating in a college preparatory program at South Dakota State University. "Perceived efficacy" was introduced as a concept useful for discussing the role of preferential policies in China and the lack of affirmative action in the US Relevant literature was reviewed.



Recently scholars, particularly those in China, have begun to shift their attention from concerns over access to issues involving how minority students experience college once admitted. Zhao Zhenzhou and Gerard A. Postiglione (2008: 136) reflect that "while there are several works that focus on university students, mostly on identity, there is virtually no recent research that focuses specifically on the cultural recognition of ethnic minorities in China's universities." Zhao and Postiglione's current research—on internationalization and multiculturalism (Zhao & Postiglione, 2008), on university media representations (Zhao & Postiglione, 2010), on minority women's empowerment (Zhao, 2011) and on nationalities' citizenship rights (Zhao, 2010b)—seeks to fill that gap.

Another lack is that few studies, in either Chinese or English, develop a strong comparative framework for investigating educational attainment and ethnic minorities. One example might be a comparative study of minority boarding schools in China and in the US, focusing on their dual functions, often as providers of quality education, but sometimes as implementers of assimilationist agendas.

Comparative sociologists of education and ethnicity have much to learn from both the Chinese and the American experiences. There is great potential for developing theoretical and policy-relevant insights (Cherng, Hannum, & Lu, 2013). This paper is an early foray into what can become a fruitful field.



## Bibliography:


Alliance for Excellent Education. Accelerating the College and Career Readiness of South Dakota's Students[EB/OL]. 2011. Retrieved August 16, 2012 (http://search.ebscohost.com/login.aspx?direct=ture&db=eric&AN=ED520677&site=ehost-live).

Bhalla, Ajit S., Shufang Qiu. *Poverty and Inequality among Chinese Minorities*[M]. New York: Routledge, 2006.

Bourdieu, Pierre. Cultural Reproduction and Social Reproduction[M]// J. Karabel, A. H. Halsey. *Power and Ideology in Education*. New York: Oxford University Press, 1977: 487-511.

Bourdieu, Pierre. The Forms of Capital[M]// J. G. Richardson. *Handbook of Theory and Research for the Sociology of Education*. New York: Greenwood Press, 1986: 241-258.

Cao, Huhua. Spatial Inequality in Children's Schooling in Gansu, Western China: Reality and Challenges[J]. *The Canadian Geographer*, 2008, 52(3): 331-350.

Chen, Yangbin. *Muslim Uyghur Students in a Chinese Boarding School: Social Recapitalization as a Response to Ethnic Integration*[M]. Lanham, MD: Lexington Books, 2008.

Cherng, Hua-Yu Sebastian, Emily C. Hannum, Chunping Lu. Sociological Perspectives on Ethnicity and Education in China: Views from Chinese and English Literatures[D]. Asia-Pacific Education, Language Minorities and Migration Network Working Paper, University of Pennsylvania Population Studies Center, Philadelphia, PA, 2013.

Choi, Sheena. Globalization, China's Drive for World-Class Universities (211 Project) and the Challenges of Ethnic Minority Higher Education: The Case of Yanbian University[J]. *Asia Pacific Education Review*, 2010, 11(3): 169-178.

Cochran-Smith, Marilyn. Blind Vision: Unlearning Racism in Teacher Education[J]. *Harvard Educational Review*, 2000, 70(2):157-190.

Dai, Yanchun, Changjiang Xu. Yunnan's Preferential Policies in Minority Education Since the 1980s: Retrospect and Prospects[M]// M. Zhou, A. M. Hill. *Affirmative Action in China and the US:A Dialogue on Inequality and Minority Education*. New York: Palgrave Macmillan, 2009: 99-116.

Daniels, Doug. Affirmative Action in Education in Inner Mongolia, People's Republic of China[J]. *Canadian Journal of Native Education*, 1984, 11(2):14-26.



Edlin, Douglas E. Learning About Equality: Affirmative Action, University Admissions, and the Law of the United States[M]// M. Zhou, A. M. Hill. *Affirmative Action in China and the US: A Dialogue on Inequality and Minority Education*. New York: Palgrave Macmillan, 2009: 227-246.

Faircloth, Susan C., John W. Tippeconnic III. *The Dropout/Graduation Rate Crisis Among American Indian and Alaska Native Students: Failure to Respond Places the Future of Native Peoples at Risk*. Los Angeles: The Civil Rights Project at UCLA, 2010.

Garrod, Andrew, Colleen Larimore. *First Person, First Peoples: Native American College Graduates Tell Their Life Stories*[M]. Ithaca: Cornell University Press, 1997.

Giddens, Anthony. *The Constitution of Society: Outline of the Theory of Structuration*[M]. Berkeley: University of California Press, 1984.

Hansen, Mette Halskov. *Lessons in Being Chinese: Minority Education and Ethnic Identity in Southwest China*[M]. Seattle: University of Washington Press, 1999.

Hayhoe, Ruth. *China's Universities 1895-1995: A Century of Cultural Conflict*[M]. New York:

Garland Publishing, 1996.

Heiss, Jerold. *The Social Psychology of Interaction*[M]. Englewood Cliffs, NJ: Prentice-Hall, 1981.

Hodges, Carolyn R., Olga M. Welch. *Making Schools Work: Negotiating Educational Meaning and Transforming the Margins*[M]. New York: Peter Lang, 2003.

Hou Hanmin. Looking at the Quality of Ethnic Minority Education in Xinjiang Province from the Perspective of the University Entrance Examination[J]. *Chinese Education and Society*, 2000, 33(1):87-91.

Hu-DeHart, Evelyn. Affirmative Action, Civil Rights, and Racial Preferences in the US: Some General Observations[M]// M. Zhou, A. M. Hill. *Affirmative Action in China and the US: A Dialogue on Inequality and Minority Education*. New York: Palgrave Macmillan, 2009: 213-225.

Huffman, Terry E. *Cultural Masks: Ethnic Identity and American Indian Higher Education*[M]. Buckhannon, WV: Stone Creek Press, 1999.

Jacob, W. James, Xinyi Wu, Sheng Yao Cheng. Chinese Minorities and Higher Education: Qualitative Findings from Students, Faculty, and Administrators[J]. *Education and Society*, 2011, 29(1): 27-44.

Kormondy, Edward J. Minority Education in Inner Mongolia and Tibet[J]. *International Review of Education*, 2002, 48(5): 377-401.



Lareau, Annette. *Home Advantage: Social Class and Parental Intervention in Elementary Education*[M]. New York: Falmer Press, 1989.

Lee, MaryJo Benton. *Ethnicity, Education and Empowerment: How Minority Students in Southwest China Construct Identities*[M]. Aldershot, Hampshire: Ashgate, 2001.

Lee, MaryJo Benton. *Success Academy: How Native American Students Prepare for College and How Colleges Can Prepare for Them*[M]. New York: Peter Lang, 2013.

Lee, MaryJo Benton, Li Hong, Luo Lihui. Minority Student Success in Southwest China: Identity Work and Its Structural Supports[M]//W. R. Allen, R. T. Teranishi, M. Bonous-Hammarth. *As the World Turns: Implications of Global Shifts in Higher Education for Theory, Research and Practice*. Bingley, West Yorkshire: Emerald Group Publishing, 2012: 345-366.

Lengerich, Ryan. Nation's Top Three Poorest Counties in Western South Dakota[J]. *Rapid City Journal*, January 22. Retrieved July 3, 2012 (http://rapidcityjournal.com/news/nations-top-three-poorest-counties-in-western-south-dakota/article_2d5bb0bc-44bf-11e1-bbc90019bb2963f4.html).

Luo, Yan, Po Yang. Chinese Higher Education: Expansion and Social Justice Since 1949[M]// H. Meyer, E. P. St. John, M. Chankseliani, L. Uribe. *Fairness in Access to Higher Education in a Global Perspective: Reconciling Excellence, Efficiency, and Justice*. Boston: Sense Publishers, 2013: 95-110.

McDonough, Patricia M. *Choosing Colleges: How Social Class and Schools Structure Opportunity*[M]. Albany: State University of New York Press, 1997.

Mead, George Herbert. *Mind, Self, and Society*[M]. Chicago: University of Chicago Press, 1934.

Mehan, Hugh, Irene Villanueva, Lea Hubbard, Angela Lintz. *Constructing School Success: The Consequences of Untracking Low-Achieving Students*[M]. New York: Cambridge University Press, 1996.

Merton, Robert K. *Social Theory and Social Structure*[M]. New York: The Free Press, 1968.

Meyer, Heinz-Dieter, Edward P. St. John, Maia Chankseliani, Lina Uribe. The Crisis of Higher Education Access—A Crisis of Justice[M]// H. Meyer, E. P. St. John, M. Chankseliani, L. Uribe. *Fairness in Access to Higher Education in a Global Perspective: Reconciling Excellence, Efficiency, and Justice*. Boston: Sense Publishers, 2013: 1-11.

Munoz, Carlos, Jr. Diversity and the New American Identity[R]. Keynote Speech at the Annual Conference on People of Color in Predominantly White Institutions, October 15-16, 1999, Lincoln, NE.



Netting, Nancy S. The Deer Turned Her Head: Ethnic Options for the Hainan Li[J]. *Bulletin of Concerned Asian Scholars*, 1997, 29(2): 3-17.

Nichols, Laurie Stenberg, Tim Nichols. 2+2+2: Collaborating to Enhance Educational Opportunities for Native Americans[J]. *Journal of Family and Consumer Sciences*, 1998, 90(1):38–41.

Noah, Harold J., Max A. Eckstein. *Doing Comparative Education: Three Decades of Collaboration*. 1998. Retrieved October 10, 2013 (http://acawiki.org/Doing_Comparative_Education:_Three_Decades_of_Collaboration).

Ogbu, John U. *Minority Education and Caste*[M]. New York: Academic Press, 1978.

Ogbu, John U. Research Currents: Cultural-Ecological Influences on Minority School Learning[J]. *Language Arts*, 1985, 62(8): 860-869.

Ogbu, John U. Understanding Cultural Diversity and Learning[J]. *Educational Researcher*, 1992, 21(8): 5-24.

Ogunwole, Stella U. *We the People: American Indians and Alaska Natives in the United States*[M]. Washington, D.C.: US Census Bureau, 2006.

Oyserman, Daphna, Kathy Harrison, and Deborah Bybee. Can Racial Identity Be Promotive of Academic Efficacy?[J]. *International Journal of Behavioral Development*, 2001, 25(4): 379-385.

Oyserman, Daphna, Larry Gant, Joel Ager. A Socially Contextualized Model of African American Identity: Possible Selves and School Persistence[J]. *Journal of Personality and Social Psychology,* 1995, 69(6): 1216-1232.

People's Daily Online. Four Million People in Absolute Poverty in Yunnan[EB/OL)] December 2, 2002. Retrieved October 11, 2013 (http://english.peopledaily.com.cn/200212/02/eng20021202_107797.shtml).

Postiglione, Gerard A. The Implications of Modernization for the Education of China's National Minorities[M]// R. Hayhoe. *Education and Modernization: The Chinese Experience*. New York: Pergamon Press, 1992: 337-357.

Postiglione, Gerard A. The Education of Ethnic Minority Groups in China[M]// J. Banks. *The Routledge International Companion to Multicultural Education*. New York: Routledge, 2009: 501-511.

Rick, Lynn Taylor. District Still Dealing with High Native Dropout Rates[J]. *Rapid City Journal*, July 8, 2012. Retrieved August 16, 2010 (http://rapidcityjournal.com/article_d34007a7-bb40-57d2-b1af66bd41410.html).

San Juan School District. San Juan Heritage: Manuelito[M]. 2003. Retrieved July 6, 2012 (http://dine.sanjuan.k12.ut.us/heritage/people/dine/biographies/manuelito.htm).

Sautman, Barry. Expanding Access to Higher Education for China's National Minorities: Policies of Preferential Admissions[M]// G. A. Postiglione. *China's National Minority Education: Culture, Schooling, and Development*. New York: Falmer Press, 1999:173-210.

Snow, David A., Leon Anderson. Identity Work among the Homeless: The Verbal Construction and Avowal of Personal Identities[J]. *American Journal of Sociology*, 1987, 92(6): 1336-1371.

South Dakota Board of Regents. *Fact Book: Fiscal Year 2011*[M]. Pierre, SD: South Dakota Board of Regents, 2011.

South Dakota State University-Flandreau Indian School. *Memorandum of Understanding*. 2000.

Steele, Claude M. A Threat in the Air: How Stereotypes Shape Intellectual Identity and Performance[J]. *American Psychologist*, 1997, 52(6): 613-629.

St. John, Edward P., Shouping Hu, Amy S. Fisher. *Breaking Through the Access Barrier: How Academic Capital Formation Can Improve Policy in Higher Education*[M]. New York: Routledge, 2011.

Stryker, Sheldon. Further Developments in Identity Theory: Singularity Versus Multiplicity of Self[M]//J. Berger, M. Zelditch Jr., B. Anderson. *Sociological Theories in Progress: New Formulations*. Newbury Park: Sage Publications, 1989: 35-57.

Swail, Watson Scott, Laura W. Perna. Pre-College Outreach Programs: A National Perspective[M]// W. G. Tierney, L. S. Hagedorn. *Increasing Access to College: Extending Possibilities for All Students*. Albany: State University of New York Press, 2002: 15-34.

Tierney, William G. *Official Encouragement, Institutional Discouragement: Minorities in Academe—The Native American Experience*[M]. Norwood, NJ: Ablex Publishing, 1992.

Tierney, William G. Power, Identity and the Dilemma of College Student Departure[M]// J. M. Braxton. *Reworking the Student Departure Puzzle*. Nashville: Vanderbilt University Press, 2000: 213-234.

Trueba, Henry T., Yali Zou. *Power in Education: The Case of Miao University Students and Its Significance for American Culture*[M]. Washington, D.C.: Falmer Press, 1994.

US Census Bureau. American Indian and Alaska Heritage Month: November 2011[EB/OL]. 2011. Retrieved August 15, 2012 (http://www.census.gov/newsroom/releases/archives/ facts_for_features_special_editions/cb11-ff22.html).

Wang Ge, Linda Tsung, Ki Wing-wah. The Pains of Becoming Trilingual in China: An Ethnographic Case Study of a Naxi College Student[J]. *The Asia-Pacific Education Researcher*, 2012, 21(2): 257-266.



Wang, Tiezhi. Preferential Policies for Ethnic Minority Students in China's College/University Admission[J]. *Asian Ethnicity*, 2007, 8(2):149-163.

Wang, Xiaobing, Chengfang Liu, Linxiu Zhang, Renfu Luo, Thomas Glauben, Yaojiang Shi, Scott Rozelle, Brian Sharbono. College Education and the Poor in China: Documenting the Hurdles to Educational Attainment and College Matriculation[J]. *Asia Pacific Education Review*, 2011, 12(March): 533-546.

Wiseman, Jacqueline P. *The Other Half: Wives of Alcoholics and Their Social-Psychological Situation*[M]. New York: Aldine de Gruyter, 1991.

Yi, Lin. *Cultural Exclusion in China: State Education, Social Mobility and Cultural Difference*[M]. New York: Routledge, 2008.

Yu, Haibo. *Identity and Schooling Among the Naxi: Becoming Chinese with Naxi Identity*[M]. Lanham, MD: Lexington Books, 2010.

Zhang, Hong. Research on Minority Education During Higher Education Changing to Marketability in China: The Example of Yunnan Province[M]// R. W. Heber. *Issues in*

*Aboriginal/Minority Education: Canada, China, Taiwan District*. Regina, SK: Indigenous Studies Research Centre, 2004: 71-79.

Zhao, Zhenzhou. Ethnic Mongol Students and Cultural Recognition: Case Studies of Three Chinese Universities[J]. *Chinese Education and Society*, 2007, 40(2): 26-37.

Zhao, Zhenzhou. *China's Mongols at University: Contesting Cultural Recognition*[M]. Lanham, MD: Lexington Books, 2010a.

Zhao, Zhenzhou. Practices of Citizenship Rights Among Minority Students at Chinese Universities[J]. *Cambridge Journal of Education*, 2010b, 40(2): 131-144.

Zhao, Zhenzhou. Empowerment in a Socialist Egalitarian Agenda: Minority Women in China's Higher Education System[J]. *Gender and Education*, 2011, 23(4): 431-445.

Zhao, Zhenzhou, Gerard A. Postiglione. Making Globalization Work for Chinese Higher Education by Building Bridges Between Internationalization and Multiculturalism[M]. *Asian Ethnicity*, 2008, 9(2): 133-150.

Zhao, Zhenzhou, Gerard A. Postiglione. Representations of Ethnic Minorities in China's University Media[J]. *Discourse: Studies in the Cultural Politics of Education*, 2010, 31(3): 319-334.

Zhu, Zhiyong. *State Schooling and Ethnic Identity: The Politics of a Tibetan Neidi Secondary School in China*[M]. Lanham, MD: Lexington Books, 2007.

Zhu, Zhiyong. Higher Education Access and Equality among Ethnic Minorities in China[J]. *Chinese Education and Society*, 2010, 43(1):12-23.

# 从中国西南部到美国中西部：少数民族和高等教育

玛丽乔·本顿·李

（南达科塔大学社会学与农村研究系，美国布鲁金斯　57007）

**摘　要**：本文主要研究中国西南地区云南省和美国中西地区南达科他州的少数民族以及少数民族的教育成就。在中美两国，高等教育的公平和获取方式备受关注，关注焦点是学术成就和族群认同。关注的主要问题是“少数民族（种族）学生怎样在高等教育中实现其族群的认同”以及“在社会大环境下，怎样支持他们实现学术成就”。本文以中国少数民族学生在云南师范大学和美国印第安学生参与南达科他大学的预科项目为例，引用“效能感”的概念讨论中国对少数民族的优惠政策以及美国对少数种族缺乏正面、平等对待的问题。

**关键词**：云南省；南达科他州；少数民族；教育成就；效能感

# Motivation for Overseas Study: Chinese Students at Arizona State University

Li Xiaojie[1] Li Wei[2]

(1 Mary Lou Fulton Teachers College, Arizona State University, Tempe, USA, 85287-5503; 2 School of Social Transformation, School of Geographical Science and Urban Planning, Arizona State University, Tempe, USA, 85287-5503)

**Abstract:** There is a global trend towards the internationalization of higher education to meet the needs of a globalizing workforce and higher education sector as an industry. Academic degrees from developed countries are often valued more in the global labor market, and as such, more students intend to go to higher education institutions in those developed countries. In order to examine the trend and the reason behind the drastic growth of Chinese international students in the US in general, and at ASU in particular, this paper aims at identifying Chinese students' motivation in choosing a study destination. Primarily using survey data and follow-up interview information, the data reveals some emerging characteristics of student mobility patterns in the global education exchange. It also serves as a useful reference for ASU and its peer universities in the US to further develop their enrollment marketing strategies towards China, while providing references for Chinese students and parents when considering studying overseas.

**Key Words:** Higher Education; Oversea Study; Motivation

There is a global trend towards the internationalization of higher education to meet the needs of a globalizing workforce and higher education sector as an industry. Academic degrees from developed countries are often valued more in the global labor market, and as such, more students intend to go to higher education institutions in those developed countries (King & Ruiz-Gelices, 2003). On the other hand, some of these countries (e.g., the US, the UK, Australia, and Canada, among others) either establish branch campuses overseas or proactively recruit full fee-paying students from overseas (Ziguras & Law, 2006). This trend has intensified after the 2008 global economic recession has damaged and slowed the domestic economy of the developed countries. At the same time, some populous developing countries' fast economic growth has enabled large number of students to go abroad to earn academic degrees at their own or their families' expenses, in addition to the traditional routes of overseas studies being financed by either the home country or the receiving country's governments or institutions (Li & Yu, 2013; Lu, Zong & Schissel, 2009). Taking the People's Republic of China for example, in part due to its booming economy, studying overseas has seen fast growth over the past decade. Nearly 340,000 Chinese students went to study in a foreign country in 2011 while this number was only around 39,000 in 2000. The US has been the leading destination for Chinese students who study overseas. In 2011, the number of Chinese students in the US made up 22% of the total study abroad population of China (Wang, 2012). In the meantime, China has become the top international student source since 2008/2009 academic year and sent a total number of 235,597 students in 2012/2013 to the US; this is equal to 29% of the entire international student population in this country (IIE, 2013).



Given that there are only three public 4-year universities in the State of Arizona (Arizona State University, hereafter ASU, Northern Arizona University and University of Arizona), it is not a traditional leading destination to receive the most international students among the 50 states in the US, as in the case of California and New York (IIE, 2013). However, the number of Chinese students has increased dramatically in recent years. Chinese students accounted for 32.4% of all international students in Arizona last year and this ratio was higher than most other states including even California and New York. Moreover, compared to the ratio of 21.2% in 2010, there was an 11.2 percentage point increase in just three years, which means that Arizona is rapidly becoming an appealing study destination for Chinese students. When examined by institution, ASU takes the lead in recruiting Chinese students. The number of Chinese students at ASU rocketed from 972 in 2010 to 2,473 in 2013 (2013 ASU enrollment data), and hence the share of this population out of the total number of Chinese students in Arizona has accordingly risen from 43.0% to 57.3% (calculated based on IIE, 2013).

In order to examine the trend and the reason behind the drastic growth of Chinese international students[1] in the US in general, and at ASU in particular, this paper aims at identifying Chinese students' motivation in choosing a study destination. Primarily using survey data and follow-up interview information, the data reveals some emerging characteristics of student mobility patterns in the global education exchange. It also serves as a useful reference for ASU and its peer universities in the US to further develop their enrollment marketing strategies towards China, while providing references for Chinese students and parents when considering studying overseas.

## 1. Conceptual Framework and Literature Review

In order to examine the specific drivers of international students' mobility, this paper adopts the classic "push-pull" theory in migration research and its implication in international education, which was brought up by McMahon (1992) to explain the international study pattern during the 1960s to 1970s, especially the dominating flow from Third World countries to the United States. According to McMahon, "push" factors are the characteristics of a sending country that propel students to study internationally. Primarily, a country that has a weaker economy or less educational opportunities was found to have a greater number of overseas students. On the other hand, "pull" factors are the variables that draw students to a particular nation. A stronger economic tie of a sending nation to a host nation facilitates the flow of students between the two countries (1992). McMahon's study emphasized that the economy is an influencing force to shape overseas study mobility.

Unlike McMahon's study that addressed the issue mainly at a country's level, Mazzarol and Soutar (2002) conducted a cross-national study to extend the "push-pull" model from a country's level to an institutional level. They indicated that a student's decision on the final destination has three stages: "push" factors first make them decide to pursue overseas education, while "pull" factors mainly influence the following two stages: selecting a host country and selecting an institution. According to this study, the most important "push" factor was that overseas programs and courses were better than locals. As for the "pull" factors, having better knowledge or awareness of a country is generally the most important factor for students to choose a host country, and institution's reputation and whether students' previous qualifications can be recognized are two major factors that motivate students to select a particular institution (Mazzarol & Soutar, 2002).

Following the important development of the "push-pull" model by Mazzarol and Soutar, there have been many studies that observed students' study abroad motivations using this approach. Among these studies, there is one also targeting Chinese students similarly to our present research. Bodycott (2009) let the students rate the factors that push them to study abroad and attract their decision making about a study destination. As a result, higher quality education is the most important factor and on-site accommodation is the highest rated feature in choosing a destination. This study also included parents, presenting a very different perspective in the value of overseas study. The major finding of this study is very interesting in that parents' decision was "influenced more by factors grounded in cultural, political and socio-economic pragmatism," while students cared more about "tangible qualities of the experience of studying abroad."



Even though many studies addressed the issue of international students' motivations in choosing an overseas study destination, there are few focusing on the flows of Chinese students to the US higher education institutions. Given the changing global economic order and rising Chinese economy in recent decades, it would be interesting to see how things have changed from what McMahon (1992) found as the increasing number of Chinese students abroad is definitely associated with a rising Chinese economy. Based on the existing literature and the gap, we aim at specifically exploring the issue of Chinese students' motivation for studying abroad. Using ASU as a case study, we focus on addressing the following research questions:

Why do Chinese students choose to study in the US?

What are the major factors that motivate Chinese students to select ASU as their study abroad destination? And how do these factors influence their decision?

## 2. Research Methods

The empirical work for this study took place at four campuses of ASU (Tempe, Downtown, West, and Polytechnic), from January to April of 2013. It consists of a questionnaire survey and follow-up in-depth interviews. The questionnaire survey was open to and distributed among Chinese students who were holding an F-1 or J-1 visa (including Optional Practical Training or OPT) and officially enrolled at the time. The questionnaire was first written in English and then translated into Chinese. Only the Chinese version was shown to the participants. The follow-up interviews were also conducted in Chinese and the transcripts were translated into English by the authors.

A total of 300 student participants successfully completed the survey. Data was collected via both online and in-person methods. The survey questionnaire invitation link was distributed via email and Chinese social media outlets QQ and microblog. The invitation link guided the students to the online questionnaire, which was created using Google Docs. One-third of the responses was received online, and the rest were collected using the printed version based on a convenient sampling with segmentation. Most of the participants were found and invited to participate in the survey at the two libraries (one each humanity/social sciences and natural sciences), dining halls, and computer center of ASU's Tempe campus, as this is the main campus hosting the majority of Chinese students. There were also 30 students invited at one of the Chinese New Year events held at the First Chinese Baptist Church. All the students who completed the printed questionnaire were required to confirm that it was their first time participating in the survey. As demonstrated in Table 1, 297 out of 300 participants held an F-1 visa (including OPT), which means they were either seeking or completed a degree at ASU. Among these 297 respondents, there were 157 undergraduate students, 102 master's students and 38 doctoral students. 43.3% of respondents were majoring in engineering and 33.3% were studying business. More than half of the respondents only had stayed at ASU less than a year, 11.0% for 1 year, 20.0% for 2 years, 8.7% for 3 years and 5.3% for 4 years or more.

Due to the web survey's inherent self-selection nature and the convenient sampling for the in-person survey, we are keenly aware that the survey respondents are not randomly chosen, and as such, we cannot claim the survey results are representative of all ASU Chinese students. On the other hand, given the multiple data selection modes and methods, and that the number of survey respondents counts for 17.6% of all Chinese students at ASU at the time of the survey, they reveal certain trends in Chinese students' motivation in choosing the US in general and ASU in particular.

Table 1 Characteristics of Survey Respondents



| All Chinese student respondents (N=300) | | | | | | |
|---|---|---|---|---|---|---|
| Visa type | F1<br>99.0% | | | J1<br>1.0% | | |
| Degree level* | Undergraduate<br>52.9% | | Master's<br>34.3% | | Doctoral<br>12.8% | |
| Length of stay | Under 1 year<br>55.0% | 1 year<br>11.0% | 2 years<br>20.0% | 3 years<br>8.7% | 4 years or over<br>5.3% | |
| Major | Engineering<br>43.3% | Business<br>33.3% | Natural sciences<br>7.3% | Social sciences<br>7.3% | Design and arts<br>6.3% | Other<br>2.3% |
| How did they come | Applied through an agent<br>34.0% | Applied by themselves<br>44.3% | Joined a collaborative program<br>18.0% | Transferred from another American university/college<br>3.3% | Other<br>0.3% | |

* Including data from the 297 F-1 visa holders only.

In order to supplement and substantiate the survey results, follow-up interviews were conducted upon the completion of the survey stage. The participants of these interviews were randomly chosen from the students who completed the questionnaire and volunteered for further involvement. An interview invitation was sent to every fifth qualified respondent and five interviews were successfully completed. These interviews were guided by semi-structured questions, conducted in Mandarin, and covering the same topics in the questionnaire aiming at better understanding the reasons and considerations behind the quantitative survey data.

The specific portion regarding overseas study motivation in the questionnaire consisted of four questions. A total of 11 influencing factors were brought up based on existing literature, and the respondents were asked to rate these factors in Likens scales from very important to not important at all. The following section represents some key findings based on both the survey and interviews.

## 3. Empirical Findings



### 3.1 The US as the Top Choice of Overseas Education

Overseas study is seen as a process of cultural capital accumulation in the form of a Western university degree (Waters, 2006; Findlay, 2011). Consistent with the literature on the desirability of a foreign degree, the US remains the top choice among international students. In our survey, 67% of survey participants claimed that the most important reason why they choose to study in the US was to obtain a foreign degree, while another 25% mostly wanted to enhance their knowledge about American society and Western culture. Even though a better understanding of Western culture has been considered as an important "pull" factor for international education in general, especially among Chinese students (Mazzarol & Soutar, 2002), a foreign degree is a more important practical reason and better represents the value of Chinese students' investment in studying in the US.

Historically the US has been a primary international graduate student hosting country. The emerging trend of Chinese students seeking overseas education at a younger age has significantly increased in recent years. At the national level the share of Chinese undergraduate students has risen to 39.8% in 2012/2013, while the share of graduate students has shrunk to 43.9%, even though the total number of graduate students is still growing (IIE, 2013). At ASU, undergraduate students barely surpassed the number of graduate students in 2012, by fall of 2013 their percentage already jumped to a surprising 59% (calculation based on ASU enrollment data). This closely mirrors the rapid growth of the Chinese economy and increasing wealth-accumulation among middle-class families who can afford to send their children for an overseas degree-seeking study (Li & Yu, 2012), as majority of undergraduate students are full tuition- and fee-paying. This phenomenon is contradictory to what McMahon (1992) found out 20 years ago. While a graduate-level US degree enjoys an extraordinary worldwide reputation, a US bachelor's degree is also favored by Chinese students. In the interviews, undergraduate students reported almost the same belief as graduate students that the US is still providing the best education in the world and a US degree would make them more competitive compared to the students who do not have one.



While 28.7% of all undergraduate survey respondents are considering to pursue a higher-level degree in the US after graduation, another 51.6% of them planned to return to China in the future with a US bachelor's degree. Unlike graduate students, undergraduate students showed less desire for either staying in the US for a couple of years after graduation (40.1% of undergraduate and 59.3% of graduate students) or immigrating to the US (7.6% of undergraduate and 12.9% of graduate students). Therefore, this may well be a reflection that undergraduate and graduate students may have different career goals and life plans, but seeking a US degree, no matter at which level, is a highly favorable choice for Chinese students.

In addition to a US degree as the major "pull" factor, "push" factors may also play an important role in drawing students to study in the US.

Heated competition to get into higher education institutions in China "push" students who have no hope in getting into the top-tier universities to look for overseas opportunities of elite HEIs or HEIs offering elite courses. One of the undergraduate students (interviewee A) in the interview stated,

> If I took the college entrance exams in China, going to a second tier university could have been the best result for me. However, I met the ASU's requirements and even got admitted by the highly ranked business school. For me, this is much better than going to college in China.

While the severe competition for top HEIs diverts undergraduate students to study overseas, graduate students who have had higher educational experience in China may be "pushed" by unsatisfying academic or working environment. A doctoral student (interviewee B) who obtained both her bachelor's and master's degrees in China recalled,

> When I was working on a project as a master's student, I had to spend time dining and drinking with government officials to have [our] requests approved. It's unfair that you can hardly work in China without investing a lot of time in building and maintaining such social networks.

This student did not indicate whether or not she was planning to return to China after completing her degree. It is obvious that moving out of her home country could be a solution for her to pursue a better working environment, and a US doctoral degree might be able to provide her leverage in future job market for lacking strong social networks if she goes back to China.

### 3.2 Institution Selection

Table 2 summarizes the reasons used by Chinese students in choosing ASU as their destination institution. The first column shows the 11 factors that the survey questionnaire asked students to rate based on their influence among students' destination selection. Column two shows the mean value of their responses (*m*) from very important to unimportant. Overall, the three leading factors that bring students to ASU are quality or ranking of the program of their major (*m*=4.50), safety concerns (*m*=4.04) and employment opportunities in the US after graduation (*m*=3.82).

Table 2 Reasoning behind Destination Institution Selection

| Reasons | Mean |
|---|---|
| 1. Academic-Quality or ranking of the program of their major | 4.50 |
| 2. Location-Safety concerns | 4.04 |
| 3. Location-Employment opportunities in the US after graduation | 3.82 |
| 4. Financial-Tuition and living expenditures | 3.62 |
| 5. Academic-Admission requirements | 3.53 |
| 6. Financial-Scholarship, TA and RA opportunities | 3.42 |
| 7. Location-Climate, neighborhood | 3.14 |
| 8. Location-Convenience (access to food and transportation, etc.) | 2.67 |
| 9. Social links-Existing population of Chinese international students | 2.57 |
| 10. Social links-Know some people who are students, faculty or staff at ASU | 2.54 |
| 11. There is a collaborative program that I could join | 2.20 |

5=Very important, 4=Important, 3=Moderately important, 2=Of little importance, 1=not important.



**Quality or ranking of study major as top priority**

As stated above, reaping a foreign degree is the highest motivation of Chinese students to study at ASU or in the US in general. Therefore, it is not surprising that achieving academic growth has been given priority in their university selection and degree-seeking process. In expecting this result, prospective Chinese students tend to evaluate the quality or ranking of the programs in their desired major field. Research, including this study, has demonstrated that many Chinese students intend to eventually return to China. Because of this, the quality and ranking of where their degree is earned becomes critically important because it determines how their degree will be recognized in their home country.

In the case of ASU, undergraduate and graduate students did not show much difference in considering this factor. If we examine the mean scores by major, the students who were majoring in natural sciences score lower than average ($m$=4.18), but the students who were studying business and engineering score relatively higher ($m$=4.54 and 4.52 respectively). This finding shows that business and engineering students give more consideration to the program quality, and it aligns with the fact that ASU has national renowned top 30 programs in these two areas (ASU, 2012). Therefore, the quality or ranking of a program could influence Chinese students' choice in a destination institution.

**Safety concerns**

Receiving country policies toward the foreign-born population in the name of national security can be an important consideration that impedes international students to flow to a certain host country. The US tightened its visa policy for international students after September 11th 2001. On the other hand, personal safety could also influence students' decision in overseas study destinations at a cultural level. Chinese people hold a relatively strong belief that the state needs to protect security in the society, so they are more likely to feel uncomfortable and insecure with the context of the US society where individuals are more responsible for their own protection (Marginson, Nyland, Sawir & Forbes-Mewett, 2010).

Constant tragedies directly affecting Chinese students in the US have aroused concerns about American campus security and safety in general. This has become alarming to both Chinese students and parents. For instance, two Chinese graduate students were shot to death at the University of Southern California of Los Angeles in 2012 and a female Chinese master's student became one of the three victims in the Boston marathon bombing last year.

In addition to the tragedies themselves, media may play a big role in sensitizing this concern, especially among parents. An undergraduate student (interviewee C) reported in the interview "my parents get to know about the US from the media, and those terrifying news make them really worry about my safety." Therefore, students who desire to study in the US tend to choose a safe place according to their own knowledge and perception about the US. A student (interviewee D) put it this way, "I think Phoenix is relatively safe because it doesn't have bad reputation regarding security problems as in other big cities like Chicago, New York or Los Angeles."

**Future employment opportunity in the US**

Even though the majority of students in the survey have the intention to return to China in the future, nearly half of all respondents hoped to have some full-time working experience in the US before returning. It shows that the Chinese students who study in the US are not only seeking the education, but also looking for enhancing the value of their education by working in the host country after graduation. The high rate of intending to return may also infer that long-term stay in the US is difficult, thus the actual preference to work in the US has been to some extent disguised.

Chinese students consider employment opportunity in the US when they are making decision on their destination university. They examine the location from the perspective of career development potential instead of merely picking a place that has a pleasant climate ($m$=3.14). As for how Chinese students perceive the potential job market in Phoenix, an engineering graduate (interviewee E) student stated,



> Phoenix metropolitan area is big, which means it needs people here. More importantly, Arizona is in proximity to California where I could enjoy the prestige of abundant working opportunities. Silicon Valley is always a dream place for engineering students like me.

It is obvious that this student considered the size of and work opportunity in the Phoenix metropolitan area, the 6$^{th}$ largest in the nation, is an advantage in choosing ASU; moreover, the proximity of AZ to Silicon Valley is considered as an additional plus for him when picking a US higher education institution.

**Self-financing among undergraduate and master's students**

Consistent with the trend that more than 90% of the total Chinese students who study abroad pay tuition and fees by themselves (Wang, 2012), scholarship, teaching assistant (TA) and research assistant (RA) opportunity provided by the host university does not fundamentally influence students' choice. However, these self-financed students are mainly undergraduate and master's students, while 92% of the doctoral participants in our survey reported having a TA or RA job at ASU, which they could count on in covering living expenses. This figure mirrors the recently released data by the US National Science Foundation that out of the total 13,971 PhD degrees conferred to temporary visa-holder foreign students in the US in 2012, 92.5% cited RA- or TA-ship, fellowship or grants were their primary financial sources (calculation based on NSF 2014).

Master's students, similarly to undergraduate students, do not expect the university to support them financially due to the scarcity of funding for them. It is unsurprising that they are the most sensitive group to the expenditure incurred on schooling. For this group, the mean score on the factor of tuition and life expenditure was 3.84, higher than the overall score of 3.62. Even though ASU tuition and living cost in Arizona in general are lower than both East and West Coast major metropolitan universities. ASU non-resident tuition and fees have increased by roughly 30% in responding to the significant cut in state appropriation since 2008, while the national average of this increase is only 19% (College Board, 2013). If this trend continues, ASU is under the risk of becoming less appealing than its peer universities to the self-financed students, especially to those at their master's level.

**Existing population of Chinese students**

Statistical data demonstrates that both in the US and the UK, there is a positive relationship between the size of the foreign student population and the academic status of a university (Findlay, 2011). However, the size of the existing foreign student population does not necessarily serve as a primary motivation for future international students to choose an institution that hosts a great percentage of international students. In the case of ASU, existing Chinese students population is not an important consideration for Chinese students ($m$=2.57). This result is, to some extent, surprising because publicizing the relatively large population of Chinese students has been constantly used as a marketing strategy to recruit new students. As for how Chinese students perceive the population of their compatriots, an undergraduate (interviewee C) claimed:

> A lot of Chinese students mean that our life could be easier because the previous students would support you in many ways—giving you advices on what courses to take, how to rent an apartment, where to find the best Chinese food in town and so on. You would not feel you are alone. But on the other hand, I do not like the universities that particularly enroll thousands of Chinese students very much because I feel that they just want to generate revenue from Chinese students. And you have less chance to practice English or get to know more about American culture if your classroom is filled up with Chinese faces.

**Collaborative program: Not necessarily a desirable shortcut**



Collaborative programs partnering with some top-tier Chinese higher education institutions are an important part of ASU's international initiatives. Through these programs, such as 3+2, Chinese undergraduate students from the partner universities have the opportunity to pursue a master's degree from ASU in an accelerated way. Usually, these programs are only open to the students who major in the STEM (science, technology, engineering and math) fields and require them to maintain the major at master's level. The students in such programs also need to meet the admission requirements and pay the same tuition as other international graduate students.

In addition to the tuition revenue, ASU is also clearly benefiting from the stable inbound flow of talented STEM students from top-tier universities in China. Taking the Huazhong University of Science and Technology (HUST) as an example, more than 60 students have come to ASU through the 3+2 program every year since it started in 2007. The completion rate of a master's degree from ASU was 85% by 2012. Around one-third of the students who completed the program continue to seek a higher-level degree in the US (interview of the founder of the ASU-HUST 3+2 program).

However, this well-designed path for overseas study does not seem to be a strong motivation for Chinese students to choose ASU. Among the students who joined such programs, the mean value of this consideration is only 3.30, which means they do not just value the "shortcut" provided to them. Even though attending a collaborative program could save their time in school, the requirements remain the same as mentioned above. Therefore, many future students in such programs still evaluate the potential educational value similarly to other students. Moreover, as the internalization of Chinese higher education, students, especially from top-tier institutions, usually have various options for overseas collaborative programs. "I chose ASU because I thought it is the best among all the available choices that I had at that time in terms of university ranking, program reputation and cost," said a master's student, who joined ASU through his alma mater HUST (interviewee E).



## 4. Summary and Conclusion

The most significant "pull" factor behind the fast growing number of Chinese students, especially undergraduate students, in both the US and ASU in particular over the past five years is found to be the perceived value of a US degree. For both undergraduate and graduate students, the US is believed to provide the best education in the world and a US degree is highly favored independent of students' future plans after finishing their study. In addition, the relatively higher competition for top-tier universities and the perhaps more unsatisfied academic environment in China could be two "push" factors to drive the students' flow from China to the US.

As the data showed that ASU is becoming a very appealing destination for Chinese students, we examined the reasons behind this fact. The high ranking of an academic program plays the most important role in attracting students.

In addition, Chinese students also give high consideration to a safe place with potential working opportunities in the future. ASU is perceived to be advantaged in both of these aspects. Since the majority of undergraduate and master's students self-finance their education, these two groups are relatively sensitive to tuition and living expenditures. On the other hand, some factors were found not to influence students' choices in selecting an institution. The existing population of compatriots was found to not greatly influence Chinese students' choices, and collaborative programs do not necessarily lead them to a specific institution.

As the student mobility pattern from a specific country to another is usually shaped by macro factors, such as economic status, quality and availability of higher education in the two countries, the students' motivations in selecting ASU have some implications for the university's future marketing strategies in recruiting Chinese students. As advertising the rankings is normally emphasized, ASU should pay more attention to supporting Chinese and other international students' career development in the US. Therefore, ASU could actively promote on-campus jobs to future Chinese students, which is an important alternate way of financing their education. A recent study also indicated that on-campus employment is statistically positively connected to foreign student retention at two Midwestern university systems (Kwai, 2009, cited in Fischer, 2014). More importantly, advocating the potential local job opportunities could be very effective in enhancing a university's image. Instead of advertising the large Chinese community, it may be better for ASU to showcase its efforts in integrating the Chinese students into the mainstream campus culture, which would present Chinese students a picture of the intangible value of a study abroad experience.



## Acknowledgement

*We are grateful to our survey respondents and interviewees for participating in this study; for Sichuan University (SCU) and ASU to co-host the 2013 International Conference on American and Chinese Southwest Studies in Chengdu, China where we co-presented an early version of the paper. We thank all conference participants who provided feedbacks at the conference, Jay Chen and Susie Huang at SCU for their hospitality, Kathryn Mohrman at ASU for her sponsorship, Denis Simon at ASU for supervising the survey, Wan Yu at ASU and Zsolt Marcet for their assistance in manuscript preparation.*

## Bibliography:

Arizona State University. Rankings[EB/OL]. Retrieved from: http://annualreport.asu.edu/rankings.html.

Bodycott, P. Choosing a Higher Education Study Abroad Destination: What Mainland Chinese Parents and Students Rate as Important[J]. *Journal of Research in International Education*, 2009, 8(3): 349-373.

College Board. *Trends in College Pricing*[EB/OL]. 2013. Retrieved from: https://trends.collegeboard.org/sites/default/files/college-pricing-2013-full-report-140108.pdf.

Findlay, A. M. An Assessment of Supply and Demand Side Theorizations of International Student Mobility[J]. *International Migration*, 49(2): 162-190.

Fischer, Karin. *Helping Foreign Students Thrive on US Campuses*[EB/OL]. 2014. Retrieved from: http://www.nytimes.com/2014/03/03/world/americas/helping-foreign-students-thrive-on-us-campuses.html?emc=edit_tnt_20140302&tntemail0=y&_r=0.

Institution of International Education. *Open Doors: Report on International Educational Exchange*[M]. New York: IIE, 2013.

King, R., Ruiz Gelices, E. International Student Migration and the European "Year Abroad": Effects on European Identity and Subsequent Migration Behaviour[J]. *International Journal of Population Geography*, 2003, 9(3): 229-252.

Li, W., Yu, W. Between China and the United States: Contemporary Migration Policies and Flows[J]. *AAPI Nexus: Asian Americans and Pacific Islander Policy, Practice and Community*, 2013, 10(1): 1-20.

Lu, Y., Zong, L., Schissel, B. To Stay or Return: Migration Intentions of Students from People's Republic of China in Saskatchewan, Canada[J]. *Journal of International Migration and Integration/Revue de l'integration et de la migration internationale*, 2009, 10(3): 283-310.

Marginson, S., Nyland, C., Sawir, E., Forbes-Mewett, H. *International Student Security*[M]. Cambridge: Cambridge University Press, 2010.

Mazzarol, T., Soutar, G. N. "Push-pull" Factors Influencing International Student Destination Choice[J]. *International Journal of Educational Management*, 2002, 16(2): 82-90.

McMahon, M. E. Higher Education in a World Market[J]. *Higher Education*, 1992, 24(4): 465-482.

National Science Foundation, National Center for Science and Engineering Statistics. *Doctorate Recipients' Primary Source of Financial Support, by Broad Field of Study, Sex, Citizenship, Race, and Ethnicity: 2012*[R]. Special Report NSF 14-305. Arlington, VA. 2014. Retrieved from: http://www.nsf.gov/statistics/sed/2012/pdf/tab35.pdf.

Wang, H. Overview of *the Report on the Development of China's Study Abroad* (中国留学报告2012综述)[M]. Beijing: Center for Globalization and China and Social Science Academic Press (in Chinese), 2012.

Waters, J. L. Geographies of Cultural Capital: Education, International Migration and Family Strategies Between Hong Kong District and Canada[J]. *Transactions of the Institute of British Geographers*, 2006, 31(2): 179-192.

Ziguras, C., Law, S. F. Recruiting International Students as Skilled Migrants: The Global "Skills Race" as Viewed from Australia and Malaysia[J]. *Globalisation, Societies and Education*, 2006, 4(1): 59-76.

# 海外留学动因研究：在亚利桑那州立大学的中国留学生

李晓洁[1] 李 唯[2]

(1亚利桑那州立大学玛丽·卢·富尔顿教师学院，美国坦佩 85287-5503；2亚利桑那州立大学社会变革学院、地理科学和城市规划学院，美国坦佩 85287-5503)

**摘 要**：为了适应全球化劳工需求和高等教育产业化，高等教育国际化已成趋势。发达国家的文凭在全球劳动力市场上往往被认为含金量更高，正因如此，越来越多的学生倾向于去其他国家接受高等教育。为了研究中国在美留学生，特别是在亚利桑那州立大学的留学生急剧增加的成因以及发展趋势，笔者采用调查数据和追踪采访的方式收集和分析数据，从而揭示了留学生在全球教育交流移动模式上的一些特征。同时，本文为亚利桑那州立大学及美国其他同类大学提供了有用参考，以便其针对中国市场调整招生营销策略，同样地，也为中国学生和家长提供有效的择校参考。

**关键词**：高等教育；海外留学；动因

# The Promises and Challenges of Teaching History through Television

Eduardo Pagán[1]

(School of Historical, Philosophical, and Religious Studies, Arizona State University, Tempe, USA, 85287-5503)

**Abstract:** Famed American journalist Edward R. Murrow held a complicated view of television, even while the industry was still in its infancy and its scale and potential could only be imagined. It was, on the one hand, a powerful medium that could teach, explore, and enlighten the public. Yet it was, on the other hand, chiefly a form of entertainment. The question was, for Murrow, which would it become? What would the nation want of television, to be educated or to be entertained? Despite the limitations of the medium, more scholarly historians need to engage the medium to present their work and teach the nation about the past, and more networks need to produce history-themed shows. There is clearly a demand for it.



**Key Words:** History; Television; Education

*This instrument can teach, it can illuminate; yes, and it can even inspire. But it can do so only to the extent that humans are determined to use it to those ends. Otherwise it is merely wires and lights in a box. There is a great and perhaps decisive battle to be fought against ignorance, intolerance and indifference.*

*We are in the same tent as the clowns and the freaks—that's show business.*

— Edward R. Murrow

1 Eduardo Pagán is also the Vice Provost for Academic Excellence and Inclusion at Arizona State University.

Famed American journalist Edward R. Murrow held a complicated view of television, even while the industry was still in its infancy and its scale and potential could only be imagined. It was, on the one hand, a powerful medium that could teach, explore, and enlighten the public. Yet it was, on the other hand, chiefly a form of entertainment. The question was, for Murrow, which would it become? What would the nation want of television, to be educated or to be entertained?

From 2007 until 2013, I worked as one of the hosts for *History Detectives* shown on the Public Broadcasting Service (PBS). From this experience I have come to deeply appreciate the power of television to educate. But I have also learned how television's imperative to entertain places very real limitations on how deeply and broadly subjects can be explored. Indeed, this popular show was eventually cancelled not because it lacked new material or ratings, but because a team of new executive producers at PBS wanted to create shows that played to a different and younger audience, like those on cable television.

The essence of the show focused on source analysis and research methods as hosts pursued answers about the historicity of artifacts presented by viewers. This many not seem an exciting topic to some, but *History Detectives* was shot in a way that brought the viewer along on the investigation, and in the process, uncovered little-know information about American history. This one-hour show first aired over the summer months of 2003, and after that it went into reruns until the next summer when a new season of episodes aired. This was the pattern that the show followed every year since then, until 2013 (IMDb, 2014). Each episode contained between three and four stories, and these stories could run anywhere between twelve to seventeen minutes long. Until the final season, each episode also contained "interstitials" at the end of every story, which were a minute-long side-stories that focused on a historical method, moment, or figure that was related to the main story.

# 1. Origins of the Show

Who came up with the idea for the show was perhaps the greatest mystery that we never solved. Gwen Wright relates how the idea evolved from early discussions with television producers for a show called *American Attic*, which eventually became *History Detectives* (YouTube, 2007). However, an executive producer at Lion Television[1]—one of the production companies that filmed the show—related to me the show developed from a colleague who was looking through his grandparents' attic one day and he began to wonder what stories these artifacts could tell, and how his grandparents might have intersected with significant historical moments associated with those artifacts. Another story came from Oregon Public Broadcasting (OPB)[2]—the partner production company with Lion—that the story simply grew out from a creative free-flow of ideas.[3] However the show originated, OPB partnered with Lion Television and pitched the show concept to PBS.



The Public Broadcasting Service, or PBS, as it is more commonly known, is a non-profit American broadcast television network. It first started out in 1952 as National Educational Television, and was launched as the Public Broadcasting Service in 1970 (Archive, 2012). Its original name illustrates the vision for PBS, that it was to serve as source that, even then, resisted the trend in television to merely entertain. Its shows would not be produced or evaluated on ratings, but on content and quality (PBS, CPB). Presently, the PBS network has 354 member television stations that hold a collective ownership with communities throughout the United States (Ledbetter, 1998; Dornfeld, 1998). For example, in the Phoenix area, where I teach at Arizona State University (ASU), KAET is operated by ASU and serves as the local PBS affiliate (Azpbs). Some of the most well-known television shows from PBS are *Sesame Street*,

1 http://www.liontv.com/Usa/Home.

2 http://www.opb.org/.

3 An executive at Oregon Public Broadcasting also shared with me that the name of the show came from a contest held among the staff, which lends support to the "free-flow" account of how the show originated.

*Antiques Roadshow*, and *Downton Abbey*.

## 2. Show Hosts

The show began with four hosts: Wes Cowan, Elyse Luray, Gwen Wright, and Tukufu Zuberi. Wes is an anthropologist by training and served for a time as the curator of Archaeology at the Cincinnati Museum of Natural History and Science before he opened a very successful antiques dealership in Cincinnati, Cowan's Auctions. He has frequently appeared on another popular show on PBS, *Antiques Roadshow* (2014). Elyse graduated from Tulane University with a degree in Art history and was the youngest vice president in Christie's Auction House before she transitioned to full-time television work as an appraiser on *Antiques Roadshow* and *History Detectives* (Elyse Luray, 2014). Gwen Wright is an award-winning architectural historian at Columbia University, and Tukufu, a Sociologist by training with a specialty in Africa, is the Lasry Family Professor of Race Relations at the University of Pennsylvania (Gwendolyn Wright, 2014; Sociology at the Universities of Pennsylvania, 2014).

Over the next 4 years the show built a steady following, eventually becoming one of the highest-rated shows on PBS. But the producers of the show wanted to continue evolving the show's direction, so in the summer of 2007 I received an email one day from an executive vice president at Oregon Public Broadcasting. It simply asked if I was interested in becoming a guest host for *History Detectives*.

I had watched the show before and liked it, but I was suspicious about this invitation that arrived by email. It is not every day that one receives an invitation from a television show to become part of the cast. I had very limited television experience, and I was so suspicious of the invitation that I almost deleted the email. But before I did that, I decided to see if I could at least verify that the message might be legitimate. So I started my own investigation of who this executive vice president was, and whether he had any credible relationship with the show.

Even though I was able to verify that this executive vice president was with the show, I was still suspicious. Phishing attempts can look very real. But I decided to respond with a tentative interest to see where this all went. So we agreed to a date when he would fly into town and we would do a test shoot.

Once that was done, the producers at PBS invited me to become a guest host for the 2007 season. After that, I was invited to become a regular part of the cast.

## 3. Behind the Scenes

How does the show get made? First, it all begins with a question.

The show depends a good deal upon the historical questions submitted by our viewers. Through internet sites at PBS.org and Facebook, viewers can submit questions about a historical artifact, most often one they have in their possession. Within any given year, the show receives between 7,000 to 8,000 story submissions annually. While that number may seem impressive, the truth is that not all of those stories fit within the premise of the show, and we are budgeted to film only 26 stories per season.



The show's hosts can submit story ideas, too, although this does not mean that a host's idea has a better chance of making it on air than a viewer-submitted idea. All story ideas undergo the same level of scrutiny for whether they allow us to explore American history with greater depth, and whether there is enough information, in the form of documentation, to do a credible job of investigation.

The credit for doing the work of vetting the story submissions goes to a small team of researchers. Production assistants at both Lion Television and Oregon Public broadcasting sift through the submissions to look for stories that are both compelling and documentable. At times this process can take up to a few years until all of the pieces fall into place, and at times the documentation can be found in a matter of months (PBS, 2012).

Once story ideas were vetted for fit and viability, our researchers then set about to prepare a story "pitch," which is a proposal for a story. First, for a pitch to be compelling, all of the documentation needed to tell the story, as well as the experts who can speak to that documentation or to the artifact's historical content, must be complete. Then the actual pitch was crafted. It is a short proposal of about one single-spaced page in length, that succinctly outlines the mystery to be solved, the documentation, the experts to be interviewed, and the particular aspect of American history to be explored.

These story pitches were circulated and widely discussed among the program staff, and the show's executive producers were the ones who give final approval to a story idea. Sometimes story ideas would be sent back to the researchers with further questions about documentation or even about whether the story is interesting or not.

Once story ideas were approved by the show's executive producers, then the production staff got involved in coordinating all of the logistical details required to send a crew out on the road. Reservations for hotels and air flights had to be made, filming locations had to be reserved, and so on. They even had to find times of the year when the weather will allow us to film outdoors.

My role in the pre-production process was somewhat like overseeing an undergraduate independent study. I was not involved in doing the actual research myself, but I advised research staff about experts to contact based on my knowledge of the field. At times my role in the story development process was to also help the television production staff understand the historiography on a given historical moment, as well as the nuances of historical interpretation.

This also became important sometimes during the actual production, when we are out filming the investigation. The film crew is made up of people who have technical expertise in their respective areas of photography and sound, but they don't necessarily know what is historically significant. And it was not uncommon to discover surprises when we were out filming. Sometimes someone would reveal something to us that we didn't know, or sometimes they would not commit to saying something on camera that they were willing to talk about off camera.

While on the road filming the investigation, the crew travelled light. A typical production crew consisted of the producer (who was also the director); the associate producer, who was the one that originally drafted the story proposal; the director of photography (who also took care of all the lighting); the director of sound, and the production assistant. Usually the production assistant was the only who will not travel with the crew because they are locally based and they help us find things like where to eat and where to find resources in the local community.

## 4. Production

Once we began filming the investigation of an artifact, the show was filmed in a way that brought the viewer along on the investigative trail, until the moment that we found the answers we were looking for.

The entire process of being out in the field lasted between 5 and 6 days. On most filming days, call time, or the time that we actually began the day, was usually at 7:00 am. Some days, call time was much earlier. On most days, the filming ended by 10:00 pm, but sometimes the filming could also go much later. There was one shoot that I was on where we had to be on our feet for 20 hours, beginning the day at 4:00 am in New York City and finishing just past midnight in Portland, Oregon. Thankfully, that was not a normal day!



Given the demands of filming, meals were often whenever we could find a break in the filming process, which meant that more often than not, our lunches and dinners were often very late and often cold. There were a few times when we finished so late in the evening that all of the local restaurants were already closed.

Most of our travel was usually by plane into a major city, combined with a long drive to a remote location, or wherever our investigation takes us.

When the production was finished, we usually had about 5 hours' worth of raw footage for a story that will last about 15 minutes long. To put that in perspective, the final story that is shown on television used only up to 5% of what we filmed, and the other 95% of what we filmed is never seen.

All this footage gives the film editors lots of material to work with, which is a good thing. We all look and sound like geniuses because the editors pick only the very best moments of our work on camera.

## 5. Post Production

Once we finished production, the work was not yet over. All of what we shot had to be transcribed and time stamped, and the producer and associate producer then used that transcription to begin editing those five hours of footage into what is known as a "rough cut," which is simply a rough draft of the final product. Part of that rough cut included the addition of music, additional sound effects, and graphics to enhance the story.

Then executives at the PBS Corporation reviewed the rough cut and sent back suggestions and feedback to refine the story. Once the rough cut became a fine cut, then an actual script is produced for the narrative "voice over," and then the host went to a sound studio to read the narration. But even then we continued to be involved in the process, and often I would suggest a phrasing that sounded more natural, or more accurate.

The final cut then went back to PBS Corporation for their final review. Sometimes they would request more revision, or something they would approve the story as is. Once it received that final approval, the story was then ready to be aired on television.



## 6. Promises and Challenges in Working with Television

Some might wonder why I, as an academic historian, devoted part of my time to working on television. About a decade ago, I had worked with another television show on PBS called *The American Experience*, which is another history-focused show (PBS).[1] The producers wanted to feature a moment in history that I had written a book about, and so I was quite involved in that production, both as a lead historical consultant and also as an on-screen expert. When that episode aired, I realized that more people tuned into to see that episode—about two million viewers—than would ever read my book.

1 http://www.pbs.org/wgbh/americanexperience/.

I also realized what a powerful medium television can be. Through the use of images, graphics, and sound, important ideas and concepts can be conveyed in ways that I could only describe with words through traditional publications.

At the same time, however, there are some significant challenges to working with television, which can be limiting. First, American television is a business—even a publically supported network like PBS, which receives some of its operating budget from taxpayers. Ultimately, television is in the business of attracting viewers, and most often that is accomplished through some form of entertainment. So as a business, television does not exist to advance complex ideas or to encourage more sophisticated thinking, which is what we strive to do as academic scholars. To be sure, there have been many powerful documentaries and in-depth analyses of complex issues aired in the history of American television. But those types of shows are relatively rare in comparison to the overabundance of situation comedies, game shows, soap operas, and so-called reality television shows that populate the airwaves.

This is not to say that television is in itself intrinsically anti-intellectual, only that American television executives and producers fear the simple television remote. They fear it because with a simple touch of a button, a viewer can switch to another show, or simply turn the television off entirely if they find what they are watching to be too tedious, or too boring. Thus American television tends to eschew complexity in favor of a streamlined narrative, and this is the second challenge in working with television: how do you keep the viewer watching? The most common approach to this in American television is to keep introducing new and more interesting information in order to keep the viewer watching. Sometimes that can take the form of creating tension in a storyline, or perhaps an element of mystery, which shapes (or sometimes distorts) what and how information is conveyed. But the basic format of almost all American television shows, from situation comedies to historical documentaries, is that a problem or a conflict is introduced at the beginning of a show, and information builds until a resolution is ultimately provided at the end of a show.

Third, television shows most often run between 30 and 60 minutes long, with time allotted for the commercials of sponsoring corporations. What that means is that complex stories can sometimes be simplified in order to fit the allocated time. Or perhaps that there are some stories that are deemed too complex for television because there are too many pieces to show and too many elements that the viewer has to remember within the medium's timeframe.

## 7. "Pancho Villa Watch Fob"

I ran headlong into these challenges with my very first story for *History Detectives*, called "Pancho Villa Watch Fob" (PBS, 2007). One of our viewers, Deidre Kolste, was given an old, commemorative watch fob by a neighbor before he passed away. He told her that he had survived Pancho Villa's raid on Columbus, New Mexico as a child, and that this fob was made as a memento of that event. Deidre wasn't familiar with that conflict and wanted to know more about the story, and especially whether it was true that he was actually there.

To me, one of the very interesting things about this story was that there are some great differences about who actually raided the town. There is no doubt on the part of American historians that Mexican revolutionary Pancho Villa led the raid. But there is credible evidence, which is given greater weight by some Mexican historians, that Pancho Villa could *not* have led the raid. Not only was he nowhere near New Mexico at the time of the attack, according to some of his contemporaries, the actual raid itself was a military blunder of great proportion that was uncharacteristic of his strategic abilities (Barrera, 1972).[1] Further, there were numerous reports at the time that German operatives were actively trying to keep the United States pinned down in a confrontation with Mexican forces in order to prevent American soldiers from entering the European theater of the First World War. So the raid was not conducted by Pancho Villa's forces, some contend, but rather by mercenaries hired by German operatives (Peterson&

1 See for example Alberto Calzadíaz Barrera, *Por Qué Villa Atacó Columbus: Intriga Internacional* (México, Editores Mexicanos Unidos, 1972).

Knoles, 1977; Katz, 1998).[1]

I worked hard to convince the show's producers that in order to tell a more complete story about the raid, we had to acknowledge these competing historical interpretations. This is the approach that academic historians embrace; we strive to explore all sides of an issue in the name of objectivity. But the producers feared that the introduction of competing theories would only complicate the story too much for viewers. And so, at the end of the day, we did not explore the question of who actually raided the town, nor did we introduce alternative interpretations of the event. The best that I could get was a very brief mention in the narrative voice over that historians still debate the question of who was responsible for the raid.

This might seem strange to those unfamiliar with television production, that I, as the on-screen host, held so little sway over the story. The truth of the matter is that the hosts of the show are responsible for producing the raw footage, but, like many other productions, they are not involved in the editing process or the production of the story. The assembly of the final product lay in many other hands, and the final voice in what the story contained—perhaps the only voice that mattered—came from the executives at PBS who underwrote the show.



1 Jessie Peterson and Thelma Cox Knoles, eds., *Pancho Villa: Intimate Recollections by People Who Knew Him* (New York: Hastings House, 1977) includes the memoirs of Dr. R.H. Ellis who served as Villa's medical chief of staff and as an observer for President Wilson. Ellis was adamant that Villa had nothing to do with the raid and claimed that he had proof that the Germans organized and financed the raid, hiring soldiers who fought with Carranza to pose as Villistas. If true, the raid links with the famous Zimmerman Telegram of 19 January 1917 that revealed Germany's larger efforts to drive a wedge between the US and Mexico and to arrange an alliance between Mexico and Germany. The publication of that telegram in US newspapers furthered the loss of neutrality towards Germany and played a significant role in Congress's passing a declaration of war against Germany on 2 April. Friedrich Katz, *The Life and Times of Pancho Villa* (Palo Alto, CA: Stanford, 1998) cites two Americans who interviewed Villa after the raid. Although Villa was circumspect on his exact role in Columbus raid, he promised that he would reveal his location on the day of the raid, witnessed by three Americans.

# 8. "Navajo Rug"

Finally, the expense of telling a more complete story may simply be too great for the budget that a show has to work with.

One of our viewers in season 8 contacted us about a very interesting Indian rug. Bob Peterson is a collector of beaded handbags made by American Indians. One day as he was looking through a popular online auction site, he found a rather curious Indian rug for sale. He was not a collector of rugs, but there was something about this particular rug that stood out to him, and he thought that it might be something of importance. So together with a few other collectors, he purchased the rug for $8,000 in US currency (PBS).

When he contacted *History Detectives*, he wanted to know whether we could determine if the rug was an authentic rug, as well as an historic rug. In other words, was it truly made by Indian artisans, and was it truly an old rug? Further, he wanted to know if we could determine what the symbols mean on the rug, and who might have woven the rug?

One of the challenges in answering this last question is that if the rug was truly an historic rug, and not a contemporary reproduction, then determining who would weave it is a very difficult thing to do. Early Indian rug weavers did not sign their work. But they did leave behind important clues based on unique weaving patterns. So we had a place to start.

Weaving has always been an important part of Navajo life, from the earliest days of their existence (M'Closkey, 2002). The knowledge of weaving was given to them by Spider Woman and Spider Man, two sacred deities who helped the Navajo in this sphere of existence. Every part of weaving is highly symbolic of harmony and balance.

Their rugs became very popular across the country at the turn of the 20th century, and rug making became an important economic endeavor for the Navajo. In order to make rugs that were appealing to American consumers, American traders urged Navajo weavers to develop more colorful rugs with interesting designs. It was around this time that one particular design, the "*Yeibechei*" rug, was created.

One Navajo weaver named Yanapah is considered to be the originator of the *yeibechei* rug. She was born in the Gallegos Canyon area of New Mexico, and was the daughter of a prominent Medicine Man. Like many young women, she began weaving at the age of sixteen. She unfortunately died in her early twenties and is believed to have produced perhaps four rugs in her lifetime. Of those four rugs, only two are known, and the other two are missing. They are highly valued rugs partly because we know who wove it, and partly because they were the first of a design that is popular today.

Even though the *yeibechei* design is widely used today, it was considered to be highly controversial when it was first produced. The *yeibechei* are human representations of what the Navajo call *yei*. The *yei* are demigods, or non-human beings, that can be either a spirit, a god, a demon, or even a monster. The presence of the *Yei* can be invited through acts of representation, and Navajo Medicine Men commonly invited their powerful presence through sand paintings created during their healing ceremonies (Griffin-Pierce, 1992; Witherspoon, 1977; Reichard, 1950).



Representations of the *yei* are considered by the Navajo to be very powerful, and they must be handled very carefully. Neither *yei* nor *yeibechei* were ever meant to be permanently displayed. To do so would be to invite harm.

The way that the Navajo think about the power of the *yei* is similar to how people of the modern period think about using electricity. As a source of power it must be handled with great care. But if one is careless around electricity, then it can be very destructive, if not deadly.

I had never authenticated a rug before as a historian, and this is one of the things that I truly enjoyed about working with the show. Not only did I learn more about particular moments of the past, I also learned more about research methods that were outside of my discipline. We began the process of authenticating the rug by locating specialists who have expertise in this area. We found a textile specialist with the Smithsonian Institution who also specialized in Navajo rug weaving. We also located a practicing Medicine Man who had taught at Arizona State University in the past and who was willing to work with us to understand the symbols on the rug. When the investigation was completed I was confident that the rug is one of the missing Yanapah rugs. But the central question, why would she weave such a powerful and controversial design, was never fully answered during the production of the story.

It was not until the crew had wrapped the production and we were on our way to the airport that it hit me: Yanapah never intended for that rug to be sold. We had the provenance to document that her husband sold it only after she died. We had historical evidence that the marriage was an arranged one, and there was evidence that suggested that the marriage may have been a deeply unfulfilling one for Yanapah. Indeed, her husband, an English trader, may have been abusive. Suddenly the power symbols woven into the rug made sense: the dark warrior figure who held the power of lightning and thunder in his hands and feet, and the war symbols that surrounded him, all spoke of pain and anger. In weaving that rug, Yanapah reached into her heritage to create a resource that could provide her protection, and perhaps a measure comfort through that protection, when she needed to call upon greater powers. This rug was her very personal way of coping with a difficult domestic situation.



As I excitedly shared this insight with the crew, we realized that it was too late to go back and re-film some of the key scenes where I could have explored this interpretation with our experts. It simply would have cost too much money to reschedule another shoot. And so the edited story revolved around whether the rug was an authentic Yanapah rug or not, and we left the question of why she would have woven such a controversial rug open.



## 9. Conclusion

Despite some of the complications of working within the confines of television, I still believe that it is a powerful teaching tool. More viewers will tune in to history-themed shows in a single night than a popular book will sell in an entire year.[1] The visual medium can convey themes and messages in a shorter space of time than any book can. And, if done well, history-themed television can, at times, educate viewers better the traditional learning environment of the classroom. Frequently viewers would comment on the *History Detectives* Facebook page that they learned to appreciate history through this show.

Despite the limitations of the medium, more scholarly historians need to engage the medium to present their work and teach the nation about the past, and more networks need to produce history-themed shows. There is clearly a demand for it.

## Bibliography:

Alberto, Calzadíaz Barrera. *Por qué Villa atacó Columbus*[M]. México: Editores Mexicanos Unidos, 1972.

Antiques Roadshow. C. Wesley Cowan[EB/OL]. 2014.

Archive. 2012. Retrieved February 4, 2014 (http://web.archive.org/web/20120822192909/).



Azpbs. Fifty years[EB/OL]. (http://www.azpbs.org/50years/).

CPB. The Public Broadcasting Act of 1967, as amended[EB/OL]. (http://www.cpb.org/aboutpb/act/).

Dornfeld, Barry. *Producing Public Television, Producing Public Culture*[M]. Princeton: Princeton University Press, 1998.

Griffin-Pierce, Trudy. *Earth is My Mother, Sky is My Father: Space, Time, and Astronomy in Navajo Sandpainting*[M]. Albuquerque: University of New Mexico Press.

Gwendolynwrighthistory. Gwendolyn Wright[EB/OL].2014. (http://www.gwendolynwrighthistory.com/index.php).

IMDb. History Detectives[EB/OL]. 2014. Retrieved January 17, 2014 (http://www.imdb.com/title/tt0375341/?ref_=fn_al_tt_1).

Jessie, Peterson and Thelma Cox Knoles. *Pancho Villa: Intimate Recollections by People Who*

1 Lee Iacocca's memoir sold over a million copies in one year, compared to the 2.5 million average viewership of *History Detectives*. See http://jeffreykrames.com/2009/03/04/how-many-books-do-you-have-to-sell-to-be-a-bestseller/.

*Knew Him*[M]. New York: Hastings House, 1977.

Katz, Friedrich. *The Life and Times of Pancho Villa*[M]. Palo Alto, CA: Stanford, 1998.

Ledbetter, James. *Made Possible by: The Death of Public Broadcasting in the United States*[M]. New York: Verso, 1998.

Luray, Elyse. History Detectives[EB/OL]. 2014. (http://www.elyseluray.com/).

M'Closkey, Kathy. *Swept Under the Rug: A Hidden History of Navajo Weaving*[M]. Albuquerque: University of New Mexico Press, 2002.

PBS. Pancho Villa Watch Fob[EB/OL]. 2007. (http://www.pbs.org/opb/historydetectives//video/1143720703/).

PBS. History Detectives[EB/OL]. (http://www.pbs.org/opb/historydetectives/video/1176774004//).

PBS. History Detectives[EB/OL]. 2012. (http://www.pbs.org/opb/historydetectives/video/2260076830//).

PBS. Mission Statement[EB/OL]. (http://www.pbs.org/about/corporate-information/).

PBS. The American Experience[EB/OL]. (http://www.pbs.org/wgbh/americanexperience/).

Reichard, Gladys. *Navajo Religion: A Study of Symbolism*[M]. Princeton: Princeton University Press, 1950.

Sociology at the Universities of Pennsylvania, Tukufu Zuberi[EB/OL]. 2014. (http://sociology.sas.upenn.edu/tukufu_zuberi).

University Libraries. Retrieved February 4, 2014 (http://www.lib.umd.edu/NPBA/subinfo/net.html).

Witherspoon, Gary. *Language and Art in the Navajo Universe*[M]. Ann Arbor: University of Michigan Press, 1977.

YouTube. PBS "History Detectives" Host/Historian Gwendolyn Wright[EB/OL]. 2007. Retrieved February 4, 2014 (http://www.youtube.com/watch?v=8yy7goPV70M).

# 通过电视进行历史教学的希望与挑战

爱德华多·蒲甘

（亚利桑那州立大学历史、哲学及宗教研究学院，美国坦佩 85287-5503）

**摘 要**：美国著名记者爱德华·R. 默罗对于电视行业有着复杂的看法，尽管该行业仍处于起步阶段，其规模和潜力难以想象。一方面来说，这是一个能教育、探索和启发公众的强大媒介。但从另一方面来说，它主要是一种娱乐的方式。对于默罗来说，问题是它将会变成什么。对于电视行业，大众的期望是什么？是教育还是娱乐？尽管电视媒介有其局限性，但越来越多的历史学者需要通过这一媒介来展示他们的工作成果并向整个民族讲述他们的历史，也需要更多电视台参与到历史主题节目的制作上来。这一需求是显然存在的。

**关键词**：历史；电视；教育

# 美国研究学科建设中的中美区域对比研究

陈　杰

（四川大学外国语学院，四川大学美国研究中心，四川成都　610029）

**摘　要：**美国研究是一个研究内容广阔、研究方法开放的学科领域，其跨学科和跨国界研究的发展趋势对我国现有的学科体制和运作模式提出了挑战。中美区域对比研究是以跨国界的全球化视野聚焦中美两个或多个具体区域，它既体现了美国研究的学科特点和学科发展趋势，又突出了研究的重点和特色。中美区域对比研究，在学理上具有可行性，并具有积极的现实意义。四川大学开展中美西南区域对比研究的实例说明，中美区域对比研究能够充分体现美国研究学科特性，符合学科发展趋势。

**关键词：**美国研究；区域对比研究；学科建设；四川大学美国研究中心



## 1．引言

近年来，国别与区域研究越来越受到政府决策部门和学术研究机构的重视。作为国别与区域研究的一个重要领域，美国研究的重要性自不待言。目前，随着中国的崛起，中美之间如何建立新型大国关系，不仅是涉及中美两个大国的问题，而且是关系到整个世界格局的重大问题。因此，在当前，美国研究不仅具有重要性，而且更具紧迫性。于是，我国美国研究的学科建设，就不单单是旨在创造知识和传播知识的学术研究，它更具重大的现实意义，那就是要为国家和高层管理输送人才，要为国家和地方政府提供决策咨询，具有重大的使命感。

然而，必须认识到，美国研究的跨学科性质，对传统的学科体制带来了冲击，也对我国高校传统的科研运作和人才培养模式提出了挑战。为面对挑战，本文拟在分析美国研究学科特性和发展趋势，并在我国美国研究学科现状的基础上，论述在美国研究学科建设中区域对比研究的重要性和可行性，并通过教育部国别与区域研究培育基地——四川大学美国研究中心开展中美西南区域对比研究的实例，为我国的美国研究学科建设提供一些启示。

## 2．美国研究学科的特殊性和发展趋势

美国研究，顾名思义，是对美国的研究。作为一门学科（academic discipline），美国研究有自己的研究对象和相应的方法论，但其特殊性在于：一，美国研究学科的研究对象包括美国社会的历史、文化、政治、经济、外交等各个方面，具有极大的包容性；二，与研究对象的分散性相适应，美国研究学科的研究方法具有极大的开放性。美国研究，即便从最狭义的角度来看，也覆盖了人文学科（文、史、哲）和社会学科诸多领域，其研究方法也理应包括人文学科和社会学科的各种研究方法。因此，美国研究不仅是一门学科，更是一个广阔的研究领域。



为了更好地理解美国研究学科的特殊性，有必要简要回顾美国研究的学科发展史。美国研究作为一门学科，诞生于20世纪30年代的美国，研究内容主要是对美国文化进行整体性阐释，具体而言主要是从文化的角度去审视美国社会的价值观和行为模式，其目的主要是彰显美国价值观的独特性和优越性。美国研究在美国的兴起，得益于第一次世界大战以后美国国力的上升和文化自信度的提升，它在某种程度上就是美国文化自觉的一个标志。经过几十年的发展，美国许多大学都建立了美国学系或者美国研究的硕士生和博士生培养项目，相关课程多而全，涉及人文社会科学及其他领域的许多方面，如加州伯克利大学的美国研究课程多达400门。欧洲、南北美洲、亚洲许多国家的大学也有美国研究机构，其中不少机构培养硕士、博士研究生。可以看到，美国研究从一开始就具有跨学科特点，特别表现在文学与历史的交融，其研究方法也融合了人文学科和社会学科的研究方法。

从20世纪七八十年代开始，随着后结构主义和文化研究的兴起，美国研究经历了研究范式的转变。研究不再侧重对精英文化和美国文化整体性的阐释，

而是扩展到对美国社会各个方面的研究，特别是大众文化、族裔文化、消费文化、媒体、性别等。这一发展模式与这一时期兴起的文化研究相呼应，涉及的学科几乎涵盖了人文和社会科学的各个分支，研究方法更是无所不包。从对同一性的关注，到对多样性的重视，这是20世纪80年代以来美国研究的一个显著特点。在2004年美国研究协会年会上费希金主席谈及很难对美国研究下一个确切的定义，“今天有多少到会的学者，也许就有多少不同的定义”，但他同时强调，美国研究的一大吸引力，也恰恰在于其研究对象、视角和方法的包容性和开放性。

随着全球化时代的到来，美国研究学科发展也呈现出新的趋势，即国际化，或称跨国界研究趋势。这种变化是基于以下共识：首先，美国研究的目的在于从多方面了解美国社会和美国文化的多重含义；其次，多元文化社会中的美国身份不是一个可以清晰划定边界的概念。过去强调同一性的“美国身份”让位于多元文化身份。因此，单从内部观察不足以达到这一目的，需要将视野投射到美国之外，需要跨文化和跨国界的视野，需要在研究中更多地引入多元和比较的视角。另外，美国研究还必须倾听美国之外的声音，美国需要通过他国学者的研究来反观自身。

综上诉述，美国研究学科是一门颇具特殊性的综合学科，其突出特点是研究内容的包容性和研究方法的开放性，尤其体现在跨学科和跨国界两个方面。



## 3. 国内美国研究学科建设现状和问题

我国美国研究的快速发展，可以说起始于中美邦交正常化的20世纪70年代，由政府发起，最初主要是开展美国政治和外交方面的研究，带有比较鲜明的意识形态特点。随着中美关系的发展和演变，美国研究在高校和研究机构日益得到重视。目前国内的社科院美国所、北京大学、清华大学、中国人民大学、复旦大学、南开大学、北京外国语学院、上海外国语学院、东北师范大学等多个单位设有美国研究方向的博士点，涉及美国政治、外交、中美关系、社会、经济、历史、文化、文学、传媒、法律等方面的研究。在美国研究人才培养方面，我国高校主要由两大类院系承担。第一类是嫡属国际政治的国际关系院系，侧重中美关系和涉及美国的国际问题热点研究。第二类是嫡属外国文学的外语院系，绝大部分是在研究生层面培养美国文化方向的硕士和博士。

虽然美国研究在国内方兴未艾，但是，作为一门学科，美国研究的学科建设，严格说来，还处于起步之时。目前我国尚无完整的美国研究学科体系，绝大多数美国研究要么侧重于国际问题研究和热点问题研究，要么侧重于人文学科方面的文化和历史，应用性研究与基础性研究脱节的情况比较严重。目前，在教育部和国家哲学社会科学办公室公布的学科类别中，还找不到“美国研究”这一学科名称。就目前国务院颁布的学科目录来看，美国研究的跨学科研究性质使之很难被划分到某一特定的学科门类。美国研究人才培养的开展，大都在一级学科政治学或者外国文学名下，这显然不符合美国研究的跨学科性质。就笔者所知，包括四川大学在内的一些国内高校，正在或者已经完成美国研究二级学科的申报工作（属自主增设目录外二级学科），但一般还挂在外国文学一级学科名下，而且尚未开始招生。

如果说缺乏学科体系和学科定位是美国研究学科建设中的首要问题的话，那么，美国研究学科建设的第二大难点就在于它的跨学科性质对我国高校传统的学科划分、课程设置，甚至教学和人事管理，都提出了挑战。目前，在早已实行跨系选课的美国高校，美国研究的学位课程可以分散在许多不同的院系。但是，在我国大多数高校，这仍然是一个需要付出许多努力和时间才能解决的问题。



最后，美国研究学科建设的难度，除了在学科定位和人才培养方面之外，还在于科学研究方面。如前文所述，美国研究是一个广阔的研究领域，它具有“大而全”的特点。“大”，是指美国研究的领域广大；“全”，是指美国研究涉及的学科全面。这就对学科研究提出了一个问题：如何兼顾美国研究的广度和深度？笔者认为，美国研究浩瀚的研究领域绝非某一个研究机构或大学所能穷尽，而且，“大而全”的研究势必导致肤浅的重复研究。因此，在高校和其他学术机构从事美国研究学科建设时，研究的重点和特色是必须认真加以考虑的问题。于是，美国研究学科建设中的中美区域对比研究，作为一个既可兼顾美国研究的广度和深度，而又颇具研究重点和特色的研究领域，成为笔者重点考察的对象。

## 4. 中美区域对比研究的必要性和可行性：以中美西南区域对比为例

事实上，在美国高校等科研机构，区域研究早已成为美国研究学科建设中的重要话题，如开展得如火如荼的边疆地区研究（Border studies）。而中美区域对比研究也不是什么新鲜事物，即便是本研究报告讨论的中美西南区域对比研究，也已经有一些美国学者涉猎其间。只不过由于该研究领域极为广阔，研究的广度和深度都还亟待开拓和挖掘。

所谓中美区域对比研究，简单来说，是以美国某一区域作为研究对象，将其与中国某一具有可比性的区域进行对比的一种跨学科和跨国界研究。显然，作为一个学科领域，它必须具备两大要素：一是研究对象的可比性，二是研究视角和方法的跨学科和跨国界性。需要注意的是，这两大因素是相互关联的。也就是说，是否具有可比性，在某种程度上是由研究视角和研究方法所决定的。笔者拟从这两个方面的关系入手，揭示这种研究对于美国研究学科发展的必要性和可行性。

很明显，中美西南部区域具有许多可资比较的相似性因素，包括：两者同处西南边陲、多样的地形地貌、多民族、重要贸易通道、受外来文化影响程度、经济和旅游资源，等等。然而，如果这些相似性因素是彼此孤立的，那么即便因素再多也无法构成可比性的学理依据。根据比较文学的研究方法论，平行研究的可比性可以来自于对一般规律的揭示。如果将此理论运用到中美西南部区域对比研究，那么研究的目的必须首先是“求同”，即必须首先忽略具体的差异，而寻找差异中蕴含的共性。与这个思路不谋而合的是，新墨西哥和中国西南部的云南，均位于边疆地区。美国历史学家霍尔早在2009年就提出了区域对比研究中的差异最大化策略（variance maximizing strategy）。这种研究方法有意选取貌似互不关联的研究对象，在对比中囊括但暂时忽略所有差异因素，以期勾勒出一个带有普遍性的范畴。落实到中美西南部区域对比研究中，这样的带有普遍性的范畴就是，从地缘政治的角度看，两者都处在边缘的地位。以更为具体的区域为例。美国西南部的新墨西哥是难以界定的流动概念，边疆各有不用，但构成边疆的一系列因素却是共同的。因此，通过比较源于不同文化根源的两个边疆地区，我们即可对构成边疆的基本因素有更好把握，从而有利于更好地理解边疆的本质。当我们使用“边缘”一词时，我们的研究已经涉及社会学科中使用的“边缘化理论”，这一理论关注的是一个国家或地区在一个世界体系（world-system）中所处的地位和影响。从中心与边缘的关系上讲，中美西南部地区在历史上都经历过融入一个更大的世界体系的过程，而且在这一演变过程中，它们作为边缘与中心的关系是一种互动的、相互影响的关系。研究中美西南部区域在各自的历史长河中如何在融入与边缘之间徘徊，如何与政治文化中心构成互为影响的关系，我们就可以从两者的比较中得出一些带有普遍性和规律性的结论，而这种结论必定比单一的区域研究得出的结论更具说服力和理论指导意义。

以上所述仅是中美区域对比研究的一个维度，即“求同”的、宏观的维度，其目的是找出带有普遍性的规律。中美区域对比研究的另一个维度当然是微观的“求异”。“求异”是在“求同”的基础上进行的，它应该是在规律（理论）指导下的一种演绎。这时，在“求同”阶段没有得到优先重视的具体因素成为重要的研究对象，包括各自区域的历史、地理、经济、人文等具体的社会文化状况和它周边的大环境状况，也即那个处于中心地位的世界体系的发展阶段和态势。之前在运用差异最大化策略进行求同研究中处于次要因素的历史、地理、社会结构等具体因素，在深入的对比研究中往往成为首要因素。就新墨西哥和云南相比，云南作为边疆的时间更长，历史上面对的较自身更为强大的世界体系更多，而且与周边的世界体系的交流更具多样性。通过比较这样的差异，我们也许可更好地理解为什么新墨西哥地区没有云南地区所保持的那么丰富的多文化特征。又如，在“求同”研究中，我们会强调中美西南部区域在地理环境、民族多元化、贸易通道、旅游资源等方面的相似性，但是在“求异”的研究中，我们就会更多关注它们之间的差异性，并进而追溯差异的成因以及对未来的影响。例如，新墨西哥和云南都十分强调民族自治区的旅游事业发展，把旅游业作为经济支柱，但是两者的做法却有很大的不同。印第安人保留地的赌博业成为自治区经济越来越不可或缺的重要部分，但赌博业的发展也会引发一系列问题，比如它会对现行的美国制度体系产生怎样的影响，自此可以生发一系列的研究课题。中美西南区域对比研究可能涉及的重要的具体问题不一而足。比如从文明进程来看，两个地域在各自国家的文明历史中的发展都相对滞后，这种情况对于区域身份的形成有何影响，这些影响中有哪些是共同的，哪些是有差异的，差异的原因是什么；又如，从国土资源来看，两个地域均有广阔的未开拓地区，均面临开发和环境保护的矛盾，应如何相互学习和借鉴；再如，从民族来看，两个地域都是多民族地区，在对少数民族的政策方面，应如何相互学习和借鉴。

笔者无意对具体的研究内容和方法做深入阐述，只是想借中美西南部区域对比研究这个话题，来说明中美区域对比研究可以作为我国美国研究学科建设中的一个重要组成部分。我们知道，一个学科的发展必然涉及研究内容在广度和深度上的延伸，涉及研究视角和方法的更新，涉及人才培养的跟进。从以上分析我们可以看出，中美区域对比研究在内容上包含社会、历史、文化、政治、经济等各方面的课题，具有极大的深度开发的潜力。在研究视角上，它既需要全球的视野，也需要聚焦地方的眼光；它既是历史的，也是当代的，因为它用当代的眼光来看待历史，同时用历史的眼光来审视当代；它既是跨国界的，又是区域的，因为我们是用中国学者的视角去观察美国，同时又通过研究美国来反思自身。在研究方法上，中美区域对比研究是跨学科的，它必然会使用社会科学和人文研究的理论方法，甚至不排除自然科学的实验和实证方法。然后，中美区域对比研究会关注自身的理论建构，发展出自己的跨学科方法论和研究范式和模型。总之，中美区域对比研究，在学理上具有可行性，并具有积极的现实意义；而且，它符合美国研究跨学科和跨国界的特性，有利于我国美国研究学科建设的发展。



## 5. 四川大学美国研究中心的实例和思考

四川大学美国研究中心（以下简称“中心”）成立于1985年，隶属外国语学院，研究人员主要来自英文系，以从事美国文学、文化研究为主，因此它不是一个跨学科的研究机构，这对美国研究学科建设构成很大的制约。从2012年开始，中心成为教育部下属的国别与区域研究培育基地，为中心拓展学科建设提供了契机。在被教育部列为国别研究培育基地之后，中心积极整合相关资源，并在同美国亚利桑那州立大学等学校的合作基础上，将研究重心聚焦于中美西部地区的文化、经济、政治、历史和社会等对比研究，中心自此确立了以中美西南部区域对比为研究重点的目标，并朝着跨学科的方向迈进，力争早日建成跨学科的美国研究学术平台。

中心之所以选择中美西南区域对比研究作为重点研究领域，除了前文所述原因之外，主要还是基于中心实际情况的考虑。首先，地缘因素。中心位于我国西南部，把美国西南区域作为研究重点，并与中国西南部进行比较研究，可以服务国家和地方，具有极大的现实意义。其次，综合性大学的优势。区域对比研究需要多学科和跨学科研究人员的参与，四川大学作为国家重点综合性大学在这方面具有资源优势。第三，与美国高校的合作。中心与美国亚利桑那州立大学建立了长期的合作关系，有利于区域对比研究的开展。

自确立了以中美西南区域对比研究为中心的重点和特色以来，中心在以下几个方面开展了卓有成效的工作：

（1）以科研项目牵头，整合校内资源，组建跨学科的研究团队。

中心利用四川大学作为综合性重点大学的多学科优势，发挥科研平台的作用，通过发布中美西南部区域对比研究项目的方式，聚集了一批分散在不同学科中而又涉及美国研究的中青年研究人员。第一批课题分为两个课题方向：美国西南部边疆研究——政治、地理和文化，以及四川和亚利桑那州的经济现状和未来发展。首批立项的18个课题围绕上述两个方向，既有基础性研究，又有应用型研究，涉及政治、经济、文化、历史等多个学科领域。



（2）开展对外交流与合作。

在科学研究的开展和科研人才的培养中，对外交流与合作是必不可少的。交流与合作分为两个方面。第一个方面是与国外高校科研机构和同行的交流与合作。以中心开展中美西南区域对比研究为例，四川大学与地处美国西南部的亚利桑那州立大学建立了良好的交流与合作关系。每年都会有相关学者从亚利桑那州立大学到四川大学讲学，每年也有四川大学的学者和学生到对方大学去交流、进修或攻读学位。为促进中美西南区域比较研究，2013年两校共同主办了首届中美西南区域对比研究国际研讨会，吸引了国内外相关领域学者的参与。2014年初，中心专门组织了一个中美西南区域对比研究研讨班，赴亚利桑那州立大学学习和考察。研讨班成员来自文学、语言学、政治、经济、管理等不同学科，且均为中心发布的中美西南区域对比研究项目的主持人。他们在美期间分别与各自领域的美方学者进行了深度的交流，为将来的合作奠定了基础。为了更好地开展中美区域对比研究，中心还将拓展与国外相关科研机构的交流和合作机制，增强人员互访和师生交流。

交流与合作的第二个方面是与国内地方高校和科研机构，以及地方政府和企业的交流与合作。首先是校际交流与合作。这是科研和人才资源整合的重要方面，特别是对于中美区域对比研究而言，不同地区的高校在进行区域对比研究时，必定会考虑到本地区的特色而使得研究的重点有所不同。四川大学在开展中美西南区域对比研究时，就特别重视与西南三省高校的交流与合作。四川大学美国研究中心于2013年在成都召开中美西南区域对比研究国际研讨会，也是在这方面的一个有益尝试。本次会议吸引了西南三省高校的研究人员的参与，进一步充实了中美西南对比研究的科研队伍。基于2013年成都会议的成功经验，中心已同云南大学商定，在2015年6月在昆明举办相同主题的国际研讨会。除了与高校和科研机构的交流与合作之外，与地方政府和企业的合作也非常重要，这也是中心正在进行的一项重要工作。这里涉及美国研究除基础性研究和理论研究之外的另一个方面，即应用型研究。应用型研究以理论研究为基础，以服务国家和地方为目的。与政府和企业的合作，类似于人们常说的产学研的结合，有利于发挥美国研究机构的智库功能，也有利于培养社会需要的应用型人才。同时应用型研究也容易获得地方政府支持，特别在需求和资源方面。合作的方式应该是多样的，以项目合作为主要方式，具体可包括为政府决策部门提供咨询报告，参与撰写企业项目的可行性报告，学生到企业和政府部门实习，等等。

（3）建立美国研究二级学科，开展硕士学位项目。

以美国研究二级学科的设立为支点招收美国研究硕士研究生，不仅对于整合分散的师资和科研力量，而且对于培养美国研究的后备人才，均具有至关重要的作用。正如在论述我国美国研究现状中所言，我国目前的美国研究人才培养的学位项目主要集中在中美关系和美国文学文化方面，严格来说都不能很好地反映美国研究的跨学科性质，对于培养中美区域对比研究的后备人才的要求来说，更是差距甚大。针对这种情况，四川大学已着手启动美国研究二级学科建设，突破口应该是开展二级学科下的美国研究硕士学位项目。比较稳妥的做法是先从小规模试点开始，头三年每年的招生规模控制在15人以内，且生源来自具有人文学科和社会学科背景的学士学位获得者。课程设置方面，除学位论文以外，开设一门专业必修课——美国研究理论与方法，其余均为选修课。学位项目的师资，包括授课教师和导师，应来自具有不同学科背景的涉及美国研究的系所。为了加强对中美西南部区域对比研究后备人才培养的力度，在选修课和学位论文选题方面，应有意识地突出这一特色。在项目头三年运转完成之后，应跟踪毕业生的就业情况，有意识地建立起校友网络，并通过校友开拓与政府部门和企业的联系渠道，以促进产学研的结合，促进应用型研究的开展。同时，经过第一个三年的项目运作，可考虑在课程设置中增加可替代学位论文的实践性课题选项，而这些实践性课题最好聚焦中美西南区域对比研究。

## 6．结语

美国研究是一个研究内容广阔、研究方法开放的学科领域，跨学科和跨国界研究是美国研究学科的发展趋势。鉴于美国研究学科的特殊性，在学科建设中应注意突出重点和特色。中美区域对比研究是以跨国界的全球化视野聚焦中美两个或多个具体区域，它既体现了美国研究的学科特点和学科发展趋势，又突出了研究重点和特色。同时，它结合了理论研究和应用研究，与国家和地方的政府决策和经济发展具有紧密的联系，更易于发挥决策咨询的智库作用。



四川大学美国研究中心在开展中美西南区域对比研究过程中，以中心作为平台，积极发挥综合性大学的跨学科优势，筹建美国研究二级学科，扩大对外交流与合作，服务于地方发展的需要，对于中国西部地区高校建设特色学科，对于西部地区加强与美国西南部地区在多方面进行区域合作和交流，均具有重要意义。

四川大学开展中美西南区域对比研究的实例说明，中美区域对比研究能够充分体现美国研究学科特性，符合学科发展趋势。同时，中美区域对比研究，既从中国学者的视角来看待美国，又通过研究美国来反观中国。这种跨国界的视野有助于在美国研究学科建设中凸显中国特色，有助于我们建立具有中国特色的美国学。综上所述，在美国研究学科建设中开展区域对比研究，具有理论价值和实际意义，可以作为美国研究学科建设中的一个可行的研究重点。

## 参考文献：


四川大学美国研究中心. 全球化时代的美国[M]. 成都：四川大学出版社，2010.

Cullen, Jim. *The American Dream: A Short History of an Idea That shaped a Nation*[M]. New York: Oxford University Press, 2002.

Fishkin, Shelley Fisher. Crossroads of Cultures: The Transnational Turn in American Studies: Presidential Address to the American Studies Association[J]. *American Quarterly*, 2005, 57: 17-57.

Hall, Thomas D. Lessons from Comparing the Two Southwests: Southwest China and Northwest New Spain/Southwest United States[J]. *Journal of World-Systems Research*, 2013, 19: 24-56.

Halttunen, Karen. Groundwork: American Studies in Place: Presidential Address to the American Studies Association[J]. *American Quarterly*, 2006, 58: 17-57.

Kammen, Michael. *In the Past Line: Historical Perspectives on American Culture*[M]. New York: Oxford University Press, 1997.

Levine. Lawrence W. *The Unpredictable Past: Explorations in American Cultural History*[M]. New York: Oxford University Press, 2003.

Lipsitz, George. *American Studies in a Moment of Danger*[M]. Minneapolis: University of Minnesota Press, 2001.

Luedtke, Luther S. *Making America: The Society and Culture of the United States*[M]. United States Information Agency, 1992.

Mergen, Bernard. *American Studies Bibliography*[M]. George Washington University, 2003.

Takaki, Ronald. *A Different Mirror: A History of Multiculturalism*[M]. Boston: Little, Brown and Company, 1993.

# On the Sino-US Area Study in the Disciplinary Restructuring of American Studies in China

Chen Jie

(College of Foreign Languages and Cultures & American Studies Center, Sichuan University, Chengdu, China, 610029)

**Abstract:** The trans-disciplinary and transnational tendency of American studies poses a challenge to the existing academic institution and its operations. Sino-US area study, by availing of a transnational and global perspective in comparing and contrasting two or more US areas with their Chinese counterparts, promises a feasible and significant approach to the disciplinary restructuring of American Studies in China. The Chinese and American southwest studies carried out by the American Studies Center of Sichuan University has proven to be an inspiring effort in this regard.



**Key Words:** American Studies; Sino-US Area Study; Disciplinary Restructuring; American Studies Center of Sichuan University